The Executive's Guide to Management Accounting and Control Systems

Seventh Edition

Brandt R. Allen
Luann Lynch
University of Virginia
Darden Graduate School of Business Administration

THOMSON

Australia · Canada · Mexico · Singapore · Spain · United Kingdom · United States

The Executive's Guide to Management Accounting
And Control Systems
Seventh Edition
Allen ~ Lynch

Executive Editors:
Michele Baird, Maureen Staudt &
Michael Stranz

Project Development Manager:
Linda de Stefano

Marketing Coordinators:
Lindsay Annett and Sara Mercurio

**Production/Manufacturing
Supervisor:**
Donna M. Brown

Pre-Media Services Supervisor:
Dan Plofchan

Rights and Permissions Specialists:
Kalina Hintz and Bahman Naraghi

Cover Image
Getty Images*

The Adaptable Courseware Program
consists of products and additions to
existing Thomson products that are
produced from camera-ready copy.
Peer review, class testing, and
accuracy are primarily the responsibility
of the author(s).

ISBN 0-759-39475-X

International Divisions List

Asia (Including India):
Thomson Learning
(a division of Thomson Asia Pte Ltd)
5 Shenton Way #01-01
UIC Building
Singapore 068808
Tel: (65) 6410-1200
Fax: (65) 6410-1208

Australia/New Zealand:
Thomson Learning Australia
102 Dodds Street
Southbank, Victoria 3006
Australia

Latin America:
Thomson Learning
Seneca 53
Colonia Polano
11560 Mexico, D.F., Mexico
Tel (525) 281-2906
Fax (525) 281-2656

Canada:
Thomson Nelson
1120 Birchmount Road
Toronto, Ontario
Canada M1K 5G4
Tel (416) 752-9100
Fax (416) 752-8102

UK/Europe/Middle East/Africa:
Thomson Learning
High Holborn House
50-51 Bedford Row
London, WC1R 4LS
United Kingdom
Tel 44 (020) 7067-2500
Fax 44 (020) 7067-2600

Spain (Includes Portugal):
Thomson Paraninfo
Calle Magallanes 25
28015 Madrid
España
Tel 34 (0)91 446-3350
Fax 34 (0)91 445-6218

PREFACE

This book is designed for managers or people who aspire to managerial positions. The contents provide the basis for what a manager needs to know about accounting and control systems. As you can see, it is a short book. Its purpose is not to include everything that might be considered important, but rather to provide a foundation on which to build.

Management accounting can be regarded as the map whose objective is to reflect the territory —the reality of costs. Just as the information an airline pilot needs to know about the ground will be different from what the automobile driver, or hiker, needs to know about the same piece of ground, so too does the user of accounting data have different information needs for different purposes. In this book, we pay a lot of attention to the relationship between information and the manager's job, because different functions such as pricing or monitoring performance require different kinds of information.

Tech booms and busts, globalization, and widespread refocusing of enterprises have put intense pressure on managers to innovate and excel. Management accounting has become more than a benign scorekeeping exercise. In fact, a good management accounting system actively contributes to a firm's competitive success. Not knowing your costs can indeed hurt you; having good information and using it well can directly improve performance.

Mastering the fundamentals of management accounting is important, and this text pays strong attention to providing a good understanding of the basic processes and logic. But management accounting is evolving in response to changing technology and competitive pressures. The built-in assumptions and generally accepted accounting practices need to be reexamined. Change in accounting processes is sometimes called for, but not always. If we know the basic processes, we are better equipped to test whether those processes will continue to serve management well or whether they must be changed.

Management accounting is one part of a management control system. The total control system is made up of other elements and it shows how a control-system design can provide strong support to the effectiveness of management.

ORGANIZATION OF THE BOOK

The book has three sections. The first focuses on cost information, and how it can be developed and organized for use in management decisions. Included is the cost planning and review cycle, as well as the concepts of activity-based costing and strategic costing. Here we establish a systems view and the need to develop a continuing process of generating relevant cost information.

Section two addresses the use of cost information in management decisions. The art of shaping cost information based upon the context or decision at hand, called relevant cost analysis, is described together with an introduction to activity-based management. This section also describes the fundamental analysis used by companies to evaluate proposed capital expenditures.

The last section of the book describes important elements of the management control system, which includes the previously discussed management accounting system, budgeting, incentives, and performance measures. Other elements are also involved, such as the planning and review functions, the direction and strength of motivation, and the organization structure. Analysis shows that it is not so much the elements by themselves, but their interaction that is a key concern in developing a good system.

INTENDED AUDIENCE

The book is designed for use in a number of settings. We have used it in our first-year MBA accounting course and in numerous executive education programs. It has also been used in undergraduate accounting courses. Prior study of financial accounting helps, but it is not necessary if students review the two appendices: one on the basic accounting processes and one on understanding financial statements.

There are questions and problems at the end of each chapter. They are designed to give practice in using the main techniques and concepts discussed in the chapter.

ACKNOWLEDGEMENTS

This is the seventh edition of *The Executive's Guide to Management Accounting and Control Systems*. For three decades, this book has helped executives, operating managers, and MBA students understand how to use internal financial systems to implement their strategies. It's about costs and costing, planning and budgets, performance measurements and incentives, decisions and decision-making. And most importantly, it's about people and how systems keep them on track, get them to do the right things, and avoid doing the wrong things. It's all about direction, motivation, and action.

Although Professors William Rotch and C. Ray Smith are not authors of this edition, we wish to acknowledge their essential contributions to it. Were it not for Bill and Ray, this book would not exist. They took the lead with the first edition and played a vital role in each successive edition. As the Johnson and Higgins Professor of Business Administration, Bill taught courses in management accounting, management control, and strategic costing for 35 years at the Darden Graduate School of Business Administration at the University of Virginia. He also served as Dean of the Faculty and the Director of the Tayloe Murphy International Business Studies Center. C. Ray Smith is the Tipton R. Snavely Professor of Business Administration Emeritus at the Darden School. In addition to teaching financial and managerial accounting and real-estate finance and development for 42 years, Ray was interim Dean of the Darden School 3 times, Associate Dean for the MBA Program, Associate Dean for Executive Education, Associate Dean for Administration, Executive Director of the Darden School Foundation, and Administrative Director of the Institute for Chartered Financial Analysts (now the CFA Institute). We dedicate this edition to Bill and Ray.

The revision of this seventh edition has been assisted by many people. Students in several schools of business and a number of executive programs have made suggestions. We wish to acknowledge the assistance and support of E. Richard Brownlee II, Mark Haskins, Robert Sack, Mary Margaret Frank, and Paul Simko, professors here at the Darden School of Business who have used the text for a number of years.

Manuscript preparation was expertly done by Debbie Quarles, Kathy Shelton, Marie Payne, and Benjamin MacMahon and a thorough editing job by Catherine Wiese, Jamie Miller, Beth Woods, and Amy Lemley. For all their help, we are most grateful.

Brandt Allen
Luann Lynch

TABLE OF CONTENTS

SECTION I
DEVELOPING COSTS FOR MANAGEMENT DECISIONS

1   Exploring the Uses of Cost Information
2   Costing Products and Processes
3   Standard Costing Systems
4   Variable Costing

SECTION II
USING COSTS IN MANAGEMENT DECISIONS

5   Relevant Cost Analysis
6   Managing Costs
7   Evaluating Capital Expenditures

SECTION III
MANAGEMENT CONTROL SYSTEMS

8   Using Control Systems to Improve Performance
9   Preparing and Using Budgets
10 Measuring Performance

Appendix A: Basic Accounting Processes Used in Preparing Financial Statements
Appendix B: Understanding Financial Statements
Index

SECTION ONE

DEVELOPING COSTS FOR MANAGEMENT DECISIONS

CHAPTER 1

EXPLORING THE USES FOR COST INFORMATION

WHY BEGIN WITH USES OF COST INFORMATION?

Why do we start discussing uses before we have said anything about how cost information is developed? We start here because the use being contemplated affects the way cost information should be prepared. Indeed, "different costs for different purposes" is the expression we often hear. Contrary to financial accounting, there are no "generally accepted accounting principles" to prescribe how managers must compile cost information to use in making strategic and operating decisions.

To illustrate: If we are considering a one-time order that will increase our manufacturing volume by 3%, the costs relevant to that decision will be the incremental costs of a small additional volume. Those will be material, labor, and *some* overhead costs, perhaps including an overtime premium if overtime production is needed. Some costs such as heat or rent on the factory won't change very much, so those costs need not be included in this analysis. On the other hand, if the proposal is to double production, we may have to heat and rent additional space, so those kinds of costs become relevant to the larger proposal. Or if we are developing costs for measuring the plant superintendent's performance, we will identify those costs we want him or her to control or influence. That may well be a different set of costs from those that are relevant to the product decisions. And if we are considering selling or downsizing the plant, we must use an entirely different set of costs.

So the use of cost information is where we begin. Looking at the overall picture, we see three general functions for which cost information is used:

1. Financial accounting for the preparation of a variety of financial statements, such as the income statement, balance sheet, and cash flow statement for external reporting. For this function, the data compiled must comply with an authoritative set of generally accepted accounting principles.

2. The development of costs that support management decisions, such as pricing, product mix, outsourcing, and strategic planning, to name a few. This function requires us to determine which costs are relevant for particular decisions and which are not.

3. Management control systems that help management to keep things on track, to avoid bad things, and to encourage good things. Included here is variance analysis arising from budgets and standard costs, as well as a variety of issues relating to measurement and the evaluation of managerial performance. Again, this function requires us to determine which costs are relevant for the decision at hand.

This book is concerned with financial accounting only to the extent that the mandatory nature of financial accounting often determines the database from which costing and control systems derive their numbers.[1] We will see that the financial accounting framework is often unsuited for the other uses of cost information; in fact, sometimes costs based on financial accounting data give entirely wrong signals for management decisions.

---

[1] For those who wish to review the basic accounting processes and the information content of financial statements, we have included two appendices on those subjects at the end of the book.

Our concentration will be on the second and third functions noted above. Those two functions are not entirely separate, of course, since decision-related costs can also serve the control process. Generally, however, decision-related costs focus on costing an outcome, such as a product, service, or a defined action choice, and the control-related costs are more concerned with behavior and the process of management.

If you have already learned about financial accounting practices, be warned that we are now moving into uncharted waters. When we move outside the financial accounting framework, we move outside a set of rules. The relevant rule or test becomes the usefulness of cost information for management. When developing product costs, for example, we may measure past and present costs to see how we are doing, but future costs are the only costs that managers can influence. Furthermore, we are not confined to manufacturing costs, the costs that financial accountants would add to inventory. We can include marketing costs, distribution costs, and, in fact, any significant cost caused by the development and sale of that product. In defining cost, we need not conform to the concept of "expense" used for the income statement or "expenditure" used for the cash flow statement. Consider, for example, how the present value of a future expenditure may be a relevant cost of today's decision or how an opportunity cost—the benefit foregone because of an action chosen—will be a relevant cost of that action. Neither of those numbers will appear on financial statements, yet both can be important in evaluating a course of action. Management accounting, therefore, focuses on the management decision as a guide to what is relevant and significant.

WHERE MANAGERS USE COST INFORMATION

In this section, we describe several areas in which managers use cost information. We also note some of the distinctive characteristics of the cost information that are relevant for each use.

Planning

A firm's planning function, whether long or short range, relies on cost information. For example, plans for marketing strategy need data on cost–volume relationships. Development of facilities and evaluation of capital projects require projections of costs and savings; even financial forecasting uses cost estimates. It must be remembered, of course, that costs of past activities will not necessarily apply to the future, and when past costs are used in planning, they must be adjusted to reflect estimates of future conditions.

Pricing

Part of the input to a pricing decision will usually be the cost of the product or service. But the cost of a product or service can be difficult to estimate. First, if a company produces only one product, the total cost of the product will be fairly easy to obtain by dividing total cost for a period by units produced during that period. But most manufacturing companies produce more than one product, and some of the costs incurred will support the production of all of them, or in some cases just a few of them. Allocating such common costs is, therefore, a challenge. Indeed, it is a growing problem, because as business becomes increasingly technology-driven, a growing percentage of costs are indirect and pertain to more than one product. Second, costs can change with changes in volume. Changes in selling prices usually influence the number of units sold and consequently the number produced. Different levels of production will, in turn, mean different costs per unit produced—while some production costs vary with volume, others remain relatively fixed. Computing unit costs at different levels of production will therefore require knowledge of which costs vary with volume and to what extent.

Pricing decisions in service businesses are also influenced by costs. For several reasons, development of useful cost information is more difficult in service businesses. One reason is the low consistency or homogeneity of service business output. Though the content of some services may be fairly consistent and precisely described (for example: a hamburger), other services can vary greatly (for example: hospital treatments or bank loans). Thus, the work that goes into the service can be difficult to define, and therefore, the cost of a service is often difficult to measure. Another difficulty in costing services arises from the frequently high proportion of indirect and common costs. In the restaurant business, one hears that the direct food costs of an entrée should be no more than 25% of the menu price. The other 75% should cover cooks, servers, management, rent, and utilities—and provide a profit. Photocopying or communication services may have more than 90% indirect costs. Nevertheless, service businesses need good cost information as much as any other businesses do. Unless management has some idea of how its costs relate to its prices, it may find itself in the unexpected philanthropic activity of an orderly donation of its assets to its customers.

It should be noted here that the influence of cost on price varies in different kinds of businesses. First, often the market or marketing strategy determines price. McDonald's once reduced the price of the Big Mac to $0.99 not because the company figured out a lower-cost method of producing it, but because Burger King lowered its price, and whatever distinctiveness there might be about Big Macs, McDonald's management believed them to be close to a commodity in the eyes of consumers.

Second, in other businesses, the value of a product or service varies with different groups of customers. Scarcity can raise the value and the price a customer is willing to pay if the customer really needs the item (for example: snow shovels in a blizzard). Consider seats on an airplane. Passengers are likely to have paid many different fares for the same economy-class seat. In those situations, price is not determined by cost plus a desired margin, but rather it is an amount determined by value to the customer.

Third, some products are unique so there is not a going market price. In those instances, cost has a big influence on price. Companies in this situation may set price simply by adding a desired markup to its costs.

The varying influence of cost on price in different businesses can be represented by a continuum showing different levels of influence.

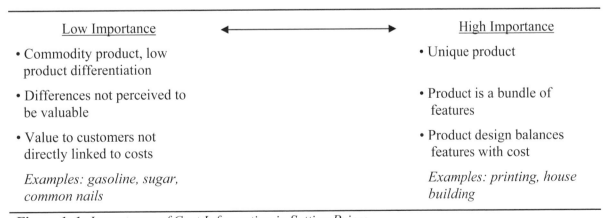

Figure 1–1: *Importance of Cost Information in Setting Prices*

A special case on the low-importance end of the continuum is the system called "target costing," in which price is set first as determined by the market, then profit is subtracted, and the remainder is the target cost. Cost management teams then work out how the product can be produced at the target cost. More will be said on this in Chapter 6.

Product or Service Profitability

Whether or not costs are used to help set prices, management will want cost information to help measure the profitability of particular products or services. Here the actual costs of the work done and items sold will be important. Also, estimates of future costs will be needed to evaluate the profitability of alternative product mixes or of new products or services not yet offered.

Process Improvement

Just as product costs help in decisions affecting a product, process costs are needed to evaluate process efficiency or proposed changes to a process. For example, one multistage machine may replace several single-stage machines. The cost information needed to evaluate that change is the cost of that process, which may be only a small part of the total cost for a variety of products. Or consider a bank that offers a collection of services, each of which is often made up of several processes. Evaluating the efficiency of these processes requires focusing on the intermediate steps rather than on the service provided at the end.

Processes are similar to activities. In recent years, activity-based costing, which is explained in the next chapter, has led to activity-based management. The latter is a way of analyzing both the efficiency and the effectiveness of activities and processes. These concepts are reviewed in Chapters 2 and 6.

Measuring Performance

Evaluating performance of individuals or groups of people is important, and to do that, management needs to be able to measure activity in terms of cost and output. Frequently, standards are established in terms of budgets or standard cost per unit, and actual performance is measured against these standards. These applications are explained in Chapter 3 (Standard Costing Systems), Chapter 8 (Using Control Systems to Improve Performance), and Chapter 9 (Preparing and Using Budgets).

THE VALUE OF COST INFORMATION

Theoretically, the cost and effort required to develop cost systems or to compile cost information should be less than the value of the information produced. Sometimes that balance is clear, as it is in the construction industry, in which cost information has a high value as the basis for bids. But often cost information is not the dominant factor or is not precisely persuasive in influencing decisions: not dominant because of other important factors, and not precisely persuasive because measurements may be only estimates and approximations. For example:

1. In pricing decisions, market forces often have more influence than costs. Here, the value of cost information is less in its role in setting prices and more in its role in helping management determine a target cost based on a market price.

2. The cost of holding inventory cannot be measured precisely. The direct costs of storage space, capital tied up, spoilage, and handling are easy enough to compute. But managers have

discovered that not holding inventory has many benefits. Companies using just-in-time techniques have reduced inventories and benefited from faster production, earlier discovery of production errors, and better customer service. Managers know those benefits are there, but measuring them is difficult. Indeed, Toyota installed its successful just-in-time system, which reduced inventory and throughput time without even trying to compute the amount of cost savings.

3. Improving quality may cause certain direct costs to increase, but over time may cause a larger decrease in indirect costs. Fewer rejects mean lower rework cost. More reliable quality allows smaller planned overruns to make up for losses along the way. Warranty costs and the expense for post-delivery service all go down. Since the cost of improved quality has tended to be more easily measured than its benefits, the cost has been more evident. However, companies are now recognizing the many values of higher quality, even if those values cannot be precisely measured.

In situations like those, it is more difficult to weigh the benefits against the costs of developing better cost systems.

Many companies recognize the linked relationships contained in what has been labeled the value chain. The value chain represents the series of activities from the development of raw materials to presenting the product or service to the customer. A chain might consider these activities:

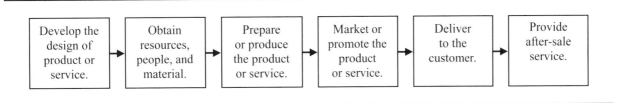

Figure 1–2: *Value Chain*

Each activity in the chain adds value to the product or service. Management accountants can add value to the chain by analyzing the cost of each stage and comparing that to estimated value enhancement. They should have a wide scope in doing the analysis because what is done in one part of the chain may affect cost and value in other parts. Consistent quality in production, for example, can enhance value to the customer. Developing a product design that is easy to produce—say, with a small number of parts—may increase the cost of the design phase, but will decrease the cost of the production phase. Thus, management accountants should be familiar with the total value chain of their company, if they want to do a good job in one of the segments.

THE NEXT CHAPTER

Chapter 2 provides the basic framework for organizing cost information. It describes how costs are assembled so that management can have a product cost for inventory, the cost of goods or services sold, or the cost of running a department. The hardest part about this process is allocating common costs, or costs that are not clearly and directly related to a product or department. These are costs such as the plant manager's salary, electricity and fuel, the quality control department, plant maintenance, and production engineering. If all those costs are to be distributed to products, some allocation method is needed; yet there is no allocation method that is demonstrably accurate or correct for those common costs. Since large amounts of costs are often involved, much time is required to develop the best method. Chapter 2 will elaborate on this challenging accounting problem.

SUMMARY

Management needs cost information to be able to predict and review the financial consequences of decisions and actions. This chapter has described various kinds of management decisions in which cost information is used not necessarily as the sole determinant, but generally as one of the key inputs. The chapter also introduced the notion that the choice and computation of cost data will depend on its intended use, an idea that will be discussed further in the next two chapters.

QUESTIONS AND PROBLEMS

1–1. Emmasville had a population of 60,000 permanent residents plus 20,000 students most of the year. Without knowing each other, Charlotte Benson and Tom Harper came to the same conclusion: Emmasville needed a purveyor of super-rich ice cream. Charlotte already ran a snack shop in which ice cream and sherbet were a part of her offerings. Tom came to his conclusion based on his two years' worth of experience delivering pizzas. Charlotte was planning to add the super rich ice cream to her existing line of foods. Tom was planning to start from scratch. Both entrepreneurs forecast sales of about 600 quarts a week.

Charlotte and Tom began working out their pricing strategies with cash flow and profit forecasts. The projected costs they used were not quite the same. Review the categories shown below, and state where you think Charlotte and Tom's figures would be similar and where they would be different. State why.

Cost per Unit of Ice Cream Sold Would Be Similar or Different. Why?

    Ingredients
    Packaging
    Labor
    Occupancy
    Administration
    Marketing
    Other

1–2. The chapter lists five areas in which managers use cost information. Can you think of others?

1–3. The importance of cost in price-setting decisions can vary. Describe two situations in which management is determining the best price for a product or service, one where cost is important and the other where cost has little influence. (Can there be a situation where cost is completely irrelevant?)

1–4. This chapter describes the notion of the "value chain" of activities, each of which is supposed to add value to the product or service. The chapter also says, "What is done in one part of the chain may affect cost and value in other parts." Based on your familiarity with a company or industry, describe two examples of that interdependence.

CHAPTER 2

COSTING PRODUCTS AND PROCESSES

INTRODUCTION

An enterprise incurs costs for many different purposes: for people, material used, electricity, supplies, repairs, new machinery, commissions, and of course for accountants. These costs need to be organized before they can be used in planning and controlling the enterprise. Sometimes costs must be organized and related to organizational units; sometimes the same costs should be related to products or services. In this chapter, we will discuss how those relationships are determined and point out ways in which the method used may affect the usefulness of the resulting cost information.

The notion of cost is powerful and useful, but subject to great confusion. People use the word in many different ways, sometimes without making themselves clear on just what they mean by cost, at least to an outsider. Organizations, like bridge players who are used to playing together, often have conventions that specify meaning—but only to themselves.

We have seen that the expected use of the cost information influences what amounts will be included in the figure labeled cost. Unlike the financial accountant, the management accountant need not be guided by generally accepted accounting principles. When computing product cost, for example, a management accountant may include marketing, distribution, development, and administrative costs that pertain to that product, whereas the financial accountant would include only the manufacturing costs that could be added to inventory. Similarly, in service businesses, the management accountant may be concerned not just with the costs incurred at the point of delivery, but with all the costs supporting the development as well as the delivery of the service.

TYPES OF COSTS

The label cost is usually preceded by a modifier, an important clue as to what the person means by cost. Examples of frequently used modifiers are variable, indirect, overhead, or actual. The modifiers help define what costs are being described, but usually uncertainties remain to be clarified. For example:

1. *Variable costs* are those that are believed to vary with some defined activity base, but the particular activity makes a difference. For example, variable costs may be costs that vary with units produced, labor hours, batches processed, or sales dollars. The costs that vary with units produced are likely to be different from those that vary with batches processed.

2. *Indirect costs* are those that cannot be easily traced to an object being costed. Sometimes the object is the product or service sold to customers, and sometimes it is an organizational unit like the plating department. Costs may be both direct and indirect, depending on the object; the cost of chemicals used in plating, for example, is direct to the plating department, but indirect (not easily traced) with regard to the items being plated.

3. *Overhead costs* are administrative and support costs. Overhead is like indirect cost in that it is not traceable directly to a product, but the term overhead tends to be applied to a wider range of costs,

including administrative, marketing, research, and finance costs. Since no general rules apply, it is important to know in each instance what costs are included.

4. *Actual costs* are not as unambiguous as one would expect. Besides actual direct costs, they often include allocated overhead. Actual costs may be actual units × actual cost or actual units × an estimated cost. They may be historic costs or replacement costs. So take care to understand just what is meant by the phrase actual.

A more extensive listing and definition of various kinds of costs appears at the end of this chapter.

THE EVOLUTION OF COST INFORMATION SYSTEMS

Many companies are modifying their cost systems in order to deal with rapidly changing competitive dynamics. Advanced technologies used in manufacturing and distribution have brought new ways of organizing businesses. For example, just-in-time systems have changed the factory, while bar coding and hand-held computers have changed distribution. Furthermore, increased competitive pressure to satisfy customer needs and preferences has directed attention away from product redesign toward customer service. Indeed, that service may be the most important competitive feature of the product.

The pace and scope of these changes in management attention have raised new kinds of requirements for cost information. These requirements are not for more accuracy, although data-processing capabilities could easily add a few more decimal places. Rather, the new requirements are that cost information systems be shaped by and integrated with the needs of a particular business.

There are three general ways in which management accounting systems are evolving.

1. Development of more *future-oriented* systems. Present systems record and analyze history quite well, but in these times of dynamic change, companies recognize the need to be able to estimate costs for a future that is different from the past.

2. Introduction of a *multifunctional and strategic orientation*. Costing systems are becoming more integrated with the total business, from purchasing to distribution, and with strong attention to customer satisfaction. Costing systems are being designed to serve strategic planning more than financial reporting. They are being called on to answer questions such as the incremental cost of one-day versus two-day delivery, or the cost of achieving a back-order level under 5%.

3. Design of systems to *strengthen a company's control, direction, and motivation*. What gets measured gets attention, so measuring costs becomes one part of a larger system that includes measures of nonfinancial quantities, quality, times, and even customer opinions.

The beginning portion of this chapter describes the basic framework of traditional cost systems. We believe it is important to understand this framework for two reasons: One reason is that this framework describes the system in use in many companies; the other is that where companies have moved beyond the traditional system, the reasons for the changes and the ways their systems have evolved are important. The traditional systems are baselines or reference points for new departures. The last section examines how cost systems have evolved beyond the traditional format.

ORGANIZING COST INFORMATION

Classification of Costs

The development of useful cost information starts with the raw data of day-by-day cost incurrence. The great variety of costs must be organized, put into categories, and summarized so that the results can be used in management decisions.

Costs are usually classified in three ways:

1. By *function* (for example: material, labor, customer service, advertising, rent);

2. By *organizational unit* (for example: machining department, shipping department, quality control section, president's office);

3. By *product or service* (for example: the output of the organization or that which is sold to customers).

Some companies, primarily small ones, classify costs only by functional type. Where there is no inventory, that is the only classification required by the Internal Revenue Service.

Some organizations—particularly service, government, and nonprofit organizations—use only functional and organizational classifications. They set up budgets by department and collect costs in the same departmental groupings. Other firms use only the functional and product categories. Job shops, for example, may collect costs of material, labor, and overhead by job, not attempting to relate those costs to departments. However, most larger companies use all three methods, so that they have data by function, by department, and by product or service.

Chart of Accounts

The way in which an organization categorizes its costs is reflected in its chart of accounts, which is a numbering scheme that codes costs by their category. For example, a small job shop might use the following system.

Chart of Accounts

Functional	*Department*	*Subclass*	*Job*	*Description*
100				Payroll
	110			Payroll in department 1
		111		Full-time hourly payroll
			111-A	Full-time hourly payroll charged to a job A
		112		Part-time hourly payroll, etc.
200				Material
		201		Material in raw material inventory, type 1
		202		Material in raw material inventory, type 2
	210			Material in department 1
		212		Type 2 inventory charged to department 1, etc.
300				Overhead
		301		Utilities
		302		Rent, etc.

In this scheme, the first digit designates the basic function; the second digit shows the organizational unit incurring the cost; the third shows a subclassification; and the letter designates the job that the cost applies to.

Obviously, the system illustrated here is very limited. More elaborate charts of accounts may have as many as sixteen digits in an account number, allowing much greater detail and more ways to summarize costs. In the next parts of this chapter, we will examine in more detail each of the three basic ways of classifying costs. Since all organizations use functional categories, we will review those first. Then we will consider classification of costs by organizational unit, including the process of allocating costs that are common to several units. Then in the next section, we will examine how the costs of products and services are developed.

Relating Costs to Functions

Most manufacturing companies put costs in the following categories. The need to categorize costs by function is driven by a company's need to comply with generally accepted accounting principles for financial accounting purposes. We will see that the categories can be helpful for management decision-making as well.

1. *Manufacturing costs.* These are made up of direct material, direct labor, and manufacturing overhead. They are sometimes called costs incurred under the factory roof or product costs. For financial accounting purposes, manufacturing costs are applied to inventory and are expensed as cost of goods sold when inventory is sold and revenue is recorded.

2. *Selling expenses.* These include advertising, commissions, and the salaries of people handling the marketing function. For financial accounting purposes, these costs are not added to inventory, but are expensed in the period in which they are incurred.

3. *General administrative expenses.* These include top management, staff salaries, office expenses, and all other expenses not directly related to production. For financial accounting purposes, these costs are expensed in the period in which they are incurred.

A merchandising firm would categorize its costs somewhat differently. The following categories are generally used:

1. *Cost of merchandise.* These include inward transportation. For financial accounting purposes, these costs are applied to inventory and are expensed as cost of goods sold when inventory is sold and revenue is recorded.

2. *Direct operating expenses.* These include the cost of operating retail or wholesale outlets, sales salaries and commissions, markdowns, etc. For financial accounting purposes, these costs are expensed in the period in which they are incurred.

3. *General administrative expenses.* These include all other expenses. For financial accounting purposes, these costs are expensed in the period in which they are incurred.

A service operation generally has little or no inventory and consequently would normally include two main categories. For financial accounting purposes, these costs generally are expensed in the period in which they are incurred:

1. *Direct operating expenses.* These are for the costs of activities directly related to providing the service.

2. *General administrative expenses.* These cover all other expenses.

Some service businesses, however, have project costs that have been capitalized, but will be expensed upon certain conditions being met. Examples can include software development cost and the cost of audit services.

Within these general categories, many accounts will provide much more detail. How much detail there should be depends on a cost–benefit tradeoff. For example, is *office supplies* detailed enough, or should paper, pencils, and computer supplies all have separate accounts? Or perhaps *paper supplies* should be broken down further, separating printed letter paper from blank copying paper. Since additional breakdown raises the cost of processing accounts, a clear benefit from greater detail should be foreseen before implementing it.

Functional cost categories are a natural first stage in gathering costs. Though these categories alone do not usually provide sufficient cost information for management's decisions, they are often useful in controlling costs. Functional costs are often used in benchmarking studies. For example, one can compare how much was spent on telephone service or Internet access. Furthermore, the categories, if detailed enough, will contain homogeneous expenses that can be handled as a group (when managers plan ahead) or that can be expected to vary predictably with changes in volume.

Relating Costs to Organizational Units

There are two basic purposes for relating costs to organizational units:

1. *For developing product or service costs.* A product may pass through several departments. A printed circuit board, for example, would pass through the preload department where special components were attached or snapped onto the board; the assembly department where the rest of the components were inserted by machine; the solder department; and finally an inspection and testing department. The cost of the work done in each department would be accumulated to develop the cost of each board. All the costs of the soldering department would be converted to a rate per hour for the soldering machine. The number of boards per hour would then determine the soldering cost per board.

2. *For control purposes.* Accounting systems do not control costs, people do. Ideally, all costs of an enterprise should be related to the person who can be held responsible. Relating costs to an organizational unit is one way of doing this. For example, the manager is in charge of the solder department for a printed circuit board manufacturer, and he is responsible for costs incurred in his department. Costs of several functional types would be under his administration: labor, supplies, machine repair, utilities, etc.

Distributing costs to organizational units is easy for some costs, but hard for others. Labor and materials costs are usually easy, because they are *directly* incurred by a department. Others, such as the cost of heat, industrial engineering, or production supervision, are *indirect* and have to be allocated to a department in some logical way. Some costs may be direct, but impractical to measure; thus they are treated like indirect costs and allocated. For example, one could use a meter to measure the electricity used by each department. Except in rare cases of high consumption, however, the cost of measuring each department is too high to be practical. Instead, the total electricity cost for the plant is allocated to the various departments, perhaps by square footage or the number of machines in each department.

Thus, there are two reasons for collecting costs by department: for product or service costing, and for control purposes. More will be said below about product and service costing. Section 3 of this book discusses designing and implementing management control systems.

RELATING COSTS TO PRODUCTS OR SERVICES

If the purpose of a firm is to sell a product or to provide a service at a profit, then many decisions depend on the cost of that product or service. Developing those costs is a process of relating input costs to output products or services. Most of the costing procedures used in service businesses are similar to those found in manufacturing businesses, except that the service is not inventoried. Indeed, many service businesses use the term "product" to describe the services they provide customers. Banks and hospitals, for example, talk about the profitability of different "product lines."

In manufacturing, generally accepted accounting principles require that the product costs that are used to put a value on inventories or cost of goods sold should be the manufacturing costs, or as we have said, costs under the factory roof. For some purposes, however, such as for a government contract, all—or substantially all—costs may be allocated to products. In those instances, the nonmanufacturing costs, such as administrative and selling costs, are allocated to products in much the same way that manufacturing overhead is allocated. Though this total allocation is sometimes appropriate, we shall confine our discussion to the more common situation in which only manufacturing costs are allocated to products. Similar principles can be used to allocate selling, general, and administrative costs to products or services when the situation warrants.

Defining the Cost Object

Defining the unit to which costs are to be applied, or the *cost object*, can sometimes be a very troublesome area of cost accounting. Where a physical product is being produced, the cost object is usually fairly clear. For example, a ton of steel, an electric motor, and a loaf of bread present few problems. However, an increasing proportion of our business activity produces services: transportation, communication, entertainment, recreation, medicine, law, finance, and education. Cost accounting in those activities is difficult, because the unit of output often is difficult to define. To a railroad, a ton-mile for coal is not the same as a ton-mile for television sets. One minute of telephone conversation in New York City is different from a minute of conversation in Charleston, West Virginia. Half-hour TV shows, surgical operations, and legal cases are not homogeneous items. Such service units don't make very good cost objects. They need further definition or breakdown into smaller segments.

What is often required in service businesses is a more flexible approach to cost accounting. Since the main unit of output cannot generally be stocked in inventory, the cost accounting system is released from having to serve balance sheet requirements. Costing units can take any form that is useful to management, and since all costs are expensed each period, changes in the system will not be constrained by the need for consistency in inventory valuation for financial accounting purposes.

Direct Costs versus Indirect Costs

Costs can be either direct or indirect. A direct cost is a cost that can be easily traced to an object being costed; an indirect cost is a cost that cannot be easily traced to an object being costed, because it is shared by several cost objects. In the previous discussion on relating costs to organizational units, we were concerned with whether costs were direct or indirect to an organizational unit such as a department. Now we are concerned with whether costs are direct or indirect to a product or service. The same costs may be direct to a department, but indirect to a product. Such would be the case with material handlers who work in just one department, but handle all the products that pass through the department.

It is important to distinguish *direct* from *indirect* costs, because they are treated differently in computing product costs. The direct cost of a product is usually easy to compute. For example, the amount of material or hours of labor that go into each item can be derived from specifications or time studies. As a result, direct costs can be easily traced to the product. The indirect costs, however, are much more trouble, because they are shared by a number of products and, hence, must be allocated.

It should also be noted that indirect costs have increased in recent years in proportion to total costs due to manufacturing processes that have become more complex and more automated, with more people working on the production system and fewer on the production line.

Manufacturing Costs: Labor, Material, and Overhead

In the next few sections, we discuss the process of developing product costs in a manufacturing setting. Later, we will examine how service businesses use many of the same processes and where they may differ. We start with manufacturing, because it seems to be easier to understand how a physical product accumulates costs.

Assigning Labor Costs to Products

Separating direct and indirect labor costs. Methods of distinguishing direct from indirect labor costs vary. In manufacturing settings, some labor costs are clearly direct to a product, such as costs for machine operators and assemblers. Other labor costs are clearly indirect, such as costs for production schedulers, industrial engineers, and plant managers. In between are costs for people like material handlers, who could be considered direct if they clocked the time they spent moving each product around the plant. This timekeeping is usually more effort than the information is worth; therefore, labor costs such as those are often considered indirect and are allocated to products along with other indirect labor costs. Thus, the separation of direct from indirect labor costs depends first on *whether the costs can be traced to specific products* and secondly on *whether the benefit that is obtained warrants the effort associated with the required bookkeeping*. In service businesses, the separation process is similar, except that there are often fewer direct costs.

Along with an employee's base wage go fringe benefits, such as vacation and holiday pay, pension costs, social security, and perhaps insurance premiums. Those increments can easily amount to 20% to 30% of base pay. Also, if the employee earns them, there may be overtime pay, shift premiums, or incentive pay. Total compensation will be well above base pay. If the person's work is classified as direct labor, would the additional increment be considered direct labor cost? Strangely enough, many companies treat such additional employment costs as overhead. They do so partly for convenience, since it is often difficult to convert lump sum payments—per person or for the company as a whole—to the costs for each hour that an employee actually worked. Companies also consider these costs to be overhead, because some costs, if considered direct (such as overtime), might unfairly penalize those products that happened to be in production when the cost was incurred.

Direct labor. Direct labor costs can be attached to products in a number of ways. One common method is for each worker to write down the time spent working on a product. Workers can do this in one of two ways.

1. A job ticket or computer readout may accompany each job, which in manufacturing may be 1 item, or a lot of 100 or 1,000 items. When work on the job is completed, a computer terminal on the floor is used to enter such information as job number, operation number, pieces or work completed, and employee number. Productive time or nonproductive time—such as downtime for machine repair or time spent waiting for the next job—may also be entered. The information then automatically goes into computer memory, so that a scheduler or salesperson can recall at any time the status of work-in-process.

2. When several employees work on the same job, workers enter the jobs worked on during the day on their time cards or into a computer terminal. To collect labor hours by job, an accounting clerk or a computer sorts the reported time by job number.

Indirect labor. For labor costs that are not direct, such as the costs of machine adjusters or material handlers, a different system must be used to allocate those costs among different products. One method is to add up all indirect labor costs for a month, or a year, and to determine the ratio of indirect labor costs to direct labor costs for the same period. If department A's indirect labor costs were $20,000 last year and direct labor was $40,000, indirect labor could then be computed for each product at 50% of the actual direct labor cost.

Some manufacturing labor costs are not even direct to production departments. Costs of engineering, maintenance, scheduling, warehousing, and plant security are examples. Since those costs are also applied to products, they too are allocated, first to the production departments and then, along with other departmental indirect labor costs, to the products. We will discuss further the various ways of allocating indirect labor costs to products in the section of this chapter that describes the allocation of overhead.

Assigning Material Costs to Products

Separating direct and indirect material costs. Material costs include both raw materials and purchased parts. After the initial introduction of material, when work starts on a product, other material may be added at later stages. In an automobile manufacturing company, for example, a large number of purchased parts are added in the final stages of assembly.

It is usually easier with material than with labor to decide whether it should be considered a direct cost. If the material ends up in the final product, it will usually be considered direct. If it is applied only to one product, but is destroyed in process, it would also generally be considered direct. But if the material is difficult to trace, is used on a number of products, or is a small part of total cost, it may be considered indirect material and part of overhead that will be allocated among different products. Indirect material may be called *supplies* and can include such items as lubricants, cleaning materials, grinding wheels, and glue.

Direct material. Materials are often bought or requisitioned from storage directly for a specific product. The purchase order, requisition slip, or job ticket will record the information relating the material to a job or product. In that way, the amount of material going into each product (or batch or job) is measured or counted.

Indirect material. Sometimes materials are put into production without being related to a specific product. Steel rods or sheet metal may be put on the production floor and used as needed. Or perhaps compounds are mixed from a variety of raw materials and sent through production, ending up in dozens of different end products. No one can say which end item a particular bit of raw material went into. In those instances, the cost of the material in the end product must be based on the quantity of each material required by design specifications to be in the product and then multiplied by the material's cost. That amount will then be added to the finished goods or cost of goods sold accounts. Determining whether the specified amount was actually used must await a check of the inventories (work-in-process and raw materials) at the end of the period.

Allocating Manufacturing Overhead to Products

What is manufacturing overhead? Manufacturing overhead,[1] which includes indirect labor and indirect material, is generally treated as a product cost, except in certain direct costing or variable costing systems that will be discussed in a later chapter. Overhead is added to the cost of direct labor and direct material to arrive at the total manufactured cost, which is used when costing inventory and calculating costs of goods sold. As products move through the production process, are worked on, and perhaps have material and components added, their cost increases. Some systems add labor, material, and overhead costs after each step; some wait until the item is finished before allocating overhead. In any case, the indirect nature of manufacturing overhead creates a special problem in discovering whatever connections there may be between the overhead cost and the benefit received by the end product—and consequently, what share of total overhead should be charged to each product.

Because manufacturing overhead is allocated to products and general administrative overhead is not, an accounting system must clearly distinguish between the two. Most costs will lie in one or the other category, or *cost pool* as it is often called, but some costs will fall into a gray area for which arguments can be made that costs should go either way.

Clearly, costs relating to running the production operation are part of manufacturing overhead. These costs would include:

1. Production supervision: supervisors and managers;

2. Indirect labor;

3. Supplies;

---

[1] The term *overhead* usually means manufacturing overhead as distinguished from general administrative (overhead) expense and selling expense. Manufacturing overhead is also referred to as *burden,* and the term *indirect costs* usually refers to the same costs that are included in manufacturing overhead.

4. Factory heat, light, power, insurance, and rent;

5. Quality control and manufacturing engineering;

6. Depreciation on plant and equipment;

7. Maintenance and janitorial services.

Clearly, costs related to running the company, but only indirectly related to running the plant are part of general administrative overhead. Some examples of these are:

1. President's salary;

2. Salaries of other officers and office staff, supplies, and cost of occupancy;

3. Financial, legal, and corporate accounting costs;

4. Research and engineering costs not directly related to production.

In the gray area are certain product development costs, costs of accounting and record-keeping, and costs that may be shared by headquarters and the manufacturing plant, such as the costs of building maintenance, utilities, security, and the computer. Some logical method must be developed to allocate those costs to either general administration or manufacturing overhead. And once the system is established, it must be followed consistently, both in planning or budgeting costs and in computing actual costs for the period.

Assigning costs to products or services. The diagram below shows the overall process by which costs are distributed and applied to a unit of product or service. We have discussed material and direct labor, which, because they are direct costs, would follow route A. All the other costs are *manufacturing overhead* and as the diagram shows, would follow different routes. Some overhead costs follow a two-stage process over route B in which they are distributed directly to a production center, and then route E in which they are distributed to products. Included in this category would be the cost of indirect labor, such as material handlers who work in the machining department. Note that while those costs are indirect to the product, they are direct to the machining department. Also included in this category is the cost of indirect material, such as lubricants and glue.

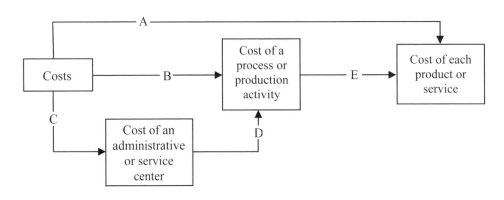

Figure 2–1: *Assigning Costs to Products*

Other manufacturing overhead costs may follow a three-stage distribution process. Route C shows costs that are distributed first to an administrative or service center; then following route D, the costs of those centers are distributed to the production centers, whose costs are finally distributed via route E to products. The accounting and payroll departments are examples of administrative centers, and the heating and maintenance departments are examples of service centers. Once costs of those administrative and service centers are accumulated, the total cost of each center is allocated to the various production departments.

For large companies, the diagram is a simplification, since they are likely to have more than three stages. Also, some companies have reciprocal systems, such as when the accounting department serves the computer department, which, in turn, serves the accounting department. But regardless of complexity, the objective is the same: to enable the measurement of product cost to reflect as well as possible the use of resources.

Methods used in allocating overhead to the production departments. Allocating an overhead cost pool to the departments being served (route D) is often carried out by dividing it in proportion to a known base. The cost of plant administration, for example, might be allocated in proportion to the number of people in the departments served. Here are some examples:

Overhead Cost Pool	*Potential Base Used*
Plant administration	Number of people in the various departments being served
Heat	Square footage of space used by each department
Equipment maintenance	Capital cost of machinery in place in each department
Electric power	Combination of square footage and machine horsepower in each department
Computer cost	Actual usage by departments

The choice of an allocation base is usually focused on one or more of the following criteria:

1. *Benefit received.* Overhead is allocated based on the benefit each department receives. This may be measured through units of service, such as maintenance hours, or through measures of the using department's characteristics that would suggest the amount of benefit received. For example, head count in using departments could be used to distribute the cost of personnel administration.

2. *Cause and effect.* If overhead varies with a measure of activity, that measure of activity is used as a base. For example, supplemental employee benefits (part of overhead) usually vary with payroll.

3. *Traceability.* If an item of overhead can be traced to a department, even though benefit and variability may be undeterminable, that department is allocated all of those overhead costs.

4. *Fairness.* For some overhead items, there is no clear benefit, cause-and-effect relationship, or traceability. In those instances, whatever method seems fair may be used.

5. *Ability to bear.* Some overhead items may be allocated in proportion to the ability of the organizational unit (for example, division) to bear those costs. For example, some corporate administrative costs may be allocated to divisions based on division revenues or division profit.

6. *Simplicity.* An overly complex procedure is both expensive and confusing. Sometimes the simplest way is best.

Allocating production department overhead to products. The final stage of distribution (shown as route E on the diagram) is from the production departments to the individual products. Since the production department's overhead cost is not direct (that is, cannot be directly related or traced to each unit of product), some way must be found to determine each product's share of that cost. The most common method is to distribute the overhead on top of a direct expense as a predetermined percentage of that expense. Labor is the most frequently used direct expense base, although occasionally, factors such as material costs, a combination of expenses, or a direct measure of activity, such as machine hours, may also be used. This base is often referred to as the *allocation base.* In recent years, a new approach to this allocation process has come to be known as activity-based costing. The last section of this chapter describes that system and how companies are applying it.

The procedure is designed to project a relationship between the overhead and the direct expense—or the measure of activity used as a base—and to use that relationship for each product. For example, consider a small manufacturing plant. Total direct labor for 2006 is expected to be $120,000, and manufacturing overhead is projected to be $180,000. For every dollar of direct labor expended on a job in 2006, $1.50 ($180,000 manufacturing overhead ÷ $120,000 direct labor) is tacked on to cover overhead. If product A requires $7.00 of direct labor, $10.50 of overhead will be added to the cost of product A. Product A's material cost of $5.00 will be added to the $7.00 labor cost and the $10.50 overhead to arrive at a total manufacturing cost of $22.50. This amount is added to inventory and the $10.50 is called *absorbed overhead.* It is the amount of overhead incorporated into inventory.

The $1.50 in overhead for each dollar of direct labor is called the *overhead rate.* To develop that number, we had to estimate the amount expected to be spent on both direct labor and manufacturing overhead. This estimate is usually made a year at a time so that the $1.50 or 150% overhead rate would be in effect for a year before being revised. This process usually starts with a sales estimate, which is then converted to required production volume. The required overhead and direct costs are then projected to meet that volume.

Comparison of absorbed overhead with actual overhead costs. One can readily see that for any specific accounting period, the amount of overhead absorbed into inventory using the overhead rate may be different from the actual amount of overhead incurred. This discrepancy would arise if either total actual direct labor or total actual overhead (or both) were different from the estimated amounts of $120,000 and $180,000, respectively. For example, in the following situation, the overhead rate was $1.50 per direct labor dollar:

	Direct Labor	Absorbed Overhead	Actual Overhead	Over- or (under-) Absorbed Overhead
Estimate for 2006	$120,000	$180,000	$180,000	$0
Estimate for each month	10,000	15,000	15,000	0
Actual for January 2006	10,000	15,000	16,000	(1,000)
Actual for February 2006	10,000	15,000	14,500	500
Actual for March 2006	8,000	12,000	14,000	(2,000)
Actual for April 2006	12,000	18,000	16,500	1,500

The right-hand column tells management whether more (or less) overhead was absorbed into inventory than was actually spent. This information tells management whether the estimated relationship ($1.50 per direct labor dollar) was born out by actual results; but if it was not, further analysis will be needed to find out why. This kind of review is called variance analysis. Variance analysis will be discussed in Chapter 3 on standard costing.

The basic purpose of allocating overhead is to arrive at a total manufacturing cost for a product. That total cost figure may be used in many ways, such as to provide a basis for pricing, to estimate costs of expected production, or to modify a product line. Those purposes, it should be noted, require that we have the cost figures before the product is actually made. Thus, we must project costs, including overhead. Of course, overhead allocation is also the basis for the valuation of inventory and cost of goods sold. Not to worry, though. The amount of over- (under-) absorbed overhead will be accounted for in the financial statements at the end of the period.

Because there are many acceptable ways of allocating overhead, and because overhead itself is an indirect cost and hence may or may not vary directly with volume or product changes, the resulting product cost figure should be used with caution in predicting overall cost changes. Chapter 4, which discusses relevant costs, will examine more fully the use of costs in various management decisions.

Job Costing and Process Costing

Having reviewed the general procedure for relating costs to products, let us now examine more specifically the two primary ways this can be carried out: job costing and process costing. Job costing systems are most useful where there are distinct units of production, such as a customer's order, a production lot of 1,000 pieces for inventory, or one office building. Work on each of those jobs has a clear beginning and ending, and frequently the job requires a unique set of operations to differentiate it from other jobs.

Process costing systems are used where production is continuous and there are no jobs requiring a different set of operations. For example, oil refineries, flour mills, electrical generating plants, and chemical processing businesses are likely to use process costing systems.

Job Costing Systems

In job costing, records are kept that show how much material and labor went toward making each job, batch, or order. Overhead may then be added on as a percentage of labor or of some other allocation base. When the job is finished, management can be fairly accurate in assessing what an item actually costs. Of course, if overhead is over- or under-absorbed during the period, the overhead applied to each job will not be correct. Aside from that limitation, however, job costing systems that record actual material and labor quantities produce fairly accurate costs per job.

The core of a job costing system is the *job sheet*. On this form are recorded the actual amounts of material, labor, and overhead expended on a job. A simplified job sheet is illustrated next:

Job Sheet

Job No. 437

Date started   4/5/06
Date finished   4/8/06

Materials:

Bar stock	250	feet at	$4.00	*Extension*	$1,000.00
Sheet stock	35	feet at	9.00		315.00
Fittings	2,024	at	0.85		1,720.40

Labor:

Dept. A	17	hrs. at	6.30		107.10
Dept. B	5	hrs. at	4.35		21.75

Overhead:

Dept. A	212% of labor dollars		227.05
Dept. B	145% of labor dollars		31.54

Total manufacturing cost:			3,422.84
Number of good pieces completed:	1,000	*Cost per piece*	3.42

Of course, the job sheet illustrated is fairly simple. And most job sheets today are maintained electronically rather than in paper form. Still, they collect the same information.

There are many varieties of job costing systems. Job costing systems can be found in both small and large operations. Job costing can be used with small jobs, as would be found in a machine shop or printing company. In such business, a worker or machine will complete one job and start another within a day or at least every few days. At the local tire shop each job is tracked. Sometimes a machine shop may have many jobs in process at one time, and each worker and machine may be devoted to several jobs during the course of a day. The objective is still the same: to record actual times and costs spent on each job.

Job costing can also be used with large jobs, such as construction projects or shipbuilding. A job in those businesses may last well over a year. The system used in the construction or shipbuilding industry accumulates vast numbers of different costs over long periods of time, often more than a year. When the project is finished, a review can be made to see how costs came out in relation to the costs estimated at the time of the original bid. Though an identical project would probably not be encountered again, parts of projects (laying brick, welding plates, or excavating dirt) are often sufficiently similar from one job to the next to make past cost records helpful in predicting costs of future operations.

Process Costing Systems

In a process costing system, the cost of running a production facility for a given length of time is divided by the number of units produced in the period to obtain a production cost per unit. The length of time is usually significant, perhaps a week or a month, but it can be any length. This type of system is most useful in situations where similar items are produced for long periods of time, such as chemical plants, oil refineries, or cement factories.

In the job costing systems previously described, production costs are collected for work done on a job, which may be one piece of work or a batch of 1,000 similar items. The job defines the limits of cost applicability. Direct material and direct labor used on the job or batch are measured and costed. Overhead is usually applied as a percentage of direct labor.

In process costing, the job is the production work accomplished during a period of time. The time period, therefore, defines the basic costing unit. The cost per unit of product is found by dividing the total cost of production during the time period by the units produced during that period.

Process costing systems tend to be used in large production facilities designed to produce one product. In such instances, all costs associated with the facility are direct to the product. Most of manufacturing overhead, for example, will be direct cost. If a flour mill produces one type of flour, all costs of the mill—direct labor, depreciation, supplies, and the superintendent—are direct costs. One should note, however, that although they are direct, they are not necessarily variable with volume.

Process costing can also be used for small operations. A single punch press may work continuously on one component used in a variety of end products made by a company. The cost of running the press for a month divided by the pieces produced would be the cost per piece.

A company is sometimes faced with a decision of whether to shift from a process to a job costing system. For example, if a paper company decides to expand its line from one grade of paper to several, and because of differing machine speeds, wants to know the costs for each grade, it will probably collect the times spent on each grade. What had been a system that computed the unit cost of a month's production becomes a system of computing the unit cost per grade. The job becomes that which was produced in the time spent on each grade.

A decision to go the other way, from job costing to process costing, may also be made on occasion. A department that produces a variety of small stamped parts that are costed by batches may find that costing is simpler if total department costs are related to pounds of stampings produced per month. If the stampings are sufficiently similar, the result will be almost as accurate as job costing, and it will no longer be necessary to record the time spent on each part.

Partially Completed Production

In a machine shop using a job costing system, there are likely to be partly completed jobs at the beginning and end of each month. In such a situation, overhead is normally absorbed by this work in process according to the amount of work done on each job. A job with 10 labor hours expended on it would absorb $15 of overhead if $1.50 per labor hour were the applicable overhead rate. If 20 labor hours are used during the following month to finish the job, it will absorb another $30 of overhead the next month and be put into finished goods inventory with a total of $45 of overhead included in its cost. Thus, in job costing systems, there is no particular problem in accounting for partially completed jobs.

With process costing systems, however, this accounting is more difficult. The actual cost of units produced is computed by relating cost inputs for the period to unit outputs for the period. If work in process changes significantly, the cost per unit computed in this way can be distorted. If an increase in work in process is not recognized, the cost per unit of output will be too high, because much of the cost incurred during the period went toward that increase in work in process, and only some of the cost incurred went into the units completed.

In process costing systems, when inventory changes are expected to be significant, *equivalent units of production* are often used to compensate. This method considers the amount of work in process and its extent of completion at the beginning and at the end of the period. If 4,000 units were three-quarters finished at the beginning of the period, they represented 3,000 equivalent units. If at the end of the period there are 8,000 units, half finished, they represent 4,000 equivalent units. If 7,000 units were completed and transferred to finished goods, the work actually done during the period was:

1. To finish the partly completed beginning inventory of 4,000 units;

2. To start and finish 3,000 units;

3. To do some work on 8,000 more units so that they are half finished. The diagram below shows this work.

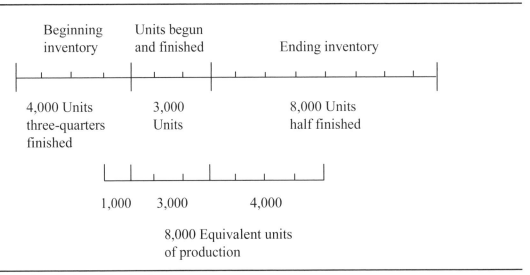

Figure 2–2: *Equivalent Units of Production*

The accounting process would compute the equivalent units as follows:

Units transferred to finished goods	7,000
− Equivalent units in beginning inventory	− 3,000
+ Equivalent units in ending inventory	+ 4,000
= Equivalent units of production for the period	8,000

Then, the costs incurred during the period would be divided by the 8,000 equivalent units of production to determine the cost per unit. Material cost will also be part of this computation. In many instances, material cost and labor cost are added at different times. Material may all be added at the start, while labor may be added during the process. Thus, the material equivalent units of production may well differ from the labor equivalent units in the same period. Consequently, labor and material are usually handled in separate computations.

Product Costing in Services Compared with Manufacturing

Having presented the basic costing processes used in manufacturing, a question emerges: In what ways is costing similar and in what ways is costing different in service businesses? To help present some specifics we will refer to three illustrative service businesses:

- Bank;

- Airline;

- Auto repair shop.

Defining the Cost Object

Defining the cost object, or the service product, is often more difficult in service businesses than in manufacturing. The service product is less tangible and sometimes has many variations to be considered. Nevertheless, a service business provides one or more services for which it expects to receive revenue, and however they may be defined, those services can be considered objects to be costed.

A bank provides a variety of services: checking accounts, mortgages, auto loans, letters of credit, and many more. Each can be considered a service product.

An airline provides passenger transportation and a number of related services, such as ticket sales, baggage handling, and, of course, passenger handling. Some of those services do not by themselves produce revenue, but act as support services. As such, they have a service product (tickets sold, bags handled, etc.) that can be costed as if it were an end product.

An auto repair shop provides a variety of repair services. Although many are standard jobs (for example, replacing brake shoes or a water pump), other repair jobs are unique for the particular problem that is being repaired. Thus, the cost objects of a repair shop are likely to be a combination of standard and nonstandard repair jobs.

Separation of Direct and Indirect Costs

Like manufacturing, services have both direct and indirect costs, although the usual absence of material cost will significantly reduce direct costs.

A bank's direct costs of checking accounts will be small since there are few people or assets devoted solely to checking accounts. The checking account service will therefore share the cost of tellers, ATMs, and transaction-processing facilities with other services. Likewise, for other services, most of the people and facilities are shared and hence are indirect.

In an airline, there can also be a separation, but what is direct or indirect depends on the cost object. What is direct for a route flown four times a day may be indirect (shared) for a particular flight. Fuel, pilot, and flight attendant costs may be the only direct costs of a flight, leaving other costs to be based on allocation.

In an auto repair shop, the direct cost of parts and labor will be a significant part of total cost. Other costs are indirect and will have to be added to the direct costs, usually embedded in the cost per part and in the labor rate applied to actual hours.

Thus, in services as in manufacturing, direct costs are those that can be traced directly to the cost object. It might also be noted that because in services there is no inventory of manufactured products, there is also no requirement to separate production costs from administrative costs.

Allocation of Indirect Costs

In service businesses, the allocation of indirect costs to cost objects may be more difficult than in manufacturing, but the process is similar. Figure 2–1 shown earlier applies in the service setting as well as in manufacturing. The final distribution to cost objects will use a variety of allocation bases, such as loans; accounts or transactions for a bank; tickets sold or flights for an airline; and labor hours in the auto repair shop.

Job and Process Costing in Service Industries

Both types of costing may be used in service businesses, although process costing is probably more common. The bank and airline will likely use process costing, assuming that loans and flights on a route are homogeneous. In the repair shop where jobs are not homogeneous, job costing will be used to keep track of the labor hours applied to each job.

Comparison Summary

From the foregoing discussion we can see that the basic structure of product costing systems in manufacturing and services are similar. Once the cost objects are defined, it is a matter of tracing direct costs and allocating the indirect costs to the cost objects.

Until recently, service businesses have been slow to develop costs for their services. There are probably many reasons for that, but high on the list is the difficulty of defining the service product and the work required to allocate in a reasonably accurate way the high proportion of indirect costs. Recently the availability of electronic data management together with the activity-based costing approach (described later in this chapter) have encouraged the development of service-product costs.

Matrix Costing

More and more companies are using matrix management techniques to focus attention in several related directions at once. For example, consumer products companies combine product line marketing as one dimension of the matrix with production management as a second dimension. The product line manager is at the interface between the customer-oriented marketing function and the efficiency-oriented production function. Both the production and marketing functions require cost and performance measures that will tell how that function is being performed. The product manager's job is to combine those sets of measures to reach overall objectives. The links, therefore, need to be built into the information system.

In the banking area, Citibank has developed both product profitability statements and relationships profitability analyses. Products are various kinds of loans, mortgages, deposit accounts, credit cards, and financial services. Relationships are defined by a single customer using a variety of services, or groups of customers with similar characteristics, such as demographics, location, mix of products and services used, size of accounts, and numbers of transactions. For example, all the business a customer does with Citibank will be included in that customer's relationship. Or a classification of customers, such as a retail customer located in Manhattan, may be the relationship's focus. Then by combining the product and customer perspectives, Citibank develops an "evolving process of relationship management." The process draws on a continuing analysis of competitors' moves and in turn influences pricing, marketing, and strategic investment decisions.

Each dimension of the matrix focuses on a different cost object or definition of output. Often, one dimension is product- or production-oriented, and the second dimension is market- or customer-oriented. Each orientation can influence the other, through volume–cost relationships, product- or service-design decisions, or marketing and distribution strategy. The cost system design will need to anticipate the interplay in order to provide the matrix manager with the information needed.

STRATEGIC PRODUCT COSTING AND ABC

Strategic Product Costing[2]

Strategic product costing is a process of relating costs to products and services in ways that help companies formulate and review strategy. Strategic product costing is not a brand new approach. Elements of the process have been around for a long time, although sometimes with different names. More attention is now being paid to product and service costing, however, and a shift has occurred in costing systems toward a strategic perspective. The reasons for this new attention derive from the distinctive features of strategic product costing. The three most important features are:

1. *Supports strategic decision-making.* Whereas traditional product or service costing methods have been designed for inventory valuation and financial reporting, strategic product costing is designed primarily to support strategic decision-making. The strategies may focus on products or services (for example: product-line profitability and its impact on pricing and product mix decisions); or may involve characteristics of products (for example: custom design versus standardization); distribution strategy (for example: wholesale versus retail); integration strategy (for example: make versus buy, or outsource); and marketing strategies (for example: push versus pull). A strategic choice may involve many functions; the choice between a low cost or a product differentiation strategy, for example, would have an impact on product design, production, distribution, and marketing. And most important, the strategic-costing process starts with the customer's perspective on value and gathers information that helps to provide value to the customer. Thus, strategic costing is designed to measure the cost impact of strategic choices.

   Strategic costing is not designed simply to allocate costs to products, but instead is designed to capture the causal relationship between output characteristics or activities and the costs that are caused—or at least influenced—by those characteristics; those latter are called *cost drivers*. Where direct costs are concerned, the cost driving relationship is usually clear. Production of a 6-foot item, for example, will drive twice as much material as a 3-foot item if the other dimensions are the same. Less clear, however, are the ways in which output characteristics drive indirect costs. Complexity of the product shape may drive additional design and setup time. Length of run will drive the amount of setup time per piece produced (the shorter the run, the higher the setup cost per piece). Customer relationships will drive the costs of customer service.

2. *Takes a longer-term view.* In reflecting these causal relationships, strategic costing takes a long-run view. The traditional separation of fixed and variable costs focuses on the short run;

---

[2] Parts of this section are drawn from William Rotch, "Strategic Product Costing," *Strategic Cost Analysis: Implementing Activity-Based Costing,* Frank Collins, ed. (New York, New York: Executive Enterprises, Inc., 1991), 6.

therefore, those costs that will not change much in the short run or with small changes are considered fixed and not relevant. Such a separation of fixed and variable costs is perfectly reasonable for those short-run, small-change decisions that won't change those costs designated as fixed. For decisions involving the longer term or bigger changes, however, those so-called fixed costs don't stay fixed. Strategic decisions tend to be long-run, so the costing process is challenged to discover and measure the links between strategic decisions and those fixed costs.

Thus, strategic costing identifies the ways output characteristics influence or drive costs, and does not make the traditional separation between fixed and variable costs, which assumes that units or sales volume are the cost drivers. However, when strategic costing identifies other drivers, such as complexity, runs, or customer characteristics, the notion of variability and the separation of fixed and variable cost changes dramatically. Costs are now seen to vary with a variety of cost drivers, though that variability may be over a long period of time.

3. *Focuses on costs' relevance to decision-making.* With strategic costing in manufacturing settings, the scope of relevant costs is not limited to manufacturing costs. The scope is as broad and comprehensive as the strategies. Therefore, marketing, distribution, administrative, or other costs may be relevant when considering decisions. *Relevance is determined not by what costs can be inventoried by following generally accepted accounting practices, but by the identification of links between strategic decisions and costs.*

Consider, for example, that a manufacturer of electrical fuse boxes is reviewing the profitability of channels of distribution. Except for a few large builders, most of the customers are electrical wholesalers. The manufacturer continually receives requests from small builders, however, for direct shipments that will have larger discounts than those provided by the wholesaler. Would it be profitable to sell direct?

The manufacturer typically recognizes selling and distribution expenses as a percentage of sales, using an average percentage for all sales. For small orders shipped directly to contractors, however, an average will not capture the particular cost-driving characteristics of that channel. Order-processing expense per dollar of sales would be higher on those small orders than with other orders; backorders may be more frequent; even the accounting department, usually considered a fixed administrative expense, will be affected by an increase in billing and collection activity. Even though those selling and administrative costs are normally considered fixed and not relevant to changes in strategy, they are likely to be changed over time by the cost-driving characteristics of a new distribution strategy. Strategic costing tries to identify the costs of those potential changes and to factor them into the decision-making process.

What Caused the Increased Attention to Strategic Costing?

None of the strategic costing concepts is entirely new. What, then, has caused the increased attention to strategic costing? Changes in three areas seem to have raised its importance.

1. Indirect costs have increased while direct labor has decreased, creating the potential for large inaccuracies in product costing if indirect costs are distributed using an allocation base, such as direct labor, that does not cause those costs to be incurred. Labor may be only 10% to 15% of total costs, and overhead three or four times that.

2. Managers have begun to realize that traditional costing methods can provide misleading estimates of the cost of individual products or services. If some products are overcosted and others undercosted, the errors will largely wash out and net profit will be fairly accurate. So, in the past, as long as product costing was mainly designed to serve financial statement presentation, firms

had little incentive to refine the accuracy of product costing. With new competitive pressures, firms now need more accuracy to analyze product groups or alternative strategies.

3. Improvement in technology allows the development of more sophisticated cost systems at a lower cost. So, where the cost of a more sophisticated system previously may have outweighed its benefit, that is often no longer the case.

Because of those changes, accurate costing has become more important and attainable. As product mixes changed with new competitors or new strategies, some companies discovered that more accurate costing could lead to changed strategies, enabling them to focus on the businesses that—over time—were the most profitable. Their improved cost systems actually became part of their competitive arsenal.

Activity-Based Costing

Activity-based costing (ABC) is one of the primary ways in which strategic costing is implemented. ABC is a method by which costs are related to output characteristics or activities, which in turn result from strategic choices. So ABC is a means of relating costs to strategy, or more importantly, defining how strategy drives costs.[3]

The ABC Process

There are two phases in developing the cost of products or services. One phase deals with direct or traceable costs, and the other with indirect costs. The indirect costs are distributed to products or services in at least two stages. (See Figure 2–3.)

---

[3] A number of articles have described the design of ABC systems. An early and comprehensive discussion is provided in Robin Cooper's four-part series called "The Rise of Activity-Based Costing" in the *Journal of Cost Management,* "Part One: What is an Activity-Based Cost System?" (Summer 1988): 45–53; "Part Two: When Do I Need an Activity-Based Cost System?" (Fall 1988), 41–48; "Part Three: How Many Cost Drivers Do You Need, and How Do You Select Them?" (Winter 1989), 34–54; "Part Four: What Do Activity-Based Cost Systems Look Like?" (Spring 1989), 38–49. Note also these other important articles on ABC systems: Robin Cooper and Robert S. Kaplan, "Measure Costs Right: Make the Right Decisions," *Harvard Business Review* (September–October 1988), 96–105; and Robin Cooper and Robert S. Kaplan, "Profit Priorities from Activity-Based Costing," *Harvard Business Review* (May–June, 1991), 130–135.

Applications and implementation of ABC are described in the following articles: Michael W. Roberts and Katherine J. Silvester, "Why ABC Failed and How It May Yet Succeed," *Journal of Cost Management* (Winter 1996), 23–35; Michael D. Shields and Michael A. McEwen, "Implementing Activity-Based Costing Systems Successfully," *Journal of Cost Management* (Winter 1996), 15–22; Christopher Dedera, "Harris Semiconductor ABC: Worldwide Implementation and Total Integration," *Journal of Cost Management* (Spring 1996), 44–58; Neal R. Pemberton, Logan Arumugam, and Nabil Hassan, "ABM at Dayton Technologies: From Obstacles to Opportunities; Our most difficult challenge was reducing the complexity of our processes and procedures and convincing managers of the benefits of activity-based costing," *Management Accounting* (March 1996), 20–27; Mary Lee Geishecker, "New Technologies Support ABC; Computer hardware/software innovations are helping to deliver the promise of activity-based costing," *Management Accounting* (March 1996), 42–48.

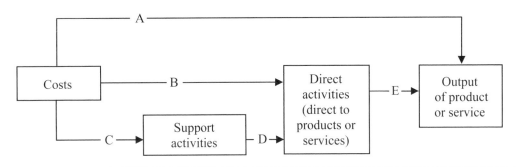

Figure 2–3: *Distributing Costs to Outputs*

Direct activities are those that can be directly related to products or services. Machining and assembly departments are traditional examples. Support activities, such as engineering or maintenance, provide support for the direct activities. The term "direct activities" is used here, because those activities work *directly* on products. The costs of direct activities are often defined in a traditional cost system as indirect to a specific product, but an ABC system tries to identify direct links to products. ABC focuses mainly on two elements of the process: definition of the direct activities, and the basis on which those activities are charged to products.

Consider the following example:

The Setup Company

The Setup Company planned to produce 10,000 units of many similar items. As shown below, the total projected costs amounted to $1,000,000, so the average cost per unit was $100. Products were generally produced in batches of different colors, and the projected costs of a large and a small batch are shown below at the right.

	Total Costs Projected for 10,000 Units	Per Unit	Item A (red) One Batch of 1,000 Units	Item B (purple) One Batch of 10 Units
Material	$ 300,000	$ 30	$ 30,000	$ 300
Labor	100,000	10	10,000	100
Overhead	600,000	60	60,000	600
Total	$1,000,000	$100	$100,000	$1,000
			$100 each	$100 each

When the company controller came back from an educational seminar, she discovered that about a third of the $600,000 overhead expense supported activities that were caused by batches—activities like setup, material movement, inspection of first pieces, and production reporting. The same batch-related activity would take place no matter how many units were run. She also noted that since 50 batches were expected, the batch-related cost per batch would be $4,000 ($200,000 ÷ 50). The remaining $400,000 of overhead would be treated as before. She then set about revising the cost per unit for a large and a small batch, allocating the remaining $400,000 of overhead as before on the basis of direct labor.

The result of her revised product costs were as follows:

	Item A One Batch of 1,000 Units	Item B One Batch of 10 Units
Material	$30,000	$ 300
Labor	10,000	100
Batch cost	4,000	4,000
Other overhead	40,000	400
Total cost	$84,000	$4,800
Cost per unit	$ 84	$ 480

This approach assumes there are two activities: One is preparing for the run of a batch of units, and the other is producing the units. The driver of the first activity is the batch, and the driver of the second activity is the units produced.

As one would expect, the revised system shows that units produced in large batches cost less per unit and units in small batches cost more per unit. What is often surprising is how much higher the unit costs are in small batches.

Note that to carry out this costing process, one has to have or gather some data that were not previously used: costs per unit of activity (in this case, cost per batch) and units of output per unit of activity (in this case, units of product per batch). Though new information may have to be generated, it often exists but must be sorted out by computer.

Defining Direct Activities

The key to such an ABC system's usefulness is in the definition of direct activities and in the links between direct activities and output. If the activities are too narrow, the full power of the system won't be captured. Such would be the case if the activity in the above example were described as "setup." Only the cost of the setup process—personnel, machines, supplies, etc.—would then be captured. The narrow definition would exclude other costs that, like setup, are incurred once per run—inspection, inventory movement, etc. A more appropriate activity in the above example would be producing a batch. That definition of activity would capture the costs of the other batch-related activity, such as material movement, inspection, and production reporting.

The definition of direct activities also must recognize the links to output (arrow E in Figure 2–3) that are keyed to output cost drivers. In the example, there are two activity drivers: the batch and the unit. The batch-making activity costs $4,000 per batch, which is the costing link between the batch-making activity and output. The unit-making activity costs $40 per piece (overhead cost), and that is the cost link between the unit-making activity and output.

Companies working on revisions of their cost systems are experimenting with many different definitions of direct activities. One basic set of activities, advocated by Professors Robin Cooper and Robert Kaplan, focuses on four levels:[4]

---

[4] Robin Cooper, Robert S. Kaplan, *Cost & Effect: Using Integrated Cost Systems to Drive Profitability and Performance* (Boston: Harvard Business School Press, 1998); Robin Cooper, Robert S. Kaplan, *The Design of Cost Management Systems*, 2nd ed. (Saddle River, New Jersey: Prentice Hall, 1999).

1. Activities driven by units;

2. Activities driven by batches or runs;

3. Activities driven by the existence of the product line, and that would not be needed if the product line were not offered (product-line sustaining activities);

4. Activities needed to support the overall business (business-sustaining activities).

The cost of the first three activities would be distributed to products based respectively on units, batches, and some measure of overall product-line activity. Since the cost of the fourth type of activity is not driven in a meaningful way by the products, it would not be distributed at all. This hierarchy is not a new idea, but in the context of strategic costing, it can have a powerful meaning.

Other definitions of direct activity are also being used. Activity caused by product complexity is one. Several companies, for example, have related costs to the number of different part numbers. A complex product, then, is one that uses many different part numbers. Because each part number drives a variety of costs—such as for recording specifications, stocking, and processing—the cost per part number is a way of costing the complexity of the product. If a standard part can be substituted for a unique part without incurring much extra cost, thereby reducing the number of part numbers, the costs that are driven by part numbers can be reduced over time.

Some direct activities are oriented to customers rather than to production characteristics. A printing company, for example, recognizes that some customers require more service than others. Some of its customers are content to submit copy and review proofs at suitable stages. Others insist on following the process step by step; one customer even sends a person to be present in the plant while the job is being run, even if that means sleeping on the site. The customer's presence forces the printing company to also have a customer representative on hand. Servicing this customer is thus more costly in relation to sales than servicing the average customer.

When customer-oriented activities are considered, the product is defined as "work done for customer X." Most sales and customer service departments know that some customers require more work than others. By developing costs for the customer service activity, the firm will know something about how much or how little it costs to serve various customers. The actual difference in costs may come as a surprise.

ABC was at first seen as an enhanced process of accounting, one that created many more pools of overhead costs to be distributed to products using a variety of appropriate allocation bases. However, many companies have recognized that the characteristics of products and services they provided for customers were really drivers of activities that in turn caused costs to be incurred as illustrated in Figure 2–4. Instead of following the traditional view that the "glob" of overhead costs had to be allocated to products and services, the attention was reversed. The arrows shown earlier in Figure 2–3 should go from right to left. And furthermore, the diagram should show a customer who has desires and preferences that influence the characteristics of output.

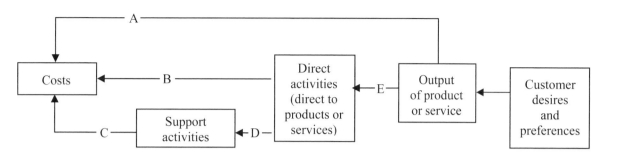

Figure 2–4: *Characteristics of Output*

Shaping the Product Definition to Match Strategic Choices

As stated earlier, strategic costing is designed to develop cost information that relates to strategic choices. The process involves identifying output characteristics that are influenced by strategy and that cause activities to be performed that drive costs in different ways. These output characteristics are not just the physical characteristics of the product, but involve the total business process of serving the customer. The two columns below show how the same basic product can be defined in different ways to capture the different cost-driving characteristics of what is provided to the customer.

One Product Definition	*Another Product Definition*
A basic product sold in one model	A basic product sold in many models
Products and services provided to customers in Virginia	Products and services provided to customers in the European Union
Products and services provided using channel A (wholesalers)	Products and services provided by using channel B (direct sales)
Products and services provided to customer X	Products and services provided to customer Y
Products and services provided with 24-hour response time	Products and services provided with 5-day response time

Analysis of the different products, both costs and revenues, can be viewed as a large matrix whose columns represent alternative product definitions and whose rows represent activities and costs. Each cell in the matrix represents the costs driven by the column's particular product. The bottom line, then, would be profitability by each defined product.

The approach is particularly suitable for analyzing the impact of strategies on the stream of activities from product development to product delivery. It also helps management focus on customers, the market, and what goes on outside a company's walls.

This format is used in various forms by a number of companies. The Citibank example described earlier showed how the bank uses a customer oriented definition. The bank's data system can identify services used by each large customer (columns); each service draws on (or drives) a set of activities within the bank (rows); and the bottom line is customer profitability. As described earlier, this information becomes an important part of a strategy called relationship management. The bank also uses a matrix in which the columns are different lines of business, and the bottom line shows the line of business profitability. Both matrices are extensions of ABC, using characteristics of customers and product lines as drivers of activities and costs throughout the bank.[5]

The Usefulness of Strategic Costing

The development of strategic cost information by using ABC has a cost. Theoretically, developing it is worth doing when the benefits exceed the cost.[6] That balance can be determined only when costs and benefits are known, however, and many companies face a kind of catch-22: until the information is developed, they don't know its cost and benefit, but developing the information requires them to plunge ahead.

Some intuitive signs can help a company decide whether to start the process of developing an ABC system. First, *diversity* is perhaps the most important component. A company that produces a homogeneous product is not likely to benefit as much from ABC, because the process aims to measure the differences in resources required by different products in ways that traditional systems do not measure. Second, if the allocation base on which a company distributes overhead to products, such as direct labor, is not a good indication of resources used by different products, ABC may provide a better measure of the way products use resources. Third, even where there are differences among products, if those differences do not involve costs of some magnitude, the new information won't be very valuable. Fourth, when the proportion of costs represented by overhead is large, then the choice of allocation base can have a large effect on the resulting product costs. So, ABC may have a larger benefit. Finally, the competitive environment can make a difference. If competition is relatively weak, improved knowledge of costs may not have a significant influence on strategy.

In summary, when a company produces heterogeneous products that use resources differently, when a traditional allocation base like direct labor is not a good indication of resources used, when overhead is a large proportion of total costs, when significant costs are involved, or where competition is present or on the horizon, ABC can produce valuable new information.

This intuitive approach is often the best way to start consideration of an ABC system. In taking a further step, many companies have discovered that a complete changeover is not necessarily required. Parts of an operation may be picked off for special treatment. The part to be analyzed might be a single production section or one function, such as setup or customer service. See, for example, the Setup Company example cited earlier. The batch-related functions would be chosen because diversity of resource use seemed greatest in that portion of the overall operation. Here are some examples:

1. One company focused on the costs associated with the number of part numbers. Overhead costs associated with handling part numbers were isolated and distributed to products according to their number of part numbers. The rest of overhead was distributed as it had been before. In this way, the company attached costs to one *known* cause of diversity.

2. Another company that made circuit boards knew that some designs required hand-insertion of components, whereas other designs allowed automatic insertion. Before the analysis was

---

[5] The system was described by Kenneth O. Danilo, controller, Northeast Banking Division Citicorp, at the American Accounting Association's Management Accounting Symposium (March 15–17, 1990) in Atlanta, Georgia.

[6] See Robin Cooper, "You Need a New Cost System When..." *Harvard Business Review* (January–February 1989), 77–82.

undertaken, no distinction had been made in costs, because both types of insertion were performed in the same department. An average cost was used. The analysis separated the costs of the two types of insertions and computed the cost per inserted component. All the other costs remained undisturbed.

3. A hospital recognized that the total cost of the nursing service represented more than half the day rate in most units. (Therefore, the money involved was significant.) It also noted that—even within a unit—some patients required more attention from nurses than others; so diversity was present. The hospital had installed a system that measured the approximate nursing hours needed per patient each day (using a measure of acuity or severity of condition), and with that information, a patient could be charged the appropriate amount. Instead of about $500 a day in the critical care unit, for example, patients were charged from $385 to about $935 a day, depending on their requirements. The rest of the hospital's cost system was unchanged.

Sometimes the cost of a strategic-costing system may be low, because most of the data to install it already exists, and programming is required to extract and sort the data. In the hospital example just cited, the acuity-rating system was already in place as an aid to staffing decisions for the nurses; an interface with the existing financial information was all that was needed for strategic costing.

In other instances, interviews may be needed to determine how much time is spent on different activities so that the link between support activities and direct activities can be identified (arrow D in Figure 2–3). This sort of data gathering is expensive, but it may uncover the absorption of unexpectedly large amounts of time by certain activities and products and, in the long run, lead to opportunities for changed strategy or reduced costs.

The more complex a cost system is, the more the system is likely to cost, and often the harder it will be to interpret the results. If the system is too simple or aggregated, however, the results may not reflect the diversity among different products. "The challenge for designers," said two people who worked on systems design for General Motors, "is to choose resource categories, activity centers, and cost drivers that provide a level of detail that matches the need managers have for information."[7]

Summary

In this chapter, we have examined the framework of how costs are organized for use by management. Costs usually appear first in functional categories, such as salaries, supplies, and electricity. A coding system or chart of accounts is used to group the costs so they can relate to management's concerns. One grouping relates costs to organizational units or defined activities. Another grouping relates costs to the products or services that the firm is providing its customers. Other groups may be used to relate customer service costs to different customers.

Costs that are direct to organizational units or to products are easily traced to those units or products. Costs that are not direct must be allocated. The chapter showed that there are often two or more stages to that allocation process. In the last stage of traditional costing systems, an overhead rate is used with a direct cost base such as labor—or some other direct input such as machine hours.

---

[7] George J. Beaujion and Vinod R. Singhal, "Understanding the Activity Costs in an Activity-Based Cost System," *Journal of Cost Management* (Spring 1990): 55.

In service businesses, the development of service product costs follows the same structure as in manufacturing: tracing direct costs to services and allocating indirect costs. Though similar, the process is often more complex because of the difficulty in defining the service or cost object and because of the high proportion of indirect costs in most service businesses.

In a matrix form of organization, cost information must be organized in several ways, so as to focus on production efficiency, product-line profitability, and customer relationships. The various dimensions need to be linked, so that the manager at the interface has the required information to make decisions that affect the several dimensions simultaneously.

In the section on strategic costing, we examined how companies relate the product-costing process to product and marketing strategy. A company's strategy shapes what it offers customers; that, in turn, affects costs. We described activity-based costing as a way to identify the cost-driving characteristics of output through the definition of activities that incur costs.

This, then, is the basic framework for costing products and services. Making the framework provide accurate, relevant cost information for a variety of management functions and decisions will be the subject of subsequent chapters.

Kinds of Costs

Categorized by what the expenditure buys:

Prime cost:	Direct material and direct labor.
Overhead:	Costs that are not prime costs (for example: support, administrative, and occupancy costs).
Burden:	Another word for overhead; usually means factory overhead.
Manufacturing cost:	Costs caused by the manufacturing activity; does not include administrative or selling costs.
Joint cost:	When a process produces two or more products and one cannot be produced without the other, the cost of that process is a joint cost of the products.
Standard cost:	A projected cost per unit of product or for other units such as machine hours or pounds of raw material purchased.
Absorbed cost:	The amount of material, labor, and overhead that is added to (absorbed by) inventory.
Product cost:	Costs that are added to inventory or cost of goods sold; manufacturing costs are usually product costs.
Period cost:	Costs that are not added to inventory, but are expensed during the period in which they are incurred. Selling and administrative costs are usually period costs.

Categorized by how cost is related to what is being costed:

Direct cost:
: Cost that can be traced to a specific cost object (for example: a product or an organizational unit).

Indirect cost:
: Cost that cannot be traced directly to a cost object, and is attributed to that cost object by means of allocation.

Categorized by what causes the cost to change:

Variable cost:
: Usually means a cost that varies with units, machine hours, or sales dollars, but variability can be caused by other things such as batches or product complexity.

Fixed cost:
: A cost that does not vary with changes in the volume of units of work completed. Some costs are fixed in the short run, but variable over a longer period of time (for example: rent or a manager's salary).

Semivariable cost:
: A cost that is partly variable and partly fixed.

Incremental cost (same as marginal cost):
: The cost of one more or one less unit.

Relevant cost:
: A cost that differs between two alternative courses of action.

Differential cost:
: The difference in cost between two alternative courses of action.

Engineered cost:
: A cost that is driven by the engineered specifications of a task or product.

Managed cost:
: A cost that is not engineered, but can be managed for the best result (for example: advertising).

Discretionary cost:
: A cost whose change or elimination will not immediately affect an operation (for example: employee training).

Opportunity cost:
: The cost of an opportunity foregone (for example: the opportunity cost of a parking lot is the net rental income obtainable from the building that is not there.)

Imputed cost:
: Usually refers to interest that is an unspecified cost, such as in a lease.

Out-of-pocket cost:
: A cash cost (hence does not include depreciation or amortization).

Controllable cost:
: A cost that a particular manager can control or influence (costs that are not controllable at one level may be controllable at a higher level).

For a more extensive discussion of costs: see R. L. Weil, P. C. O'Brien, M. M. Maher, and C. P. Stickney, *Accounting: The Language of Business*, 9th ed. (nl.: Thomas Horton and Daughters, 1994).

QUESTIONS AND PROBLEMS

2–1. *Define.*

    a. Functional cost categories

    b. Organizational unit

    c. Chart of accounts

    d. Costing unit

    e. Indirect labor

    f. Manufacturing overhead

    g. General overhead

    h. Overhead rate

    i. Absorbed overhead

    j. Overabsorbed overhead

    k. Job costing

    l. Process costing

2–2. *Chart of accounts.* Bob Sale has an expanding TV repair firm. He has just added a third location and in two of the locations has begun to sell new TV sets and video recorders. All three locations have bought and sold used equipment, in addition to the main business, which is repairing all kinds of video equipment in the shop and on house calls. Pickup and delivery is provided when requested. Currently, costs are kept in six functional categories:

    a. Parts

    b. Payroll–skilled

    c. Payroll–assistants, drivers, etc.

    d. Auto and van costs

    e. Occupancy costs

    f. Office and administrative expense

Bob would like you to set up an account numbering system (chart of accounts) that will help him develop information on:

    1. Payroll cost for the firm and by location, by classification, and per hour;

    2. Profitability by type of business: shop repair, house repair, buy and sell used equipment, and sell new equipment;

    3. Cost and profitability by location.

2–3. *Controlling costs.* You are the controller of Azzo Electrical Contractors. The firm has 70 employees and does a variety of work: new construction, renovation, and repair. There is also a small fabrication shop, an engineering department, and a sales group.

Azzo has three copy machines located to provide easy access. Everyone uses whichever machine is closest. You are thinking about replacing one of them with a larger model, and when you mention this to the president, he points out that although the firm has been growing, the cost of copying has been growing twice as fast. He wonders if copying costs are out of control.

1. In that instance, what would control of copying costs mean?

2. After talking to your friends in the controllers' society, you find three approaches used to control copying costs:

   a. Use of access codes to unlock the copy machine and record the number of copies made. Each user, or group of users, would have an access code. The access code would enable the company to record the number of copies each user makes.

   b. Use of forms that each user fills out each time he or she makes copies.

   c. Free use (as Azzo has now) with periodic admonishments to all users to be frugal.

What are the advantages and disadvantages of each system? As controller, what evidence would you look at to decide whether copying costs were in control?

2–4. This chapter discusses direct costs and indirect costs.

   a. What evidence would you look at when deciding whether a cost was direct or indirect?

   b. Are direct costs the same as variable costs?

   c. Can the same cost be both fixed and variable?

   d. Can an indirect cost be made to be a direct cost?

2–5. What is meant by costing unit or cost object? Why is it sometimes difficult to define a cost object? Describe several instances in which the cost object is clear and several in which it may be hard to define an appropriate cost object.

2–6. What do we mean when we say we distribute overhead to products on top of a direct expense? How does that work? Does it have to be a direct expense?

2–7. What does it mean when we say overhead is under-absorbed? Is that good or bad?

2–8. What is the key difference between job costing systems and process costing systems?

2–9. Why do we sometimes need to compute equivalent units of production with process costing systems, but not with job costing systems?

2–10. Assume (1) 20,000 units were present at the beginning of the month, three-quarters finished, (2) 230,000 units were completed during the month, and (3) leaving 15,000 units in progress, two-thirds completed. How many equivalent units were produced?

2–11. *Product costing.* Joan ran the 3 S Cafe in a busy shopping center. Her soups, salads, and sandwiches were highly appreciated by patrons throughout the area. While the cafe had been moderately successful, Joan thought her pricing was pretty unscientific. Edith, an accountant friend of hers, suggested computing the cost of items to be priced. "That won't be easy," said Joan. "I could make a leap at computing the cost of ingredients, but what about the other costs—for space, helpers, supplies, utilities, and that fellow I've hired to deliver?"

Edith asked for some information and said she would think about what would be the best way. First, she learned that the 3 S Cafe was open 9:00 a.m. to 3:00 p.m., six days a week. Joan employed two helpers for eight hours each day and the delivery fellow for six hours each day. The soups were made between 9:00 and 10:00 in the morning, and the salads and sandwiches were made as they were ordered. There was a drink machine that was serviced by the Pepsi man.

The weekly expenses, not including food, looked like this:

Payroll for three	$1,150
Joan's salary	500
Space	350
Supplies	90
Utilities	60
Insurance	50
Other	200
Total	$2,400

Food costs were about $800 a week. Revenue had been running close to $3,500 a week, including the delivery business: $500 for soups, $2,000 for sandwiches, and $1,000 for salads. Soups sold for about $4.00, sandwiches for $5.00, and salads for $2.00. Joan estimated that food ingredients cost $1.00 for soups, $0.94 for sandwiches, and $0.60 for salads.

With this information, Edith decided she could compute the total cost of a soup, a salad, and a sandwich, but she would have to choose an allocation base on which to distribute the operating expenses. Should it be on the base of ingredients cost (i.e., as a percentage of food cost) or a certain amount per order of each item? Edith also wondered about the delivery business, which amounted to around $1,000 in weekly sales. Since delivered prices were the same as those in the cafe, Edith wondered if that business was profitable since it incurred the delivery expense of wages plus some transportation expense. She guessed those expenses came to around $300 a week.

What is the cost of soups, sandwiches, and salads using each of the two allocation bases Edith is considering? Which allocation base would you choose? What does the resulting cost information tell you? How would you measure the profitability of the delivery business?

2–12. *Activity-based costing.*

Part A

Cutty Manufacturing Company made two products: standard A and special B. The direct material costs of A and B were $60 for A and $80 for B. Direct labor was $50 for A and $70 for B. Planned production and sales was 1,000 units for A and 500 units for B.

Total manufacturing overhead for the period was expected to be $170,000, and all other expenses for selling and administrative functions were expected to be $45,000. Standard A sold for $250 each, and special B sold for $400 each. Cutty was in the habit of distributing manufacturing overhead to the two products on the basis of direct labor, and other expenses as a percentage of sales.

Draw up a schedule showing revenue and costs for the company as a whole, and total for each product. Draw up a second schedule showing the per-unit figures for A and B. What is the overhead allocation rate?

Part B

Having learned about activity-based costing, Cutty's controller recognized that the distribution of manufacturing overhead and other expenses to the two products did not quite reflect the resources used by the products. The controller knew that special B required machine programming and quality assurance activities not needed for standard A. Purchasing and handling of some special parts were also activities required by B, and the expense of those activities was included in overhead and applied in proportion to direct labor. The controller thought they should really be considered direct product expenses. After talking with people and observing the processes, the controller decided that those specific expenses amounted to $34,000 per period. The remaining $136,000 he distributed as before, on the basis of direct labor.

The controller also realized that several customer service activities (for example, training and warranty service) pertained only to the special B product. Study showed that those activities cost about $9,000 per period, which should be charged to B. The remaining $36,000 he distributed as before, based on a percentage of sales.

Draw up two schedules as in part A: one showing revenue and costs for the company and total for each product, and one showing per-unit figures. What do the new figures tell you about product profitability?

2–13. *Costing products with setups.* Caldwell Company makes a variety of bearings for a range of different applications. About two-thirds of sales are standard bearings that Caldwell makes in long runs. The other bearings are known as specials and are generally produced in short runs for specific orders. Standard bearings were priced approximately at standard cost plus 20% general, selling, and administrative expense (GS&A) plus 10% profit. Special bearings were priced with the same GS&A add-on, but around 20% profit to reflect Caldwell's special competence in making those bearings. Currently, setup cost is considered to be part of overhead. Chan Frothingham, Caldwell's controller, is wondering how much difference it would make if he separated setup cost from overhead and charged setup hours directly to products. The setup hours would then be treated like direct labor hours except that the setup labor was paid at a higher $20 per hour rate. To answer his questions, he selected two bearings: one he called LR, which was a long run, standard bearing; and another SR, which was one of the specials. Then he collected the data noted below. What conclusions would you draw about product cost, pricing, and product mix strategy?

Total budgeted figures for the year:

> Direct labor hours–100,000 hours
> Direct labor dollars–$1,500,000
> Total overhead–$2,100,000
> Setup labor included in overhead was 25,000 hours or $500,000

Product information:

> LR: produced in 1,000 unit lots:

Direct labor per lot: 10 hrs. @ $15.00	=	$150.00
Overhead 10 hrs. × $21.00 rate	=	210.00
Total cost		$360.00
Cost per unit		0.36

> SR: produced in 20 unit lots:

Direct labor per lot: 1 hr. @ $15.00	=	$15.00
Overhead 1 hr. × $21.00 rate	=	21.00
Total cost		$36.00
Cost per unit		$1.80

> Setup time was as follows:
> LR: 2 hours per run
> SR: 1 hour per run

Material cost was as follows:
    LR: $0.50 per unit
    SR: $0.80 per unit

CHAPTER 3

STANDARD COSTING SYSTEMS

Adam left his employer, a large industrial products manufacturer, to start his own company, which was to focus on the efficient production of a specialized water pump. He designed the pump in several configurations, developed a bill of materials, and wrote the manufacturing specifications. With that information at hand, he estimated his cost per pump and priced it with a reasonable profit margin. Based on a projected volume of pump sales, he expected a six-month profit before tax of $70,000. A month after the end of the six-month period, however, his accountant told him that his profit before taxes was just over $15,000. Adam's accountant also told him that she could not tell just where the actual costs departed from Adam's estimates, and hence, it was unclear where action should be taken. To help provide needed information in the future, the accountant recommended the installation of a standard costing system.

Standard costing systems serve many of the same functions as operating budgets that will be described in Chapter 9. Like budgets, standard costs are based on plans of operation and are an expression of those plans in financial terms. And like budgets, standard costs are an important part of the planning process and enable managers to monitor results by comparing actual costs with the planned standards. Furthermore, standard costs allow managers to make the comparison in enough detail to provide important clues as to where improvements can be made.

There are, however, some important differences between standard costs and budgets. Whereas budgets are usually made for organizational units, standard costs are typically prepared for a unit of production or service output. For example, the standard cost for one of Adam's water pumps would include the standard cost of several castings. The castings department would have an annual budget for its operations and might well cast parts for several different pumps.

Standard product costs are the estimated or projected costs of producing a product. Standard costing systems use the standard product costs as an integral part of the accounting system. There are many instances in which managers estimate costs, as Adam did in the foregoing illustration, but the existence of those estimates does not constitute a standard costing system. The difference is that standard costing systems use those estimates *as part of the firm's accounting system.* Inventory valuation will use the standard cost of products, and the standard costing system will provide the differences between actual cost and standard cost by type of cost (labor, material, overhead) and, if desired, by type of product. The differences are called variances, and the analysis of variances is a key part of a firm's management control system. A standard costing system would then provide Adam with variances in enough detail for him to identify the major reasons why his profit was lower than expected.

Standard costing systems are also helpful in the planning process. If the standards are accurate, and checking their accuracy is one of the objectives of variance analysis, those standards can be used in pricing decisions and to convert unit sales projections to production requirements in terms of materials, people, machines, and dollars. Adam, of course, had estimates of those resources; a standard costing system would help him verify the accuracy of those estimates.

In addition to providing variance and planning information, standard costing systems also simplify a firm's accounting for inventories. Because inventory is valued at standard cost, an item is always carried at the same cost, regardless of when it was made or how much the material or labor put into it actually cost. The inventory value per item changes only when the standards are changed.[1]

Thus, there are three important ways in which standard costing systems assist management:

1. The automatic built-in provision of variances helps to identify areas that need management's attention.

2. The development of a database of standard costs and quantities supports pricing decisions and helps the overall planning process.

3. The use of standard product costs simplifies inventory accounting.

Installation of standard costing systems may be costly, since an investment of time and effort is usually required to establish the standard costs and to incorporate them into the accounting system. In addition, standards must be kept up to date and new standards computed for each new product. Where standard costing systems are used, however, such installation and maintenance costs are more than offset by the benefits from simpler inventory accounting and valuable control information.

Let us see in some detail how a standard costing system works. We will use as an example a company that produces drumcaps in two production steps: machining and assembly. The first example describes a simple system involving one product and one cost center. The second example makes the second production stage a separate cost center, and the third example explains how multiple products are handled.

EXAMPLE 1: STANDARD COSTING WITH ONE PRODUCT AND ONE COST CENTER

In this first example, the company treats both machining and assembly as part of a single cost center.

The first step in setting up a standard cost system is to construct a standard cost sheet for each item to be produced. A standard cost sheet is reproduced as Figure 3–1.[2]

Such a cost sheet will show:

1. The standard amounts of direct materials per unit of output (in this case per 100 drumcaps) and the standard cost of that material per unit of material input.

2. The standard hours of direct labor per 100 drumcaps and the standard labor rate per hour.

3. The amount of overhead allocated to the 100 drumcaps using the preset overhead rate for the single cost center.

The standard cost sheet is usually prepared or revised once a year for continuing products and throughout the year whenever new products are developed. Drumcaps are a standard item so this standard cost sheet was prepared in November.

---

[1] The differences in standard costs and actual costs (variances) are recorded at the end of the accounting period.

[2] It may be noticed that this standard cost sheet looks very much like a job cost sheet, an example of which is shown in Chapter 2.

Standard Cost Sheet

Prepared: 11/4/2005

Effective: 1/1/2006

Drumcaps: cost per 100

Material:

20 feet #36 rod @ $0.18/foot	$3.60	
100 washers @ $1.00/thousand	0.10	
100 nuts @ $3.00/thousand	0.30	
Total material		$4.00

Labor:

Machining 0.75 hrs. @ $8.00/hr.	$6.00	
Assembly 0.50 hrs. @ $4.00/hr.	2.00	
Total labor		8.00
Overhead		4.00
Total manufacturing cost (per 100)		$16.00

Figure 3–1: *Standard Cost Sheet*

In January, the plant produced 10,000 drumcaps, so $1,600 was added to finished goods inventory. Half of those were sold, so cost of goods sold (at standard) was $800, leaving $800 in finished goods inventory at the end of the month. There is no work in process at the beginning or end of the month.

At this point, we have no information on what our actual costs were for the month. The accountants go to work and discover the following information:

1. We used 2,050 feet of #36 rod.

2. We used 10,100 washers.

3. We used 10,300 nuts.

4. Machinists worked 70 hours.

5. Assembly workers worked 57.5 hours.

6. Manufacturing overhead was $425.

7. Prices paid for material and wage rates paid the workers were the same as the set standards.

A quick calculation tells us that what we actually used and spent was not quite what it would have been had we exactly met the standards. The accountant would usually handle those discrepancies by adding to work in process $369 for the #36 rod used (2,050 × $0.18) and transferring $360 from work in process to finished goods. This transaction leaves $9 in work in process, which should be at 0 since there is actually no inventory there. The accountant then transfers the $9 to a material variance account, leaving 0 in work in process. Finished goods and cost of goods sold stay at standard cost per 100 drumcaps.

The accountant then follows the same procedure with the other five items and ends up with the following items in variance accounts:

Item	Actual	Standard	Variance	
Material: #36 rods	$369.00	$360.00	$9.00	(50 extra feet × $0.18/foot)
Material: washers	10.10	10.00	0.10	(100 extra washers × $1.00/thousand)
Material: nuts	30.90	30.00	0.90	(300 extra nuts × $3.00/thousand)
Machining labor	560.00	600.00	(40.00)	(5 hrs. less labor × $8.00/hr.)
Assembly labor	230.00	200.00	30.00	(7.5 hrs. extra labor × $4.00/hr.)
Overhead	425.00	400.00	25.00	($25 extra overhead)

All variance accounts except the machining labor variance account have left-hand (debit) entries. The machining labor variance account has a right-hand (credit) entry. All left-hand variances are unfavorable, and sometimes are also called negative variances, because they cause a decrease in profit. The machining labor, then, is a favorable or positive variance. Unless he or she had good reason to do otherwise, the accountant would finish his or her work on variances for the month by closing them to the profit and loss account for the period. The monthly income statement that the accountant has drawn up for management shows them as separate entries (see Figure 3–2). Alternatively, the accountant might have combined them with manufacturing overhead and/or the cost of goods sold, or prorated them between cost of goods sold and inventory. Whichever way he or she handles it, management would always have in the records the amounts of the individual variances, which could be discussed with the people responsible.

Sales (5,000 drumcaps)		$1,000.00
Standard cost of goods sold		800.00
Standard gross margin		$ 200.00
Variances:		
Material–rod	$(9.00)	
Material–washers	(0.10)	
Material–nuts	(0.90)	
Labor–machining	40.00	
Labor–assembly	(30.00)	
Overhead	(25.00)	
Net variances		$ (25.00)
Actual gross margin		$175.00

Figure 3–2: *Income Statement*

EXAMPLE 2: STANDARD COSTING WITH ONE PRODUCT AND TWO DEPARTMENTS

In the previous example, the factory was treated as one large department with one plant-wide overhead rate. Let us now separate the plant into two departments, machining and assembly, to see how standard costing would apply to the two cost centers.

The total budgeted plant overhead of $400 a month must now be reexamined and distributed to the departments. In this case, $300 goes to machining and $100 to assembly. The machining department is assigned more overhead, because it uses a greater amount of equipment.[3] Since the planned volume of

---

[3] Chapter 2 (Costing Products and Processes) contains a fuller discussion of the process by which overhead is distributed to various departments.

work for each department is 10,000 drumcaps, the overhead works out to be $3 per 100 drumcaps in the machining department and $1 per 100 drumcaps in the assembly department.

A revised standard cost sheet is shown in Figure 3–3.

Standard Cost Sheet			
Prepared:	11/4/2005		
Effective:	1/1/2006		
Drumcaps: cost per 100			
Machining department:			
Material: 20 feet #36 rod @ $0.18/foot		$3.60	
Labor: 0.75 hrs. @ $8.00/hr.		6.00	
Overhead		3.00	
Total cost of machined drumcaps			$12.60
Assembly department:			
Material: 100 washers @ $1.00/thousand		$0.10	
100 nuts @ $3.00/thousand		0.30	
Labor: 0.50 hrs. @ $4.00/hr.		2.00	
Overhead		1.00	
Total cost of assembly			3.40
Total cost of 100 drumcaps			$16.00

Figure 3–3: *Standard Cost Sheet—Two Departments*

With this division of budgeted overhead between the two departments and the standards shown in the standard cost sheet, the resulting standard cost system is illustrated by the T-accounts shown in Figure 3–4, with descriptions of the 14 transactions used to apply costs and develop variances. Explanations of the numbered transactions follow.[4]

1. From the raw material inventory account, 2,050 feet of rod was taken and then added to the work-in-process–machining ($369).

2. Machinists worked 70 hours on the rods; $560 is transferred from direct labor payroll to work-in-process–machining.

3. Overhead is added to work-in-process–machining on the basis of $3 per 100 drumcaps machined ($300).

4. The 10,000 machined drumcaps are transferred at standard cost to the assembly department. The standard cost of each 100 units is $12.60 as shown on the standard cost sheet for two departments. Of those lots, 100 have a total standard cost of $1,260.

5. Of the washers, 10,100 are transferred to work-in-process–assembly ($10.10).

6. There were 10,300 nuts transferred to work-in-process–assembly ($30.90).

7. The assemblers worked 57.5 hours on assembly ($230).

8. Overhead is added to work-in-process–assembly at $1 per 100 drumcaps assembled ($100).

9. There were 10,000 completed drumcaps transferred to finished goods inventory ($1,600).

10. There were 5,000 drumcaps sold; cost of goods sold at standard cost is $800.

---

[4] The meaning and use of T-accounts are explained in Appendix A, which discusses basic accounting processes.

At that point, the end-of-month inventory is taken, and no drumcaps are found to be in process. Any balances in the work-in-process (W.I.P.) accounts then represent variances from standard and must be transferred to variance accounts.

11. The $31 credit balance in work-in-process–machining is transferred to material variance (debit $9) and labor variance (credit $40).

12. The debit balance of $31 in work-in-process–assembly is transferred to material variance (debit $1) and labor variance (debit $30).

13. Actual overhead is $315 in the machining department (some allocated, some direct) and $110 in the assembly department. The other half of this transaction consists of credits to a number of accounts, such as cash, accounts payable, accrued payroll, and accumulated depreciation.

14. Since the two overhead accounts are temporary accounts used during the accounting period, they are closed out and their balances are transferred to overhead variance ($15 and $10).

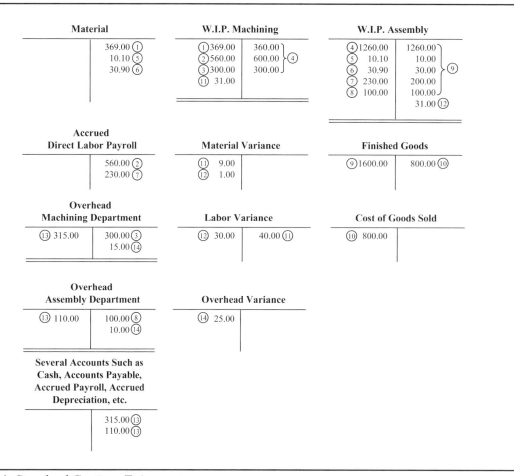

Figure 3–4: *Standard Costing: T-Accounts*

Variance Analysis

After those transactions are recorded, management has in its records the amounts of the several variances and might call for a production report such as the one shown in Figure 3–5.

Several facts should be noted about this report. The report says that production for the month was 10,000 drumcaps, a total that has a standard cost of $1,600. Column one shows the standard cost of the actual drumcaps produced by the type of expense. The second column shows what the actual costs were, and the third column shows the variance. The last column gives the variance as a percentage of standard cost. The dollar size of a variance is important, but the percentage of the deviation is also worth noting, because it can show whether the variance is a relatively small random deviation or if it is significant. Notice also that the total variance is only 1.6%, but behind that figure are larger offsetting variances in the different types of expenses.

				Percentage of Standard
Production for the month:	10,000 drumcaps			
Standard cost of actual volume:	$1,600			
Variance by department:				
	Standard Cost	*Actual Cost*	*Variance*	*of Standard Cost*
Machining department:				
Direct material	$ 360	$ 369	$ 9.00 (unfavorable)	2.5
Direct labor	600	560	40.00 (favorable)	6.7
Overhead	300	315	15.00 (unfavorable)	5.0
	$1,260	$1,244	$16.00 (favorable)	
Assembly department:				
Direct material	$ 40	$ 41	$ 1.00 (unfavorable)	2.5
Direct labor	200	230	30.00 (unfavorable)	15.0
Overhead	100	110	10.00 (unfavorable)	10.0
	$ 340	$ 381	$41.00 (unfavorable)	
Total	$1,600	$1,625	$25.00 (unfavorable)	1.6

Figure 3–5: *January Production Report*

Use of Direct Labor as a Base for Overhead Allocation

With multiple products, it is likely that overhead would be applied using direct labor as a base rather than units produced. Direct labor is used because the several products may be quite different and require different amounts of effort to produce. Under those circumstances, the overhead required would be more closely related to direct labor used than to the number of units produced. The labor base can be either the number of hours or the number of dollars of direct labor contained in the units actually processed. Using drumcaps production as an example and applying overhead on the basis of standard labor hours, we reach the following results.

1. The 10,000 machined drumcaps have a standard labor content of 75 hours. Because overhead in the machining department is expected to be $300, the rate of application would be $4 of overhead per standard labor hour.

2. In assembly, the standard assembly labor content of 10,000 drumcaps is 50 hours, so the rate used to apply the expected $100 of overhead would be $2 per standard direct labor-hour.[5]

There are other reasons why it may be easier and fairer to apply overhead on the basis of labor rather than production units. One is that the output units from a particular department may not be the same as the end product units. In the early stages of production, the units may be pounds and only in the later stages become identifiable end products. In those cases, labor content is a base common to all products, and it is often easier to establish an expected relationship between overhead and direct labor.

EXAMPLE 3: STANDARD COSTING WITH MULTIPLE PRODUCTS

Most companies produce more than one product. When such is the case, keeping track of actual costs for each product would require a job costing system similar to the one described in Chapter 2. Actual costs would be recorded on a job sheet, and variances would be available for each job or product.

The question of whether to record costs by product did not arise in the first two examples, because only one product was made. All costs were automatically the costs of that product. A standard costing system, however, does not have to record actual costs by product. A much simpler and more frequently used type of standard costing system records costs and develops variances by type of input, such as labor or material, but not by each individual job or product. Costs would also be identified by department.

For example, suppose that after the #36 rod entered the machining department, it was made into five different products. During the month, we could debit the machining department for the actual amount of rod used for all products and credit the department for the standard material content of the units actually sent on to the assembly department. At the end of the month, after being adjusted for any inventory change in the department, the material variance will be the difference between the actual input and the standard material content of all units transferred out. The variance will pertain to the whole department, and we would have no information about which products caused it. If it were important to relate the variance to the products, we would have to record actual amounts on job sheets. However, if a departmental variance is enough information, much detailed recordkeeping can be avoided.

Direct labor costs can be handled the same way. Actual total labor costs in a department are often easily available from payroll records. The difference between the actual direct labor for the month and the standard direct labor content of units transferred out will be the monthly direct labor variance. Again, we will not know which product caused the variance.

Note that the variances we have discussed thus far have been quantity variances. Material prices and labor rates have not entered the picture. Price and rate variances will be discussed in the next section.

PRICE AND QUANTITY VARIANCES

When a standard cost for a product is established and laid out on a standard cost sheet, both standard quantities and prices are set. We have seen how quantity variances can result from differences between

---

[5] Note that the example applies overhead on the basis of standard direct labor hours rather than actual labor hours. Most systems work that way, although it is possible to use actual hours as a base. More will be said about that later.

actual and standard quantities. Actual prices and rates may also differ from the standard, resulting in price and rate variances.

Theoretically two sequences can be used to compute price and quantity variances. One sequence computes price variance first, then quantity variance. The other computes quantity variance first and then price variance. Consider Figure 3–6.

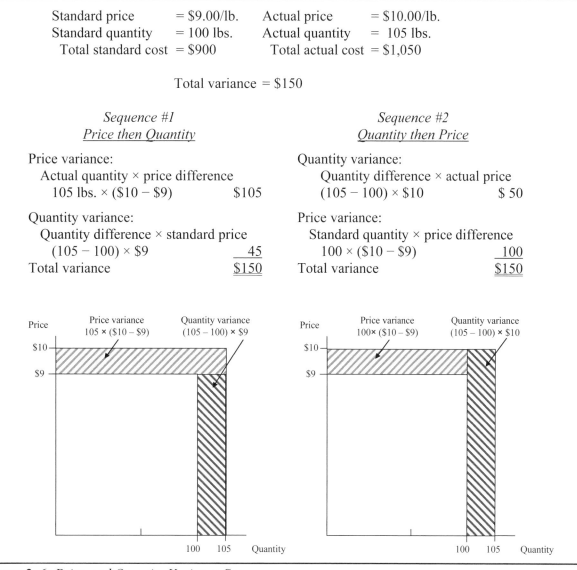

Standard price	= $9.00/lb.	Actual price	= $10.00/lb.
Standard quantity	= 100 lbs.	Actual quantity	= 105 lbs.
Total standard cost	= $900	Total actual cost	= $1,050

Total variance = $150

Sequence #1
Price then Quantity

Price variance:
  Actual quantity × price difference
  105 lbs. × ($10 − $9) $105

Quantity variance:
  Quantity difference × standard price
  (105 − 100) × $9   45
Total variance $150

Sequence #2
Quantity then Price

Quantity variance:
  Quantity difference × actual price
  (105 − 100) × $10 $ 50

Price variance:
  Standard quantity × price difference
  100 × ($10 − $9)   100
Total variance $150

Figure 3–6: *Price and Quantity Variance Sequence*

One can see that in this example, there is $5.00 that can be part of either the price variance (sequence 1) or the quantity variance (sequence 2). That $5.00 is depicted in the graphs as the upper right-hand rectangle ([105 − 100] × [$10 − $9]). Though either sequence is possible, sequence 1 is almost always used. There are several reasons for that choice. First, it allows material inventory to be kept at the standard price per unit, which greatly simplifies the accounting system, since every unit of an item in inventory will have the same cost attached to it regardless of its purchase price. Second, the operations manager may not influence the actual price paid, so the standard price is used when assessing the effect of quantity differences resulting from the operation manager's efforts. Third, material price variances are computed on the actual quantity of material, so all material is considered in assessing the effect of price differences resulting from the purchasing department's efforts. Labor rate and usage variances are also computed following sequence 1 for similar reasons.

Using sequence 1 (price variance before quantity variance), there is another timing choice that arises with material. Note that material is purchased and used at different times. Material price variances may be developed when the material is put into production, or they may be developed when the material is purchased. The latter method allows raw material inventory to be kept at the standard price per unit, which, as is indicated above, greatly simplifies the accounting system. And that method allows us to calculate the material price variance on all material purchased as soon as that information is known.

In companies that purchase large amounts of raw material at irregular intervals and at widely fluctuating prices, however, that method may produce large favorable or unfavorable price variances that distort the income statement for the period. Purchase of six months' supply of copper on December 30 might produce a price variance that would distort the year's results. Furthermore, the external accountants may worry that a favorable price variance on material purchased, but not used, will show a profit before the income has actually been realized. In most businesses, significant distortions are rare and it generally turns out to be easier to develop the material price variance at the time of the purchase.

To carry that out, the standard cost of the amount of material actually purchased is added to raw material inventory, and the difference between the actual and the standard costs is added to or deducted from the material price variance account. From then on, the raw material is always handled at the standard cost per unit.

Since labor is not carried in inventory by itself, purchase and usage of labor occur at the same time. A standard rate for each operation is noted on the standard cost sheet, and if the actual rate is different, the difference is entered into a labor rate variance account at the time that the labor cost is applied to inventory.

OVERHEAD VARIANCES

Meaningful variances for overhead are more difficult to develop than for material and direct labor. Although we can assume with some validity that material and direct labor costs will vary directly with volume, we cannot reasonably assume that overhead will do so. The standard for material and labor is a set amount per unit produced. If volume is above or below the level anticipated at the beginning of the year, the standard material and labor content will be correspondingly above or below the expected level, and the assumption is that actual material and labor costs will follow the standard amounts. In practice, that is generally true for material; however, with increasingly restrictive labor policies, labor is becoming more of a fixed cost that does not easily vary with small changes in volume. Nevertheless, most cost systems incorporate the assumption that direct labor is variable, leaving it to those who interpret the variances to decide the extent to which that assumption is correct.

Manufacturing overhead, however, is generally assumed to be a mixture of fixed and variable costs. Some costs such as depreciation are known to be fixed, while others such as indirect labor and supplies may be largely variable. One can see that costs that are fixed in total will not be the same per unit produced if production volume varies. Thus, if overhead variances are to contain a useful message, there must be a way for variances to recognize that some overhead costs will remain fixed while others will vary with volume.

This recognition is granted in an overhead budget that specifies the expected level of overhead expense at various volume levels. We discuss this process in the section on flexible budgets in Chapter 9.

Using the drumcap machining department, let us follow the sequence of steps:

1. At the beginning of the year, an estimate is made of the volume of production that the department is likely to have each month. In this case, it is 10,000 drumcaps with a standard content of 75 hours of direct labor. That figure is often called *standard volume.*

2. An estimate is also made of the amount of manufacturing overhead that the department will incur at the standard level of production. In this case, it is $300 a month for the machining department.

3. From those figures, we know that the standard overhead rate will be $4 per standard direct labor hour. This figure is also known as the *overhead absorption rate*, since work in process absorbs $4 of overhead for each standard hour of direct labor contained in units completed or transferred out.

4. Knowing that volume may not be exactly as predicted, we establish a *variable overhead budget*, which says how much overhead we think will be incurred at volumes other than standard. As described in Chapter 9, this estimate can be made in several ways, such as by examining past records to see how much actually was incurred at different volumes, or by asking people directly involved how much would be spent if volume were 10% above or below the standard volume.

Figure 3–7 shows a graph depicting the overhead absorption line ($4 per standard direct labor hour) and the budget line. The budget line shows that $240 of the $300 is fixed; a rate of $0.80 per standard direct labor hour reflects the variable portion of overhead. Because the budget may not hold for volumes that vary greatly from standard, the budget line may not be very accurate for low and high volumes.

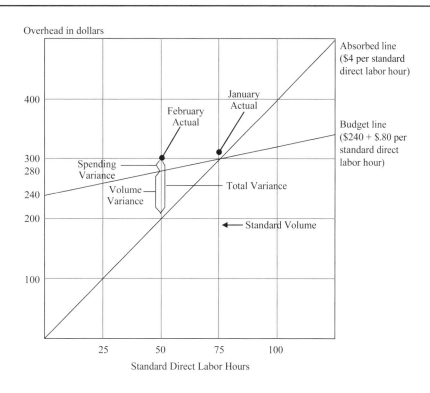

Figure 3–7: *Overhead Budget for Machining Department*

In the month of January, the 10,000 drumcaps that were machined contained 75 standard direct labor hours. Production was exactly at standard volume. The dot represents actual overhead at $315. The $15 overhead variance is represented by the vertical distance between the actual point and the point below it on the absorption line. In this case, that point is where the two lines cross since production was at standard volume.

Suppose production declines in February to 6,667 drumcaps, which have a standard labor content of 50 labor hours. Absorbed overhead will be $200 (50 hours times $4 per hour). Let us also suppose that actual overhead is $300, marked by the other dot. The overhead variance shown in the accounting records will be $100 negative or unfavorable (absorbed overhead of $200 minus actual overhead of $300).

A look at the graph tells us that overhead was only $20 above the budgeted amount for that level of production, so the negative variance of $100 may be a bit misleading. At the level of 50 standard labor hours of production, we expected to have $80 negative overhead variance; the other $20 was not anticipated. The $80 is called the *overhead volume variance*; the $20 is called the *overhead spending variance*. In that way, the total overhead variance is broken into two components: the volume variance, which is caused by volume being below or above standard volume, and the spending variance, which is the difference between actual overhead and the amount budgeted at actual volume. As the graph shows, the two variances add up to the total overhead variance. If actual overhead had been $260, the spending variance would have been a favorable $20, and the unfavorable volume variance of $80 combined with the favorable $20 spending variance would have netted out to a total variance of $60, unfavorable ($200 – $260).

Overhead Variance

Volume Variance	= Absorbed Overhead – Budgeted Overhead at Actual Volume
Spending Variance	= Budgeted Overhead at Actual Volume – Actual Overhead
Total Variance	= Absorbed Overhead – Actual Overhead
Total Variance	= Volume Variance + Spending Variance

Note that the volume variance is the *expected* difference between absorbed overhead and budgeted overhead at actual volume. If overhead came out exactly as the budget line (formula) said it should, then the overhead volume variance would tell us what the total overhead variance was. The overhead spending variance would be zero. As shown in Figure 3–8 below, the volume variance is the vertical distance between the budget and absorbed lines. And if actual volume is below standard volume (to the left), the volume variance is negative; if actual volume is above standard volume, the volume variance is positive. Since it is the fixed component of overhead that causes the budget line to be different from the absorbed line, one can see that the *overhead volume variance pertains only to fixed overhead*. A graph for fixed overhead alone would appear as in Figure 3–9.

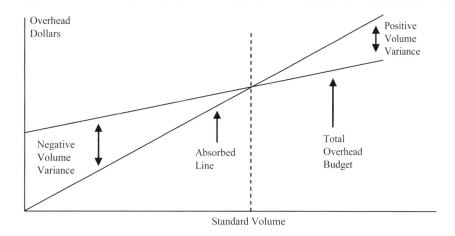

Figure 3–8: *Volume Variance with Total Overhead*

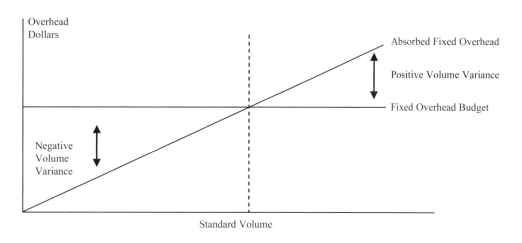

Figure 3–9: *Volume Variance with Fixed Overhead*

Note also that the overhead spending variance is the same number that would be shown by the difference between the actual overhead and a flexible budget for the machining department as described in Chapter 9, if the measure of activity used for the flexible budget was standard direct labor hours.

Volume of Activity

The volume of activity used in this analysis can be measured in terms of either units completed or standard labor hours, which express the standard labor content of units completed. If the department does only part of the work required to complete the units, then the volume of activity should reflect the partly completed units or the standard direct labor content of the partly completed work. As noted earlier, labor hours are used more frequently than units because they are a measure that can be used throughout a production process that may involve many different kinds of units (pounds, feet, parts, components, etc.) and because labor hours are often thought to be more closely related to overhead expenditures.

This discussion of the use of direct labor as the base on which to distribute manufacturing overhead to products reflects common usage. As Chapter 2 illustrated, however, labor is becoming a poor base for use in many manufacturing plants. Other measures of activity are being devised that would relate indirect costs to products more accurately. In service activities, the same is also true. The objective is the same, however, no matter what base is used to allocate overhead to the product or service output. One wishes to measure as accurately as possible the resources used by each product or service.

Overhead Efficiency Variance

Some companies use a third overhead variance called the overhead efficiency variance. To obtain the third variance, the overhead spending variance used in the two variance system just described is broken into two variances (see Figure 3–10). The overhead efficiency variance is that part of the total overhead spending variance that is caused by a difference between actual and standard labor hours. Since only the variable component of overhead is affected by different levels of activity, the *overhead efficiency variance reflects only variable overhead.* It measures the amount of variable overhead that we would expect to be caused by an over or under usage of direct labor hours and, hence, it really reflects direct labor efficiency.

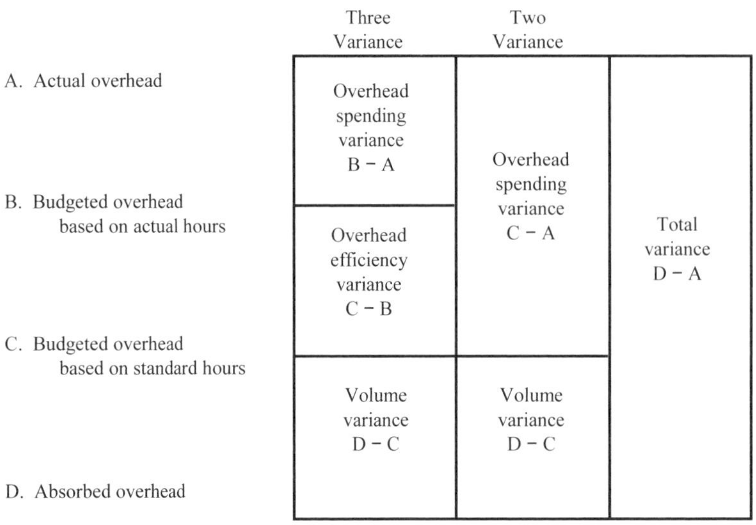

Figure 3–10: *Overhead Variance Systems*

SUMMARY DIAGRAM OF VARIANCES

In understanding the relationships that produce variances, some people like to see formulas—for example: Material Price Variance = [(Standard Price − Actual Price) × Actual Volume]—some prefer graphs such as the one shown in Figure 3–7, and others are helped by diagrams such as the one shown below in Figure 3–11.

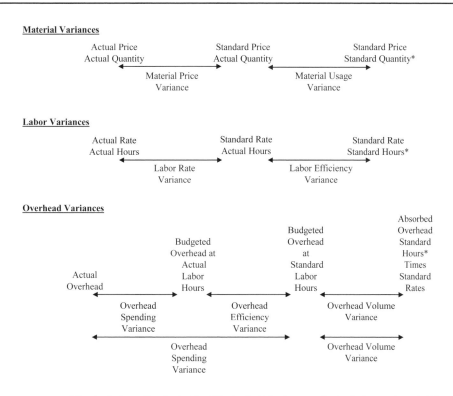

Figure 3–11: *Variance Diagram*

Note that the diagram shown in Figure 3–11 implies these formulas for calculating variances:

Material Price Variance = (Standard Price – Actual Price) × Actual Quantity

Material Usage Variance = (Actual Quantity – Standard Quantity Allowed for Actual Units Produced)
  × Standard Price

Labor Rate Variance = (Standard Rate – Actual Rate) × Actual Hours

Labor Efficiency Variance = (Actual Hours – Standard Hours Allowed for Actual Units Produced) ×
  Standard Rate

Overhead Spending Variance = (Budgeted Overhead Rate × Actual Hours) – Actual Overhead

Overhead Efficiency Variance = (Standard Hours Allowed for Actual Units Produced – Actual
  Hours) × Budgeted Overhead Rate

Overhead Volume Variance = Overhead Absorbed at Standard Hours Allowed for Actual Units –
  (Budgeted Overhead Rate × Standard Hours Allowed for Actual
  Units Produced)

INTERPRETING VARIANCES

When negative variances occur in a standard costing system, they do not necessarily mean that something is wrong. They simply compare an earlier estimate with what actually occurred. There is always the possibility that the estimate was wrong or unrealistic in the first place. The variance does mean, however, that a plan was not fulfilled, and nonfulfillment usually causes concern. If standards are used in decisions on scheduling, pricing, or product design, it is certainly important to know as soon as possible whether it is the standard or the level of performance that needs to be changed.

Variances indicate that performance was not as planned. The breakdown of variances into the labor, material, and overhead components of production costs, and the further breakdown into price and quantity or spending and volume variances, helps to define the precise nature of the difference between planned and actual performance. The variances themselves cannot indicate the reasons for the difference. But they can signal the need for management to obtain more information and can provide clues as to where management might look. For example, to investigate a material price variance, management might start by talking with the purchasing manager. Before management can take any corrective action, it must interpret the variances to find out why they occurred.

Variances usually come as no great surprise to an alert management. It is often obvious that material spoilage is high, or that there is excessive machine downtime. Direct observation or production counts will often indicate right away whether things are going properly. Two examples illustrate the use of direct production reporting. In one scenario, the manager of a glass-making plant called for a daily record showing pounds of good pieces formed. With that information he could tell quickly and accurately whether the previous day's production was up to standard. In another instance, the manager of an electrical products plant received a weekly report showing the ratio of people in the direct and indirect labor categories. Both those managers received monthly reports showing material and labor variances and usually knew in advance approximately what they would show.

Variance reports do often reveal trends or aggregate positions. Day-to-day or detailed observation may not show that certain areas are creeping toward seriously out-of-standard conditions, or that many little deviations are adding up to a large variance. Variance reports are a convenient way of summing up total performance and comparing it to the predetermined plan.

CONTROLLABILITY

Any action aimed at correcting variances must consider the problem of controllability. Unfavorable material usage variances may be caused by inexperienced or careless production operators. They may also be caused by poor purchasing that brought in poor quality material. Likewise, labor inefficiency may be either a production departmental problem, a scheduling problem, a product design problem, or a sales problem (such as selling too many small orders). Or labor inefficiency may result from a company strategy of rapid expansion that necessitated hiring and training inexperienced operators.

Separating overhead variances into volume and spending variances clarifies their controllability. A supervisor can be expected to control overhead spending variances, but not volume variances. Use of supplies and indirect labor may be controllable, and variation from the budget may indicate that his or her performance is not what it should be. Maintenance and repair, which may be considered variable and somewhat controllable by a supervisor, may on occasion vary inversely with volume. The time when work is slack and machines are idle may be the opportunity for overhaul and preventative maintenance.

Even volume variances may be affected by a departmental supervisor if managerial skill influences the department's ability to process a backlog of work.

Clearly, management's job is to look behind the variance figures to see what the causes are and to determine if or when changes should be made. Developing an accounting system that identifies variances is therefore only the beginning of management's job. Determining what action to take and acting effectively are where management really earns its pay.

STANDARD COSTING SYSTEMS AND BUDGETS

You may have noticed that budgets and standard costing systems have similarities. Both are financial representations of operating plans; budgets focus on operating units, standard costs on units of output. Both allow managers to compare actual results with the plan. Both use estimates of cost variability to accommodate different relationships between activity and cost behavior.

Both budgets and standard costing systems can give bad signals if the information provided is not carefully interpreted. For example, there will always be random variations (noise in the system) that carry little useful information. And there will always be the question whether a variance indicates that the standard is wrong.

RECENT DEVELOPMENTS

So far in this chapter, what we have described is what could be called a traditional standard costing system. Such systems simplify accounting for inventories and provide a way to compare actual results with planned results.

Although these traditional standard costing systems continue to be useful in many companies, a growing number of companies have started to abandon or significantly change their standard costing systems. New perspectives on what are key success factors have made the fixed and apparently predictable nature of standard costs less valid and sometimes misleading. There are three reasons for those changes:

1. Variance reports based on standard costs often arrive outside the time frame in which they could be useful for control purposes. Monthly material or labor variances, for example, describe what in many situations is ancient history. If the variances show a need for corrective action, it probably should have been taken weeks earlier. Furthermore, determining the cause of variances usually requires further investigation into things like down time, rejects, or poor performance due to a lack of training. That is why companies have developed focused performance measures that short circuit the need for standard cost variances. Those other measures will be discussed further in Chapter 10.

2. Many companies believe that their current emphasis on continuous improvement is restrained by a standard costing system that sets standards once a year. That process implies a fixed target, whereas the approach underlying continuous improvement puts no limits on improvement. The standard becomes "better than last time or last month." One can say, of course, that continuous improvement simply means beating the standard more and more. But that doesn't capture all the meaning of continuous improvement. Standards tend to focus on part of the total cost (labor in

department X, or material used in Y, etc.), whereas continuous improvement takes a more global view and looks at whole systems, processes, and designs.

3. Standard product costs that include some element of fixed costs tend to encourage production managers, supervisors, or department managers to use up capacity and to produce in long runs whether the whole run is needed right away or not. Idle capacity shows up as negative variances. (Labor costs are often treated as variable, though in the short run they are often fixed.) That tendency creates excess inventory, which has been shown to be much more costly than was generally realized. Bottleneck operations do need to operate at capacity, but other operations do not, and create waste if they try to. So the influences of standards and variance analysis can be counterproductive. Instead of using cost variances to measure efficiency, the alternative is to focus on other measures, such as the throughput, elapsed time, and overall operating expenses.

The reasons why a company would reconsider its decision to use a standard costing system are most valid where processes are changing rapidly and where pressure on capacity creates restraining bottlenecks. The problems are not inherent in standard costing systems, but in how variances are used and how behavior is influenced. Such systems will continue to be useful in many situations and, as is always true, managers will need to be careful in using the information they provide.

SUMMARY

In this chapter, we have reviewed the basic processes of standard costing systems. From a costing system covering one product and one cost center, we went on to more complex systems handling multiple cost centers and multiple products.

Standard costing systems require an investment of effort to establish standards for price, rate, and quantity, and they require continual updating for changes in price, methods, product design, and processes. Their value lies in providing standard costs for planning, pricing, and reviewing operations. The use of standard product costs enables the development of variances. For material there are usually price and usage variances; for labor there are usually rate and efficiency variances. For overhead there cannot be price and rate variances in the usual sense; but the total overhead variance can be separated into volume and spending variances, and occasionally a third variance, called the overhead efficiency variance, is computed. Variances from standard, though they seldom give management the reasons for deviation from plan, do provide a convenient and constant monitoring system that shows to what extent operations are proceeding according to plan.

For Adam and his pump manufacturing plant, a standard costing system would direct his attention to the main areas where actual costs deviated from his projections. He could tell whether

- Material was costing more or being wasted;

- Labor rates were higher than expected;

- More time was being taken than he anticipated.

And in the overhead area, he could learn whether

- Expenditures were above budget;

- Lower volume caused fixed costs to be higher per unit.

With that information in hand, he would be in a good position to begin improving his firm's profitability.

QUESTIONS AND PROBLEMS

3–1. Why is it true that standard costing systems automatically produce variances?

3–2. Why go to the trouble of computing separate price and quantity variances?

3–3. Are there price and quantity variances for overhead?

3–4. What causes the overhead volume variance?

3–5. What does the overhead efficiency variance tell us?

3–6. When is fixed overhead not fixed?

3–7. *Standard costs and variances*. The Alpha Company produces hammers in two production steps: molding and assembly. Each step involves a different cost center. To establish the costs of inventory and maintain control over production costs, the company uses a standard costing system and has accordingly prepared for the current year the following standard cost sheet for 100 units of hammers.

Standard Cost Sheet

Hammers: cost per 100		Effective date: 1/1/2006

Material:		
100 lbs. iron @ $0.25/lb. (heads)	$25.00	
100 wooden handles @ $0.50/unit	50.00	
		$ 75.00
Labor:		
Molding: 1.50 hrs. @ $6/hr. (heads)	$ 9.00	
Assembly: 0.25 hrs. @ $4/hr.	1.00	
		10.00
Overhead:		
Molding: @ $9 per direct labor hour	$13.50	
Assembly: @ $6 per direct labor hour	1.50	15.00
Total manufacturing cost (per 100)		$100.00

Planned production is 190,000 hammers a month. To obtain the two overhead rates, the total budgeted plant overhead of $28,500 a month was divided into $25,650 for the molding department and $2,850 for the assembly department. The molding department has a larger share of the plant overhead, because it uses more energy and requires more supervision and indirect labor. Since the total planned direct labor hours of the molding department is 2,850 hours (190,000 units × 1.5 hours per 100 units), the overhead rate of the department, therefore, is $9.00 per direct labor hour. On the other hand, the total planned direct labor hours of the assembly department is 475 hours (190,000 units × 0.25 hours per 100 units), so its overhead rate is $6.00 per direct labor hour.

In January, the company produced 190,000 units, the normal monthly production level. There was no work in process at the end of the month.

The transactions that took place during the month were as follows:

1. 199,500 lbs. of iron were taken from the *raw material inventory* account and put into *work-in-process–molding*. Price paid for iron was the same as standard.

2. Molders worked 2,736 hours on the iron. Actual wage rate paid the workers was the same as standard and the *accrued direct labor payroll* account was charged $16,416.

3. Overhead was added to work-in-process–molding (and charged to the *overhead–molding department* account) at $9 per standard direct labor hour. (Standard direct labor hours for headsets molded.)

4. The 190,000 molded headsets were transferred at standard cost to *work-in-process–assembly* leaving no work-in-process inventory in the molding department.

5. The 195,700 wooden handles were transferred to work-in-process–assembly. Purchase price of the handles was the same as standard.

6. The assemblers worked 494 hours on assembly. The wage rate paid the workers was the same as standard.

7. Overhead was added to work-in-process–assembly and charged to the *overhead–assembly department* account at $6.00 per standard direct labor hour.

8. There were 190,000 completed hammers transferred to *finished goods,* leaving no work in process.

9. There were 160,000 hammers sold.

10. The balance in the work-in-process–molding account was transferred to the appropriate *variance* accounts.

11. The balance in the work-in-process–assembly account was transferred to the appropriate variance accounts.

12. Actual overhead was $26,163 in the molding department and $2,736 in the assembly department.

13. The balances in the two overhead accounts were transferred to the *overhead–variance* account.

Using T-accounts (most of those you will need are italicized), enter the transactions for January. Prepare a production report showing the cost components of the two departments at standard and actual costs and the variances in absolute amounts and in percentages to standard costs. Indicate whether the variances are favorable or unfavorable.

3–8. *Overhead volume variance.* The Y Company has a monthly standard production volume for its product of 25,000 units. Information on the breakdown of the standard unit cost is as follows:

Direct materials	$8.00
Direct labor	
(1.25 hrs. per unit @ $3.84 per hour)	4.80
Manufacturing overhead	3.60
This is 75% of direct labor dollars.	
40% was thought to be variable, 60% fixed.	

Because the company realizes that monthly production volume can vary from the standard volume due to different factors, it follows the procedure of predicting in advance the overhead volume variance for every month. Assume that for the month of January, the company thinks production volume will be 24,000 units and direct labor hours will be 30,500 hours. What then is the predicted overhead volume variance of the company?

3–9. *Overhead volume variance.* The Modest Company manufactures an electronic product called Ren. To have good control over production costs, the company uses a standard costing system. It established the standard volume for 2005 at 40,000 units with production costs set as follows:

Direct materials		$480,000
Direct labor		120,000
Factory overhead:		
Variable	$80,000	
Fixed	100,000	
		180,000
Total product costs		$780,000

Actual production in 2005 turned out to be 42,000 units.

In January 2006, two newly hired financial analysts in the company were having a discussion on what the overhead volume variance was for the year just ended. One of them said that it was the difference between the budgeted cost at standard volume and the budgeted cost at actual volume. He then computed the variance:

Budgeted overhead cost at standard volume: $180,000

Budgeted overhead cost at actual volume:

$$\text{Variable} = 42{,}000 \text{ units} \times \frac{\$80{,}000}{40{,}000 \text{ units}} = \quad \$84{,}000$$

Fixed   =   100,000

                                                  184,000

Unfavorable volume variance $ 4,000

The overhead volume variance according to the analyst was $4,000. He explained that it was unfavorable, because overhead cost at actual volume was higher than that at planned volume.

The second analyst said she thought the overhead volume variance only concerned fixed costs, and that it was calculated as the difference between the amount of fixed costs absorbed at actual volume and the amount that would have been absorbed at standard volume. In this case, the absorbed fixed costs were $5,000 higher, so there was an unfavorable volume variance of $5,000. Her figures were as follows:

Fixed costs absorbed at standard volume:

  $100,000/40,000 = $2.50/unit × 40,000 units   = $100,000

Fixed costs absorbed at actual volume:

  $2.50 × 42,000 units   =   105,000

  Volume variance (unfavorable) $ 5,000

Which analyst was right?

3–10. *Overhead efficiency variance.* The Universal Company is a producer of Kilon. At the normal production of 20,000 units per month, the standard production costs per unit are:

Direct materials $15
Direct labor (2 hrs./unit @ $5 per hour)   10
Manufacturing overhead
    (80% of direct labor dollars):
        Variable = 37.5%   3
        Fixed = 62.5%   5

Aware that actual total direct labor hours are not always the same as standard direct labor hours for actual volume, the production manager asked the controller if the variance in total direct labor hours can be reflected in the analysis of overhead variances. The controller said that kind of analysis was possible by using a three-way analysis of overhead variances. According to the controller, there would be three kinds of overhead variances: spending, efficiency, and volume. He defined the variances as this:

Spending variance. The difference between actual overhead and the budgeted overhead based on actual direct labor hours input.

Efficiency variance. The difference between budgeted overhead based on actual direct labor hours input and budgeted overhead based on standard direct labor hours for actual volume produced.

Volume variance. The difference between absorbed overhead and budgeted overhead based on standard direct labor hours for actual volume.

In January, actual overhead was $172,000, actual volume was 22,000 units, and actual direct labor hours were 42,000. What then are the overhead spending, efficiency, and volume variances? Interpret your answers.

3–11. *The effect of variances on profit.* A company has a standard volume of 100,000 units per year for its sole product. At the start of the year that just ended, the company had 30,000 units on hand. That year, it produced 110,000 units and sold 130,000 units. Information on the product and company expenses are:

Selling price per unit $2.00
Standard manufacturing cost per unit:
    Materials $0.80
    Direct labor   0.40
    Variable overhead   0.10
    Fixed overhead   0.20
                                                                      $1.50
Budgeted general, selling, and
    administrative expenses for one year $30,000

Actual product costs and company expenses for the year involved were these:

Production costs:	
Materials	$ 89,500
Direct labor	43,000
Variable overhead	11,500
Fixed overhead	20,600
Total	$164,600
General, selling, and administrative expenses	$ 33,000

Assignment:

1. Prepare an income statement showing variances, but exclude income tax.

2. Explain the difference between actual profit and profit at standard cost using the sales volume figure of 130,000 units.

3. If the company had produced 20,000 more units at an additional cost of $26,000 (standard variable cost) and sold 130,000 units, what would profit have been? Explain the difference.

3–12. *Accounting for rejects.* The A Company is an exclusive producer of lunch boxes for a national restaurant chain. Its production process involves two cost centers: preparation and assembly. In the preparation department, cardboard is cut into specific sizes and forms and stamped with colorful designs. In the assembly department, the cut cardboard forms are folded and pasted. Before the cut cardboard forms are transferred to the assembly department, all of them are inspected. About 5% of the cardboards are usually rejected, because of some discoloration or disfigurement.

In the company's present standard costing system, no allowance for rejects is included in the standard costs. The total standard cost for rejects is segregated from the cost of good units and subsequently closed to the cost of goods sold. Consequently, rejects have to be counted. That procedure resulted in two kinds of variances: one was the cost of rejected units at standard cost per unit and the other was the difference between actual costs and the standard cost of goods and rejected units combined.

The preparation department's standard cost of production per box is:

Materials	$0.09
Labor	0.06
Overhead	0.04
Total cost per box	$0.19

The department produced 101,000 boxes in January and transferred 96,500 good units to the assembly department. The rest of the units were rejects. The production costs for the month were:

Materials	$10,250
Labor	5,970
Overhead	4,990
Total	$21,210

Therefore, the variances in the preparation department are computed as follows:

	Materials	Labor	Overhead	Total
Standard unit cost	$ 0.09	$ 0.06	$ 0.04	$ 0.19
× Production volume (boxes)	× 101,000	× 101,000	× 101,000	× 101,000
Standard costs of good and rejected units	$ 9,090	$ 6,060	$ 4,040	$ 19,190
− Actual costs	− 10,250	− 5,970	− 4,990	− 21,210
Variances	$ 1,160	$ 90	$ 950	$ 2,020
	Unfavorable	Favorable	Unfavorable	Unfavorable
Standard cost of the 4,500 rejects	$405	$270	$180	$855

The standard cost of good units charged to the work-in-process–assembly account and the standard cost of rejects charged to the rejects account are as follows:

	Charged to Work-in-Process Assembly	Charged to Rejects	Total
Number of units	96,500	4,500	101,000
Standard unit cost	$ 0.19	$ 0.19	$ 0.19
Total cost	$18,335	$ 855	$ 19,190

The company's controller is considering a change in the costing method that would involve including an allowance for rejects in the standard costs. Given that the expected volume of rejects is 5%, the new standard cost of good units would include the cost of rejects at 5% of total units produced. If the change is undertaken, there would no longer be a rejects account.

If the company undertakes the change, what would be the production costs by component (i.e., materials, labor, and overhead) that would be transferred to the work-in-process–assembly? What would be the variances by component? What are the advantages and disadvantages of the present costing method and the proposed costing method?

3–13. Describe the change in information required if a company shifts from one system to another:

  a. From an actual job costing system to a standard job costing system;

  b. From an actual process costing system to an actual job costing system.

CHAPTER 4

VARIABLE COSTING

Some years ago, the manufacturing vice president of a company making timing devices was asked by a firm across town if he could make some machined parts for the other firm, which was having trouble meeting a deadline on a government contract. The vice president knew that things were a bit slack at the moment at his plant (as was also the case with several similar plants nearby), so he said that he thought he could make the parts and would have his controller work up a price. The part would need precision-machining, one assembly step, and packing.

After asking the controller for a price, the vice president, who had been around for many years, took out his own little black book of costs and worked up an estimate. When the controller came back with his version of the cost, the vice president nearly exploded. "It's that stupid overhead in the screw machine room," he said, "I've always thought that 325% was too high. This time I'll fix you, though. I'm going to move one of those screw machines into the assembly department where overhead is only 75% and then we'll be able to make a decent bid on this job."

The controller was so shaken that he talked it over with the firm's president. Eventually the debate led to adoption of a variable costing system.

Variable costing,[1]—often called by the less accurate name, direct costing—has frequently been described and promoted as a wonderful new accounting system that provides management with radically improved tools for decision-making. When all the smoke has cleared, however, one can see that the new system does not use any innovative concepts, nor is it particularly radical in design. Its main advantage is that it is a useful discipline in cost accumulation, which, if not previously practiced, provides new, helpful information for many kinds of decisions. It is applicable to all organizations. In this chapter we refer to *products*, but that phrase embraces the output of manufacturers, service firms, nonprofits, and governments—indeed, all organizations. We will also refer to *production costs*, which for a manufacturing company are all factory costs and for a service company are all service delivery costs, such as materials, direct and indirect labor, and other delivery overheads. Excluded from production costs are research and development, sales, marketing, and corporate office costs.

In this chapter and throughout the remainder of this book, we will distinguish between *cost behavior* (costs are either fixed or variable with respect to volume) and *cost assignment* (costs are either direct or indirect). This distinction can be illustrated as follows:

---

[1] The alternative, more common system is called *full costing* or *full absorption costing.*

Cost Behavior

Cost Assignment	Variable	Fixed
Direct	A	B
Indirect	C	D

Variable costs increase or decrease in proportion to production or service level volumes. *Fixed costs* are independent of volume changes over normal ranges of operations. Semivariable costs are discussed in Chapter 5. *Direct costs* are those that can be tracked or measured by product, whereas *indirect costs* cannot and thus must be allocated to products in some fashion. In the figure, category A costs are those that vary with volume and can be measured by product. The material content of most manufactured products would fall into category A. Some materials (which we generally term *supplies*) are variable but indirect because we know they vary with volume, but we can't or choose not to try to measure or track them by product; they fall into category C. Category B, which is made up of direct fixed costs, would be something like the depreciation on a machine only used to make one particular product. That cost doesn't vary with volume, but we know which product it should be assigned to. Category D, which includes costs such as the plant manager's or office manager's salary, is fixed and cannot be traced to a particular product or service. Direct costs are measured by products. Indirect costs must be allocated, they are what we call *overhead.*

Basically, variable costing involves:

1. Categorizing all production costs (manufacturing or service delivery) as either fixed or variable. The variable costs usually consist of material, direct labor and some part of indirect labor, and those elements of overhead costs that are considered variable.

2. Maintaining product inventory or accumulated service costs at values that include only variable costs.

3. Accounting for nonvariable or fixed production costs as period expenses. They are not added to inventory or accumulated service costs (and consequently are not part of the cost of sales), but are charged off during the accounting period in which they are incurred.

4. Changing the internal financial reporting so that the company, division, and product-line income statements automatically show variable gross margins (revenues minus variable costs), figures that are essentially the same as the *contribution* (which will be discussed in the next section).

In short, variable costing takes fixed manufacturing and service delivery overhead out of current assets and cost of sales, calling it a period expense. Only those fixed costs are treated differently. It may seem like a small change, but its implications can be revolutionary.

VARIABLE COSTING COMPARED TO FULL COSTING

You may remember that full costing, whether a standard costing system or not, distributes all manufacturing or service delivery costs to the product. Variable costing distributes only variable production costs to the product or service. Variable costing is usually described as providing new information, because most companies come to the system by shifting from a traditional full costing system. Thus, comparing the two systems will highlight the choices they offer. (Later in this chapter, however, we will point out that the two systems are not really mutually exclusive.)

Cost information is valuable only in the context of its use by management. Hence, we will examine the usefulness of variable costing for the types of management decisions described in Chapter 1. We can then determine whether variable costing provides information that is more useful, accurate, or relevant than that provided by the traditional full costing system.

EVALUATING PRODUCT PROFITABILITY

To see how variable costing can assist in evaluating product profitability, let us consider two income statements for a company with a broad line of products. The company income statement in Figure 4–1 shows the same net profit under full costing and variable costing. Profits will be the same under both systems as long as the inventory remains level. (What happens when inventory changes will be explained later.) Under the full costing system, fixed and variable manufacturing costs are not separated. Under variable costing, they are separated, $40,000 variable and $30,000 fixed, a separation that allows the company to calculate its variable gross margin.

	Full Costing	Variable Costing
(inventory level unchanged)		
Sales	$100,000	$100,000
Variable cost of sales		40,000
Variable gross margin		$ 60,000
Fixed manufacturing or service-delivery cost		30,000
Full cost of sales	70,000	0
Gross margin	$ 30,000	$ 30,000
Administrative and selling expenses	20,000	20,000
Operating income	$ 10,000	$ 10,000

Figure 4–1: *Company Income Statements*

Figure 4–2 shows how income statements for one of the company's product lines would look under each system. Since in variable costing, fixed production costs are not distributed to the various products, but are instead charged off in total as a period cost, there is no entry beyond the variable gross margin. Our comparative question, then, is whether the variable gross margin is more useful for evaluating product profitability than the total gross margin is.

	Full Costing	Variable Costing
(inventory level unchanged)		
Sales (10,000 units)	$20,000	$20,000
Variable cost of goods sold		
($1.00 per unit)		10,000
Variable gross margin		$10,000
Fixed manufacturing cost		not avail.
Full cost of goods sold	15,000	
($1.50 per unit)		
Gross margin	$ 5,000	

Figure 4–2: *Product G–2 Income Statements*

The variable gross margin is really a ready-made figure representing contribution to fixed costs. This gross margin as a percentage of sales (sometimes called the profit to volume ratio or P/V) should remain constant under the various levels of volume. With that ratio, one can quickly calculate how a change in volume will affect profit.

For example, in Figure 4–2, product G–2 has a P/V of 0.5 (variable gross margin divided by sales). If sales are expected to increase $2,000, the P/V shows that the expected increase in profit is $1,000 (0.5 × $2,000 = $1,000). The gross margin of 25% of sales (after full costs) is not helpful, because total gross margin cannot be expressed to vary directly with sales volume.

One can also use the breakeven analytical framework to show the difference between the two systems. The graph shown in Figure 4–3 uses the total company figures shown earlier in Figure 4–1. The dashed line shows how total manufacturing costs will *appear* to vary with volume, according to a full costing system. In other words, the dashed line shows the total costs that will be absorbed into inventory and charged to the cost of goods sold. The other total cost line, which is dotted, shows the effect of separating fixed and variable costs, as is done under variable costing. Note that the full cost line is always below the revenue line, suggesting that there will always be some gross margin whatever the volume. Advocates of the variable costing method say that this implication is an inaccurate and misleading representation of the way costs actually behave. They point out that variable costing shows that when volume is below 50,000, revenue will be below total costs and a loss will be sustained.

This is such an important point we'll say it another way. Look again at Figure 4–3. How do costs change with changes in volume? The $30,000 of fixed manufacturing cost stays the same no matter what volume is produced, while the *total* variable cost ($0.4/unit) increases with volume. The line labeled "total costs: variable cost system" perfectly describes the cost behavior in this admittedly simple situation, while the "total costs: full cost system" line does not! It is based on the assumption that the average production volume (called standard volume or financial-planning volume) would be 100,000 units. At 100,000 units, the total cost is:

Variable cost	$40,000
Fixed cost	30,000
Total cost	$70,000

So $70,000/100,000 units is $0.70. The total cost line is $0.70/unit at every level of volume. Figure 4–3 is an excellent illustration of the problems caused by full costing: At production volumes below 100,000 units, only a portion of the fixed manufacturing costs are absorbed into inventory. The remainder is unabsorbed cost. And similarly, at production volumes greater than 100,000 units, more cost is absorbed or charged into inventory than was actually incurred (overabsorbed costs).

Classifying costs as fixed or variable certainly improves the evaluation of product profitability under varying volumes. It is dangerous, however, to ignore fixed costs entirely or to assume those costs will always remain fixed. Fixed costs have a way of staying the same for a while and then jumping up when an accumulation of capacity pressures forces a decision to expand or change a process. Theoretically, every decision should have its own classification of costs but, except for major decisions, the reclassification effort would not be worthwhile. Thus, the variable gross-margin figure aids many management decisions, but its accuracy should be accepted with caution.

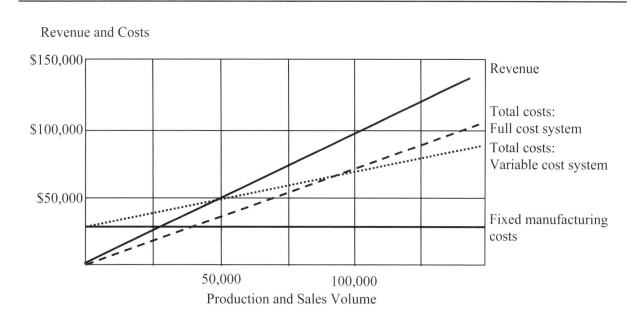

Figure 4–3: *A Comparison of Total Cost Lines*

Some companies develop two levels of variable gross margin to provide two types of contribution. The following table shows variable margin computed in the usual way. From this margin is subtracted product-related fixed costs—those costs which, although fixed in the usual sense, are directly applicable to the product. Depreciation on machinery specially designed for the product and the product manager's salary are examples. While fixed for varying sales volumes, those costs could be avoided if the product were dropped. Thus, they are variable for the decision to keep or to drop the product.

	Product A	Product B
Sales	$1,000	$2,000
Variable costs	550	1,600
Variable margin	$ 450	$ 400
Product-related fixed costs	300	50
Product gross margin	$ 150	$ 350

The two levels of contribution are useful for different decisions. The variable margin is useful for decisions on pricing, advertising, and product design. The product contribution figure is not helpful for those decisions, but does help in evaluating what kind of business to be in.

PRICING

It has been said that sales managers love variable costing, while manufacturing managers distrust it. The reason for those preferences is that with only variable costs included, product costs will be lower, and the sales manager will have an easier argument for lower prices, which lead to more sales and happier salespeople. When the manufacturing vice president in the story at the beginning of this chapter wanted to cut his overhead by moving the screw machine into the assembly department, he was acting just like a sales manager.

Most manufacturing managers, on the other hand, focus on all those overhead costs that must be covered by sales revenue and fear that if margins are narrowed too much, overhead may never be covered.

Certainly, enlightened management should have no difficulty overcoming that dilemma. One can have the best of both worlds, either by adding appropriate percentage margins onto variable costs or by using a full costing system that clearly separates fixed and variable costs so that marginal costs can be analyzed.

DETERMINING PROFIT VARIATIONS WHEN INVENTORY LEVELS CHANGE

Variable costing introduces one bothersome difference in profits, which appears only when there is a change in inventory either in work in process or finished goods.

If we start from the premise that manufacturing costs end up in inventory, cost of goods sold, or under variable costing, some costs have a third track and become a period expense, then we can see how profits will be affected by inventory changes. The following diagram portrays the distribution of costs under both systems.

From that diagram, we can see that the treatment of fixed overhead makes a difference. With variable costing, fixed overhead costs are always period costs and are expensed during the period. With full costing, they are expenses of the period only if the inventory of which they are a part of is sold. If the inventory is not sold (inventory increases), some of the period's fixed costs will be capitalized, to be expensed later when the inventory is sold. (Also, one can see that if inventory decreases, some of last period's fixed costs are expenses of this period.) The following examples will illustrate those discrepancies.

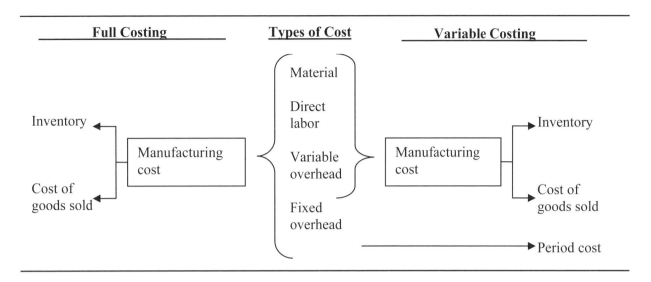

Suppose that finished goods inventory rises during the period from 1,000 units to 1,500 units of product G–2, as described in Figure 4–2. The cost of inventory would look like this:

	Full Costing		Variable Costing	
	1,000 Units Beginning	*1,500 Units Ending*	*1,000 Units Beginning*	*1,500 Units Ending*
Variable cost (at $1.00/unit)			$1,000	$1,500
Full cost (at $1.50/unit)	$1,500	$2,250		
Increase		$750		$500

One can see that $750 has been added to inventory under the full costing system, but only $500 under the variable costing system. We know that costs not in inventory must be charged to the period. The $250 difference represents fixed costs that variable costing leaves out of inventory and charges to the period. Hence, variable costing will show $250 higher charges to the period and $250 lower profits; full costing, on the other hand, will show higher profits when inventory rises during the period. Those differences are shown in Figures 4–4 and 4–5.

Figure 4–4 presents a period of G–2 sales and production in which production is constant at 10,000 units (as shown in Figure 4–2), but sales have decreased. Hence, inventory rises and profits are $250 higher under full costing. Figure 4–5 shows the effects of a reverse change in inventory. Sales have increased, inventory has decreased (production again being constant), and profits are lower under full costing.

Figure 4–6 holds sales the same as in Figure 4–5 and increases production so that inventory increases and profits rise under full costing. It is sometimes said that when inventory rises under full costing, some fixed overhead is *sold to inventory* and, hence, avoids being a cost of the period. Of course, if inventory is reduced later on, the opposite effect will result. That high-cost inventory (full cost is higher than variable cost) will become cost of goods sold during the period and profits will be lower.

	Full Costing	Variable Costing
Sales (9,500 units @ $2.00 ea.)	$19,000	$19,000
Cost of goods sold:		
Beginning inventory (1,000 units)	1,500	1,000
Variable cost of goods manufactured (10,000 units @ $1.00 ea.)		10,000
Full cost of goods manufactured (10,000 units @ $1.50 ea.)	15,000	
Less: ending inventory (1,500 units)	(2,250)	(1,500)
Total cost of goods sold	$14,250	$ 9,500
Gross margin	$ 4,750	$ 9,500
Fixed manufacturing costs	0	5,000
Net before selling and administrative	$ 4,750	$ 4,500

Figure 4–4: *Inventory Rising: Production Constant, Sales Decrease*

	Full Costing	Variable Costing
Sales (10,500 units @ $2.00 ea.)	$21,000	$21,000
Cost of goods sold:		
Beginning inventory (1,500 units)	2,250	1,500
Variable cost of goods manufactured (10,000 units @ $1.00 ea.)		10,000
Full cost of goods manufactured (10,000 units @ $1.50 ea.)	15,000	
Less: ending inventory (1,000 units)	(1,500)	(1,000)
Total cost of goods sold	$15,750	$10,500
Gross margin	$ 5,250	$10,500
Fixed manufacturing costs	0	5,000
Net before selling and administrative	$ 5,250	$ 5,500

Figure 4–5: *Inventory Falling: Production Constant, Sales Increase*

One can summarize the effects as follows:

When production exceeds sales, inventory rises, and profits are higher under the full costing system (lower under variable costing).

When sales exceed production, inventory declines, and profits are lower under the full costing system (higher under variable costing).

One can also see that under the variable costing system, profits increase or decrease along with sales volume, and are unaffected by variations in production volume (compare Figure 4–6 with Figure 4–5). This relationship exists because fixed production costs are charged to the period regardless of production or sales volumes. Under full costing, some of those fixed production costs may be left in or taken out of inventory, depending on the relative amounts of production and sales. Thus, variable costing advocates can say that since profits should reflect realized sales and not inventory changes, variable costing does a better job than full costing in presenting a reliable profit picture.

	Full Costing	Variable Costing
Sales (10,500 units @ $2.00 ea.)	$21,000	$21,000
Cost of goods sold:		
Beginning inventory (1,000 units)	1,500	1,000
Variable cost of goods manufactured		
(11,000 units @ $1.00 ea.)		11,000
Full cost of goods manufactured		
(11,000 units @ $1.50 ea.)	16,500	
Less: overabsorbed fixed costs*	(500)	
Less: ending inventory (1,500 units)	(2,250)	(1,500)
Total cost of goods sold	$15,250	$10,500
Gross margin	$ 5,750	$10,500
Fixed manufacturing costs	0	5,000
Net before selling and administrative	$ 5,750	$ 5,500

* Assuming actual fixed costs remain fixed at $5,000, production of 11,000 units would cause $5,500 to be absorbed (at $0.50 per unit), hence the favorable overabsorption of $500.

Figure 4–6: *Inventory Rising: Production Increased, Sales Constant*

PLANNING INTERDIVISIONAL SALES

When products are sold by one division to another, and perhaps after further work are sold again to a third, an interesting phenomenon arises: fixed costs appear to be variable.

If division A sells to division B, the *transfer price* will normally cover all costs and perhaps provide a profit, too. From division B's viewpoint, its purchase cost is variable; but from A's point of view, that transfer price reflects more than just variable cost. It may reflect a large proportion of fixed costs.

The same relationships will exist when division B sells to division C. Then perhaps division C sells to an outside customer. When division C is doing its cost–volume–profit analysis, costs that are variable from division C's point of view will not be variable from the company-wide viewpoint. (Division C may see 75% variable costs while in fact, for the company as a whole, those costs may be only 35% variable.) It is possible, then, that division C might make a decision that is good for it, but bad for the company as a whole. Alleviating that problem is not easy. Two steps are necessary. The first is to recognize the existence of the problem, and the second is to have available the fixed and variable split of all costs. This information would be available automatically if the company had a variable costing system, but often there are reasons why this information is not shared, even under a variable costing system. These reasons have to do with transfer pricing and are discussed in Chapter 10.

VARIABLE COSTING AND EXTERNAL REPORTING

Variable costing is not generally accepted as a basis for external reporting. The United States' generally accepted accounting principles (GAAP) require that the reported cost of a manufactured product should not omit any element of the manufacturing cost. Thus, inventory costs should include the fixed manufacturing cost.

A company using variable costing for internal purposes is therefore obligated to convert the variable cost of inventory to a full cost when preparing external financial statements. This conversion is commonly handled by adding an estimated amount of fixed cost based on an overall fixed-cost to variable-cost ratio. Similarly, the cost of sales must be adjusted.

VARIABLE COSTING USING SEVERAL LEVELS OF COSTS

Many companies recognize that some costs are fixed at one level, but variable at another. The cost of depreciation and maintenance of specialized machinery, for example, would be fixed for small changes in unit volume, but variable for a big change that would alter the amount of equipment required or for a decision on whether to drop the product.

One way to portray those levels of variability is by using a multilevel income statement. Figure 4–7 is an example used by a food company for each of its consumer product lines.

Net Sales

Variable manufacturing cost
Freight
Public warehousing

Total variable cost of sales

Variable Profit Contribution

Manufacturing nonvariable cost
Plant warehousing
Other nonvariable costs

Total nonvariable cost of sales

Delivered Profit

Advertising
Sales promotion
Marketing services–direct
Marketing write-offs
Product group
Selling direct

Total direct marketing expense

Direct Profit Contribution

Selling
Marketing services
Technical research
Administrative

Total indirect expense

New product development charge

Trading Profit

Figure 4–7: *Statement of Product-Line Profit and Loss*

An interpretation of the four levels of profit depicted in Figure 4–7 might be as follows:

1. *Variable profit contribution* is derived from sales and variable manufacturing costs including outbound freight and public warehousing costs (used only when volume is high). It is a short-run view of the contribution to all other costs.

2. *Delivered profit* recognizes nonvariable manufacturing and warehousing costs of this product, and is therefore a longer-run view of the contribution from making and selling the product.

3. *Direct profit contribution* recognizes marketing costs incurred for the product.

4. *Trading profit* recognizes expenses that do not directly support the product line, but which are incurred in support of the overall business. Selling is an indirect expense in this company, because all products share the sales organization.

The different levels of variability shown in this statement are used to provide data that can be used to answer different questions. Depending on their job, different people apply different contribution numbers to the decisions they make.

THROUGHPUT ACCOUNTING

Some companies use a version of variable costing called *throughput accounting*,[2] popularized by Eliyahu M. Goldratt, where the only variable costs are for material. All the other costs that Goldratt calls operating expenses are considered fixed. The variable contribution is then revenue minus material costs and is called throughput. When there is a constraint or bottleneck, a product's variable contribution in dollars per unit of bottleneck capacity (often hours) is used to measure the relative profitability of products. The higher the throughput per bottleneck per hour, the higher the relative profitability. The measure helps companies use the bottleneck resource effectively and often shows a high value of increasing the bottleneck's capacity.[3]

A MATRIX OF COST SYSTEM CHOICES

In this and previous chapters, we have described a number of different ways costs can be collected, organized, and analyzed. In designing a system, there are basically three separate choices, which result in eight possible combinations. The three choices are as follows:

1. Actual or standard costing systems;

2. Job or process costing systems;

3. Full or variable costing systems.

In order to emphasize the differences between costing systems, a three dimensional cost system matrix has proven useful in putting all major types in one framework. As shown in Figure 4–8, the matrix has eight compartments, four representing full cost systems and four representing the variable cost versions of the same four basic systems.

---

[2] Eliyahu M. Goldratt, *Theory of Constraints* (Great Barrington, Massachusetts: North River Press, 1990).

[3] William Rotch and Kim Constantinides, "Champion International Corporation's Hamilton Mill," (Darden Business Publishing, UVA) UVA-C-2105; and John Shank and Kim Constantinides, "Matching Accounting to Strategy: One Mill's Experience," *Management Accounting* (September 1994) 76, 3: 32–36.

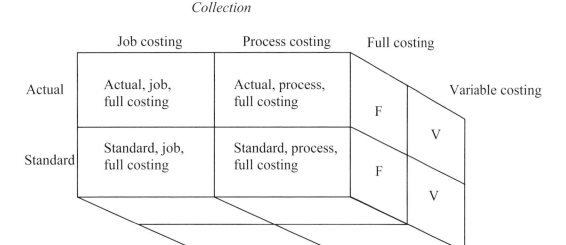

Figure 4–8: *Cost System Matrix*

Below is a brief description of the four basic types of systems. It is worth noting that the quadrant containing the standard process costing systems, has two parts, the second of which probably would not normally be described as a type of process costing system. This is a fairly common system for a company producing a variety of products, for which there are standard costs, but whose management has decided not to collect actual costs by product. Since actual costs are collected for a process by time period, it is classified here as a process costing system. With that system, variances can be developed by department or process, but cannot be related to the individual product or lot. This highlights the fact that the distinctive feature of process costing systems is the method used to collect actual costs (by time period, not by product) rather than that costs are collected by process, or that the products produced are homogeneous.

In order to clarify the tradeoffs involved in choosing between systems, it is useful to consider what changes in information gathering and reporting would result from a shift from one quadrant to another. First, shifting from a process to a job costing system would require measuring costs, or specifically, the costs of labor, material, and overhead inputs, that are associated with a job, or some unit of output less than the total produced in the accounting period. Second, shifting from an actual job cost system to a standard job cost system would require establishing standard product costs, but would allow inventories to be kept at standard cost and facilitate the development of variances.

Any one of the basic systems can be either a full cost or variable cost system. The primary purpose of this matrix, therefore, is to focus on the differences among the four main classifications, any of which can be set up as either full cost or variable cost systems.

Actual, Job, Full Costing

Actual costs collected (may use standard labor rates or standard material prices) for each job, lot, or order. Some sort of job sheet is often used. No standard quantities are used in the cost system. A standard rate may be used to apply overhead.

Illustration: A printer collects costs on each job by having the operators record times on a job ticket accompanying the work. Each job is different. Job costs are obtained by multiplying operator times by a predetermined full cost rate and totaling the cost of all operations.

Actual, Process, Full Costing

Costs are collected for a time period and related to the units produced during the time period to get actual cost per unit. Work in process may be assumed not to vary or may be computed using equivalent units of production. For the latter, the extent of the completion of work in process may be estimated to be constant (for example: all units at 50%) or may be computed from direct observation.

Illustration: A paper company producing various widths and thicknesses of paper accumulates all direct and overhead costs of running the paper-making machine and at month end computes cost per pound produced.

Standard, Job, Full Costing

Standard quantities (labor hours and material amounts) are computed ahead of time, usually at the beginning of the year. Actual quantities are collected on job sheets (or time cards), and variances can be computed right away. Variances are linked to each item or lot produced.

Illustration: A ball bearing manufacturer has computed standard costs for each size and type of bearing. Actual times and quantities are noted on the job ticket accompanying each lot. For each lot produced, actual costs incurred in each operation can be compared with standard costs.

Standard, Process, Full Costing

Costs for a department or process are collected for a time period.

If units are to be considered as homogeneous, then the number of units produced times their standard cost is the output at standard cost. Comparison with actual inputs produces variances. Equivalent units of production may be used to value work in process.

Illustration: A bottling machine fills and caps bottles all month. The predetermined standard cost per bottle is compared at the end of the month with the average actual cost per bottle.

If units are not homogeneous, then the number of each unit times its standard cost gives the standard cost of production of that unit. The total standard cost of all units is then compared to the total actual cost of inputs to produce variances. Equivalent units of production must be computed or assumed for each type of unit. Variances cannot be linked to a particular product.

Illustration: A food company assembles, cooks, and freezes various kinds of TV dinners and pot pies. Each item has a predetermined standard cost of ingredients, labor, and overhead. At the end of the month, the total actual costs of ingredients, labor, and overhead are compared with the standard cost of whatever was produced that month. For example, the total standard cost of chicken in all the items containing chicken would be compared with the actual cost of the chicken used.

Variable Costing Systems

The four variable costing systems are the same as the four full costing just described except that only variable costs are considered. Fixed costs are not attached to products, but are expensed directly in the period in which they are incurred.

SUMMARY

Variable costing is primarily used for internal management reporting. Its use obliges management to distinguish between fixed and variable costs and results in a variable gross margin (or contribution) measure of product profitability. This measure is more useful in short-run decisions, that is, those decisions that affect only variable costs. Fixed manufacturing costs are considered to be a period cost and, hence, are unaffected by volume changes. In fact, some of those fixed costs tend to vary in the longer run. Thus, variable costing data on profitability should be used carefully.

QUESTIONS AND PROBLEMS

4–1. Do you agree that the commonly used term *direct costing* is less accurate than the term *variable costing* to describe the costing system discussed in this chapter? Explain your reasoning.

4–2. Why would a company use two levels of variable gross margin, such as the variable margin and the product contribution described in this chapter.

4–3. What does the expression *selling fixed costs to inventory* mean?

4–4. What would you say to the manufacturing vice president who, as related at the beginning of the chapter, wanted to move a screw machine across the hall to take advantage of the assembly department's lower overhead rate?

4–5. How can it be that costs for one division are variable, but those same costs are fixed for the company as a whole?

4–6. Using the cost figures given in the chapter for G–2, develop two income statements, one for full costing and the other for variable costing, if sales are 10,500 units and production is 10,000 units.

SECTION TWO

USING COSTS IN MANAGEMENT DECISIONS

CHAPTER 5

RELEVANT COST ANALYSIS:
ECONOMIC ANALYSIS FOR BUSINESS DECISIONS

Skillful decision-making is an art. But that art is based on knowledge of revenue and cost behavior. Costs are meaningful only in the light of specific assumptions and conditions. Thus, many different concepts of cost exist and yield varying cost figures. Understanding those concepts and using them appropriately in problem situations is termed *relevant cost analysis*. Actually, relevant cost analysis covers revenues as well as costs. Hence, this chapter has the more general subtitle "Economic Analysis for Business Decisions."

In chapter 2, we examined what caused or drove costs. We saw that there were a number of possible drivers. In that analysis, we assumed that all costs could be driven, or in other words, that there were no "fixed" costs. In this chapter, we recognize that there can be costs that will not change in the relevant time frame or from decisions being considered. For that reason, in this chapter, we focus on relatively short-term cost analysis and particularly on the effect of volume on costs.

COST BEHAVIOR: FIXED AND VARIABLE COSTS

The cost of a manufactured product or service is composed of many different elements. Those cost elements behave differently under varying circumstances. One of the most important circumstances affecting cost behavior is the volume or quantity of goods or services produced. Some costs vary directly with volume and are called *variable costs*. For example, the cost of steel in automobiles, food in a restaurant, professional staff in a law firm, or coal for a power company are variable costs in that the quantity of steel, food, billable time, or coal used is directly related to the quantity of automobiles produced, meals served, legal services provided, or kilowatts generated. It should be noted that the total amount of variable cost changes with volume, but the cost per unit remains the same. The cost of the steel in each car will be the same whether 50,000 or 60,000 cars are produced. Other costs do not vary directly with the quantity produced and are called *fixed costs*. The plant manager's salary in the auto factory, the cost of the restaurant's or law firm's rent, and the depreciation of the electrical generator are examples of costs that do not change as the level of output changes. Some cost elements are neither fixed nor variable; those will be discussed later in this chapter.

The decision-maker must study each situation fully to determine the nature and significance of each cost element. The impact of volume on cost behavior can be seen in the following example from the Sunshine Manufacturing Company. Study this example carefully, for it will be used throughout this chapter to illustrate a number of relevant cost concepts.

Sunshine makes two types of Zingos—model A, which the company thinks costs $32.50, and model B, which costs $57.00. Figure 5–1 shows the company's analysis that determined those costs.

Sunshine Manufacturing Co.
Cost Report
(full cost basis)

		A Zingos		B Zingos
Production volume		20,000		5,000
Cost elements:				
Raw materials and purchased parts:		$8.00		$11.00
Direct labor:				
Fabrication	$1.50		$2.00	
Assembly	1.50		4.00	
Testing–packaging	<u>1.00</u>	4.00	<u>2.00</u>	8.00
Manufacturing overhead:				
Indirect labor	$2.00		$4.00	
Supplies	3.00		4.00	
Depreciation–building	6.00		12.00	
Depreciation–equipment	1.50		2.00	
Utilities and all other items	<u>8.00</u>	<u>20.50</u>	<u>16.00</u>	<u>38.00</u>
Total cost		<u>$32.50</u>		<u>$57.00</u>

Figure 5–1: *Cost Report: Full Cost Basis*

The costs shown in Figure 5–1 are called *full costs,* because they include all manufacturing costs.[1] That cost analysis covers the following elements:

1. *Raw materials and purchased parts.* Those are the estimated costs of the steel, plastic, wiring, and purchased parts included in each Zingo. They are clearly variable, because as the production level increases, more of those items must be purchased and used.

2. *Direct labor.* These cost elements reflect the labor payrolls in each of the three departments: fabrication, assembly, and packaging testing. These costs are also variable, because more workers must be added as the production level is increased. If production levels are reduced, the workforce is cut back.

3. *Indirect labor.* These costs include money spent for supervisors, material handlers, utility relief people, and cleanup crews. As explained in Chapter 2, these are indirect costs because they cannot be tied definitely to a particular product or job. Nevertheless, Sunshine considers those indirect labor costs to be variable with volume, because as production increases and more direct laborers are hired, Sunshine must also hire more supervisors, material handlers, and so on. From past experience, Sunshine determined that its indirect payroll is about half of its direct payroll. Because management expected that relationship to hold over normal operating levels, it allocated $1.00 of indirect labor for every $2.00 of direct labor used to make Zingos.

4. *Supplies.* Supplies are also variable. They include the cost of paint, packaging material, and miscellaneous items that, while difficult to measure using items produced, do vary with the level of production. The cost of supplies shown in Figure 5–1 was determined by plotting the past cost of supplies against production volume month-by-month on a graph. Volume was measured

---

[1] The alternative is called *direct costing,* or *variable costing*, in which case only variable costs are allocated to the product. That costing method was discussed in Chapter 4.

not in absolute units, but in labor dollars, because that measure reflected more adequately the larger size and production time of model B Zingos. That analysis revealed that for every $1.00 of direct labor, Sunshine spends about $0.75 on supplies for model A Zingos and $0.50 for model B Zingos. Thus, model A Zingos, with $4.00 direct labor, were allocated $3.00 of supplies per Zingo, while model Bs, with $8.00 direct labor, were allocated $4.00 of supplies.

5. *Depreciation of the building.* The factory building originally cost $3.6 million to construct and had an expected useful life of 20 years. Accordingly, $180,000 depreciation expense was charged to manufacturing each year. Depreciation was also allocated to products on the basis of volume, again measured in terms of labor content. Depreciation was a fixed cost, however. The depreciation cost per Zingo depended upon the number of Zingos produced. Accordingly, each year an estimate was made of production volume and that estimate—called planned or normal volume—was used to determine the depreciation cost of Zingos. Those calculations were as follows:

Zingo Model	Normal Volume (units)	Direct Labor Content (per unit)	Volume Expressed in Labor Dollars
A	20,000	$4.00	$80,000
B	5,000	8.00	40,000
			$120,000

Therefore,

$$\frac{\text{Yearly Depreciation Costs}}{\text{Expected Yearly Volume}} = \frac{\$180,000}{\$120,000} = 150\%$$

or a depreciation rate of 150% of direct labor. Thus, the cost of building depreciation for model A was set at $6.00 (150% × $4.00) and for model B at $12.00 per Zingo.

6. *Depreciation of equipment.* The depreciation cost for the equipment, although also a fixed cost, was allocated to products differently. Since all the equipment was in the fabrication department, Sunshine decided to allocate the depreciation cost of this equipment to products on the basis of the *volume in the fabrication department alone.* Volume was again measured in labor dollars. Sunshine's calculations were as follows:

Zingo Model	Normal Volume	Fabrication Direct Labor Content	Volume Expressed in Fabrication Labor Dollars
A	20,000	$1.50	$30,000
B	5,000	2.00	10,000
			$40,000

Because the yearly depreciation cost was $40,000, the depreciation rate was 100% as applied to fabrication labor:

$$\frac{\text{Yearly Depreciation Costs}}{\text{Expected Yearly Volume}} = \frac{\$40,000}{\$40,000} = 100\%$$

Thus, the equipment depreciation cost for model A was $1.50 (100% × $1.50) and for model B was $2.00.

7. *Utilities and all other items.* This entry included the costs of heat, light, power, telephone, taxes, the plant manager's office costs and salary, and other miscellaneous items. Those costs were essentially fixed, because experience had shown that they were insensitive to changes in the production level. Sunshine incurred costs of $240,000 per year in this category, and management was convinced that these costs would be substantially the same whether 25,000 Zingos were produced, or 10,000, or 50,000. These utilities and other costs were allocated to products in the same manner as building depreciation was. Since those costs were expected to be $240,000 per year, the overhead rate for these utility accounts was 200% of direct labor.

Thus, by stating all cost elements as a cost per Zingo, Sunshine was able to construct the full cost of each model Zingo as shown in Figure 5–1. This cost remained a good estimate as long as volume was close to the expected level. But if volume were different, a new kind of cost analysis was needed. To make this analysis the cost elements were restated as in Figure 5–2.

Sunshine Manufacturing Co.
Cost Report
(full cost basis)

	Variable Costs		
	A	*B*	*Fixed*
	Zingos	*Zingos*	*Cost*
Raw materials and purchased parts	$8.00	$11.00	$ 0.00
Direct labor:			
Fabrication	1.50	2.00	
Assembly	1.50	4.00	
Testing–packaging	1.00	2.00	
Manufacturing overhead:			
Indirect labor	2.00	4.00	
Supplies	3.00	4.00	
Depreciation–building			180,000
Depreciation–equipment			40,000
Utilities and all other items			240,000
Total Cost	$17.00	$27.00	$460,000

Figure 5–2: *Cost Report: Fixed and Variable Elements*

Thus, the variable costs for A and B Zingos are $17.00 and $27.00, respectively, and fixed costs are $460,000. It should be clear that Figures 5–1 and 5–2 portray the same basic facts. With the assumed volume of 25,000 Zingos,

	Model	*Projected Volume*
	A	20,000
	B	5,000
Total		25,000

the projected manufacturing costs would be $935,000, according to the full cost data shown in Figure 5–1.

Model	Full Cost	×	Volume	=	Total Costs
A	$32.50		20,000		$650,000
B	$57.00		5,000		285,000
					$935,000

Happily, as shown below, the same $935,000 projected cost figure could be obtained from the fixed and variable cost elements in Figure 5–2.

Model	Variable Cost	×	Volume	=	Total Variable Cost
A	$17.00		20,000		$340,000
B	$27.00		5,000		135,000
					$475,000
				Plus fixed costs:	460,000
				Total costs:	$935,000

PROFIT PLANNING WITH FIXED AND VARIABLE COSTS

Currently, A and B Zingos sell for $50.00 and $65.00, respectively. The market research group estimates that sales volume will increase to 35,000 units, if prices are lowered. The situation is as follows:

Model	Price	Projected Volume (units)
A	$50.00	20,000
B	65.00	5,000
		25,000

Market research recommends these prices and volumes:

Model	Price	Projected Volume (units)
A	$45.00	25,000
B	60.00	10,000
		35,000

If prices are lowered but volume is increased as suggested, will profits increase? That is the question to answer before making the decision to lower the price. It can be approached in a variety of ways. There is also a *wrong way* to attempt to solve this problem.

The first thing to do is to determine the profits under the current pricing system. Shown in Figure 5–3, there are three methods.

Under the *full cost method*, the full cost per unit is subtracted from the sales price to get the profit per unit, which is then multiplied by the projected volume of units to get the total profit. Under the *variable cost method*, the variable costs per unit are subtracted from the selling price to get the gross margin per unit. That gross margin is then multiplied by the project volume to get total gross profit. Under the *total sales less total cost method*, the total sales are first determined by multiplying the sales price by the projected volume. Next, the total costs (determined by either of the two methods previously discussed) are subtracted to yield total profit.

Before calculating the expected profits under the revised price and volume conditions, we will first look at the wrong way of attacking this problem to see why it's wrong. Figure 5–4 shows a projected profit of $342,500 at the new price and volume levels. Because that amount is less than the $390,000 profits under the existing conditions, we would be tempted to reject the market research group's recommendation. But Figure 5–4 is wrong. The full cost data in Figure 5–1 *cannot* be used to project the total cost at this new level of production, because those cost figures were based on the old, lower estimates of volume. Costs must be recalculated as shown in Figure 5–5, because both per-unit costs and total costs will change as volume is increased.

Because of the increased volume, the overhead rate for building depreciation drops from 150% to 100%. The overhead rates for equipment depreciation and for utilities, which are the other fixed costs, also drop. As a result, the new full costs for A and B become $27.37 and $47.06. That change illustrates two very important aspects of full costs. First, whenever there are fixed cost elements, certain assumptions must be made about expected volume, and the method of cost allocation must be determined before full cost figures can be established. Second, whenever volume changes, so do the full costs per unit.

1. Full cost method:

Model	Sales Price	−	Full Cost	=	Profit Margin	×	Estimated Volume	=	Projected Profits
A	$50.00		$32.50		$17.50		20,000		$350,000
B	65.00		57.00		8.00		5,000		40,000
									$390,000

2. Variable cost method:

Model	Sales Price	−	Variable Cost	=	Profit Margin	×	Estimated Volume	=	Gross Profits
A	$50.00		$17.00		$33.00		20,000		$660,000
B	65.00		27.00		38.00		5,000		190,000
									$850,000
								Less fixed costs:	460,000
								Total profits:	$390,000

3. Total sales less total costs method:

Model	Sales Price	×	Estimated Volume	=	Total Sales
A	$50.00		20,000		$1,000,000
B	65.00		5,000		325,000
					$1,325,000
				Less total costs:	935,000
				Total profits:	$ 390,000

Figure 5–3: *Projected Profits with Existing Prices*

Model	Sales Price	−	Full Cost	=	Profit Margin	×	Estimated Volume	=	Projected Profits
A	$45.00		$32.50		$12.50		25,000		$312,500
B	60.00		57.00		3.00		10,000		30,000
									$342,500

Figure 5–4: *Projected Profits with Revised Prices—The Wrong Way*

Note that the revisions shown in Figure 5–5 required a lengthy set of calculations and considerable time to complete. Another set of volume projections would require a similar effort. If there were many products and many possible levels of volume under consideration, nothing short of a computer could perform all the calculations necessary to budget total profit.

Sunshine Manufacturing Company
Cost Report with Revised Production Volume
(full cost basis)

	A Zingos	B Zingos	Explanation of Revisions
Production volume	25,000	10,000	
Cost elements:			
Raw materials, etc.	$8.00	$11.00	No change
Direct labor	4.00	8.00	No change
Manufacturing overhead:			
Indirect labor	2.00	4.00	No change
Supplies	3.00	4.00	No change
Depreciation–building	4.00	8.00	See note A
Depreciation–equipment	1.04	1.39	See note B
Utilities and all other items	5.33	10.67	See note C
Total Costs	$27.37	$47.06	

Note A: revised calculation of building depreciation rate:

Model	Revised Volume	Direct Labor Content	In Labor Dollars
A	25,000 units	$4.00	$100,000
B	10,000 units	8.00	80,000
			$180,000

$$\frac{\text{Yearly Depreciation Costs}}{\text{Revised Yearly Volume}} = \frac{\$180,000}{\$180,000} = 100\%$$

Therefore building depreciation cost for model A is 100% of $4.00 direct labor cost and for model B is 100% of $8.00 direct labor cost.

Note B: revised calculation of equipment depreciation rate:

Model	Revised Volume	Fabrication Direct Labor	Volume Expressed in Fabrication Labor Dollars
A	25,000 units	$1.50	$37,500
B	10,000 units	2.00	20,000
			$57,500

$$\frac{\text{Yearly Depreciation Costs}}{\text{Revised Fabrication Volume}} = \frac{\$40,000}{\$57,500} = 69.5\%$$

Model A: 69.5% of $1.50 = $1.04
Model B: 69.5% of $2.00 = $1.39

Note C: revised calculation of utilities, and so on, rate:

$$\frac{\text{Yearly Depreciation Costs}}{\text{Revised Yearly Volume}} = \frac{\$240,000}{\$180,000} = 133.3\%$$

Model A: 133.3% of $4.00 = $5.33
Model B: 133.3% of $8.00 = $10.67

With these new per-unit cost figures, the total cost at the new volume can be calculated as:

Model	Full Cost	×	Volume	=	Total Cost
A	$27.37		25,000		$ 684,250
B	47.06		10,000		470,600
					$1,154,850

Figure 5–5: *Cost Report: Revised Production Volume*

Fortunately, there is an easier way. The fixed and variable cost elements from Figure 5–2 can be used to make the total cost calculations very quickly.

Model	Variable Cost	×	Volume	=	Total Variable Cost
A	$17.00		25,000		$425,000
B	27.00		10,000		270,000
					$695,000
				Plus fixed costs:	460,000
				Total costs:	$1,155,000

Note: The slight difference between the $1,155,000 and the $1,154,850 is from rounding.

With those few figures, the project profits at the new sales price and volumes can easily be determined by any of the methods previously discussed. Those calculations are shown in Figure 5–6 and show identical results.[2]

---

[2] Again, slight differences in results are due to the fact that the revised full cost figures are rounded numbers.

1. Full cost method:

Model	Sales Price	−	Full Cost	=	Profit Margin	×	Estimated Volume	=	Projected Profits
A	$45		$27.37		$17.63		25,000		$440,750
B	60		47.06		12.94		10,000		129,400
									$570,150

2. Variable cost method:

Model	Sales Price	−	Variable Cost	=	Profit Margin	×	Estimated Volume	=	Gross Profits
A	$45		$17		28		25,000		$700,000
B	60		27		33		10,000		330,000
									$1,030,000
							Less fixed cost:		460,000
							Total profits:		$ 570,000

3. Total sales less total cost method:

Model	Sales Price	×	Estimated Volume	=	Total Sales
A	$45		25,000		$1,125,000
B	60		10,000		600,000
					$1,725,000
			Less total cost:		1,155,000
			Total profits:		$ 570,000

Figure 5–6: *Projected Profits with Revised Prices and Volumes*

These profits are much higher. Thus, in the absence of any other data, Sunshine should accept the market research group's recommendations and reduce its prices.

CONTRIBUTION

The terms *contribution* or *marginal contribution* or *contribution to overhead and profit* essentially have the same meaning. Contribution is the difference between the selling price of a product or service and its variable costs; it is the amount of funds available to cover the fixed costs and to provide profit. If the selling prices of A and B Zingos are $50.00 and $65.00, respectively, contribution is calculated as follows:

	A	B
Sales price	$ 50.00	$65.00
Less: variable costs		
Materials	8.00	11.00
Direct labor	4.00	8.00
Overhead	5.00	8.00
Total variable cost	$17.00	$27.00
Contribution	$33.00	$38.00

Contribution is not the same as profit, if there are fixed costs. The relationship between contribution and profit can be illustrated in several ways. One method is the per-unit calculation shown in Figure 5–7.

	A	B
Sales price	$50.00	$65.00
Less: variable costs	17.00	27.00
Contribution	$33.00	$38.00
Less: fixed costs*	15.50	30.00
Profit/unit	$17.50	$ 8.00

* Assuming an estimated volume of 20,000 and 5,000 units as shown in Figure 5–1.

Figure 5–7: *Profit Calculation Using Fixed Cost per Unit*

A second method shows the relationship in terms of total dollars as shown in Figure 5–8.

Contribution has many uses in business decision-making. The effect on profit of changes in selling price, unit volume, or variable cost can easily and quickly be seen by determining the change in contribution. For example, take the situation depicted in Figure 5–8:

	A	B	Total
Sales price	$ 50.00	$ 65.00	
Less: variable costs	17.00	27.00	
Contribution/unit	$ 33.00	$ 38.00	
Times: volume	× 20,000	× 5,000	
Total contribution	$660,000	$190,000	$850,000
Less: fixed cost			460,000
Total profit			$390,000

Figure 5–8: *Profit Calculation Using Total Fixed Cost*

Suppose that the unit volume of B Zingos is 8,000, rather than 5,000. What is the effect on total profit? Clearly, we would be adding an extra 3,000 units at $38.00 contribution per unit or $114,000 to profit. Suppose instead that the selling price of model B falls by $8.00. What happens to profit? Here the decrease in contribution is $8.00 per unit times 5,000 units ($40,000). We'll see other examples in this chapter of how the concept of contribution aids the decision-maker.

DECISION-MAKING: RELEVANT COSTS

The accounting rules for preparing financial statements, such as the income statement and the balance sheet, require that costs be handled in certain prescribed ways. In accordance with those rules, product and service costs are calculated as shown in Figure 5–1. Unfortunately, such cost determinations are rarely the right costs to use in a decision-making situation. One must get behind such calculations to determine what cost figures are really relevant for a particular decision. We can illustrate this process with the information we now possess concerning Sunshine Manufacturing.

Suppose that the selling price of model B Zingos drops to $55.00, due to competition. Because Figure 5–1 shows the full manufactured cost of these products as $57.00, the question of dropping model B is immediately raised. Why sell at a loss? If one works solely with the data in Figure 5–1, one has to question if the product should be dropped. Otherwise, Sunshine will lose $10,000:

New sales price	$ 55.00
Cost	57.00
Loss/unit	$ 2.00
× Projected volume	5,000
Expected loss	$10,000

But there is more to this matter than first meets the eye. One approach to this problem is to predict changes in revenue and costs. If the product is dropped, what items will be affected? A *differential analysis* can be set up as in Figure 5–9:

	Keep Model B (5,000 units)	Drop Model B	Differences
Revenue:			
Sales	$275,000	$ 0	$ (275,000)
Costs:			
Materials	55,000	0	55,000
Direct labor	40,000	0	40,000
Indirect labor	20,000	0	20,000
Supplies	20,000	0	20,000
Depreciation–building	60,000	60,000	0
Depreciation–equipment	10,000	10,000	0
Utilities and all other items	80,000	80,000	0
Total costs	$285,000	$ 150,000	$ 135,000
Net profit and difference	$(10,000)	$(150,000)	$ (140,000)

Figure 5–9: *Differential Analysis*

Thus, in summary, if model B is dropped, the relevant items are:

Loss revenue	$ 275,000
Cost savings	135,000
Net decrease in profit	$140,000

Here we see that rather than lose $10,000 by keeping model B, Sunshine would actually lose an additional $140,000 for a total loss of $150,000, by dropping model B!

How does that discrepancy arise? Note that certain cost elements have been eliminated from consideration in this differential analysis. Depreciation and utility costs have been excluded, because they are fixed costs—costs that will remain and must be incurred by Sunshine, whether product B is produced or not. Those costs will not be saved if the product is dropped. For purposes of this decision, those costs are *sunk*; they cannot be affected by the decision to keep or drop.

The decision to keep model B or to drop it is sometimes called the *keep or drop problem*. In addition to the differential analysis discussed previously, a total cost analysis of such problems may be made. Figure 5–9 shows that after all costs, there will be a $10,000 loss if model B is kept, but that $150,000 of costs will still be incurred even if the product is dropped. In the absence of a new product to take the place of B, that $150,000 of costs would have to be charged to product A. Such a reallocation of costs should not be allowed to confuse the central issue: whatever the profits are on the rest of Sunshine's business, they will be $10,000 lower if model B is kept and $150,000 lower if model B is dropped. Obviously, Sunshine would be better off by $140,000 by keeping model B, even if model B lost $10,000 at the new price.

Some managers study these keep or drop problems using a contribution basis as shown in Figure 5–10:

Sales price		$ 55.00
Less: out-of-pocket cost		
Material	$11.00	
Labor	8.00	
Out-of-pocket overhead	8.00	27.00
Contribution/unit		$ 28.00
Times: volume		× 5,000 units
Total loss if product dropped		$140,000

Figure 5–10: *Contribution Analysis*

ACCOUNTING FOR SUNK COSTS

You may still be thinking about those sunk costs that were ignored. Are they not real costs? If so, do they now show up somewhere? After all, buildings and equipment are being carried on the balance sheet as assets and must be expensed to the income statement at some time. Perhaps another example will clear things up.

Suppose that Red Ball Freight Line has just installed an $8,000 gasoline engine in one of its trucks when a new diesel engine costing $12,000 reached the market. Either engine would outlast the remaining useful life of the truck and would have a negligible salvage value. Expected fuel consumption over the remaining life of the truck would be about 25,000 gallons for the gasoline-powered engine, but only 20,000 gallons for the newer diesel engine. Both fuels were expected to cost $3/gallon. Red Ball management was sorry that it had not heard of the new diesel engine before installing the gasoline one, because the fuel savings would have more than offset the additional cost of the new engine. Indeed, it was too bad that management had not heard of the new engine sooner, but perhaps there were still savings to be had. Suppose that the extra cost of removing the gas engine and installing the new diesel one was just equal to the resale value of the gas engine—$1,000. Should Sunshine have switched? The conventional bookkeeping answer would have been no as is shown in Figure 5–11.

But that would be a bad decision. Again, look at just what differences there would be if the new engine were acquired. Clearly, the investment in the gasoline engine is sunk cost, as is shown by the out-of-pocket or cash flow analysis of Figure 5–12.

Thus, instead of showing a $5,000 loss, this cash flow analysis treats the investment in the gas engine as a sunk cost and shows a net savings of $3,000.

Actually, Figure 5–11, the bookkeeping approach, is not incorrect—just incomplete. There will be a book loss of $7,000—on the sale of the gasoline engine. But if the diesel engine is not bought and the gasoline engine is kept, *there would still be an accounting charge to income for depreciation* on the gas engine totaling $8,000.

Cost of new diesel engine	$ 12,000
Loss on sale of gas engine ($8,000 – $1,000)	7,000
Installation cost	1,000
Total cost	$ 20,000
Savings on fuel (5,000 gallons × $3/gallon)	$ 15,000
Total loss	$(5,000)

Figure 5–11: *Bookkeeping Approach—Red Ball Problem*

Cash outflows:	
Cost of new diesel engine	$12,000
Installation cost	1,000
Total cash outflow	$13,000
Cash inflows:	
Sale of old gasoline engine	$ 1,000
Savings on fuel over lifetime of truck	15,000
Total cash inflows	$16,000
Net cash flow (favorable)	$ 3,000

Figure 5–12: *Cash Flow Analysis—Red Ball Problem*

The drawback to the bookkeeping approach can be explained another way: The $7,000 paid for the gasoline engine is a sunk cost and can be ignored for purposes of decision-making. It is not a new cash item relating to the decision. It also can be ignored from an accounting point of view, because it will be a charge to the income statement no matter what decision is made: If the gasoline engine is scrapped, there will be a *loss on the sale of fixed assets* charged to income; if the engine is kept, there will be a *depreciation expense*. These outcomes are presented in Figure 5–13.

If gasoline engine is kept:	
Depreciation cost total	$ 8,000
Cost of fuel over lifetime of truck	75,000
	$83,000
If diesel engine is purchased:	
Loss on sale of old engine ($8,000 – $1,000)	$ 7,000
Depreciation of diesel engine	12,000
Installation cost	1,000
Cost of fuel over lifetime of truck	60,000
	$80,000
Difference	$ 3,000

Figure 5–13: *Accounting Results—Red Ball Problem*

To summarize then, a sunk cost is the cost associated with a past decision. In an analysis of the merits to alternative courses of action, the relevant costs are those that will be affected by the decision at hand. These are the costs that will be incurred after the decision is made. Since a sunk cost is a past event, it cannot be affected by a current decision and consequently is not a relevant cost.

That is not to say that accountants should not keep track of sunk costs that have been capitalized. They certainly should, and such costs should be written off over the proper time period, so that the firm's income statement will incorporate generally accepted and expected accounting procedures.

Some capitalized costs may even be written off or amortized according to units produced or machine hours. As such, they will behave like variable costs. However, those costs are still reflections of a past decision and are not cash or out-of-pocket costs. The point here is that when evaluating current decision alternatives, one must remember that sunk costs are sunk and will not make any difference.

DECISION-MAKING: BREAKEVEN

On the surface, calculating breakeven appears simple. Suppose that a computer rents for $5,000 per month. Variable costs for operating the computer center are $30 per hour, and computer time is *worth* (or can be sold for) $80 per hour. What is the breakeven point of operations? In this instance, *breakeven point* refers to the number of hours per month that will leave the computer center with neither profits nor losses. The solution can be quickly found by analyzing contribution or by making a graphical analysis as depicted in Figures 5–14 and 5–15.

In the analysis of contribution, we find that each hour of operation will yield $50 toward covering fixed costs. Only 100 such hours are needed before all fixed costs are recovered. We can prove that calculation as follows:

Selling price	$80/hour
Variable costs	30
Contribution	$50/hour

$$\frac{\text{Fixed Cost}}{\text{Contribution/Hour}} = \frac{\$5,000}{\$50} = 100 \text{ hours} = \text{Breakeven}$$

Sales (at 100 hrs.)		$8,000
Less:		
Variable costs	$3,000	
Fixed costs	5,000	8,000
Profit (or loss)		$ 0

Figure 5–14: *Breakeven Analysis of Contribution*

Those same relationships can be graphed as in Figure 5–15 to show the breakeven point. The steps are as follows:

1. Volume is typically shown on the horizontal axis. In this case, the unit of measure is hours per month.

2. Dollars are generally plotted on the vertical axis.

3. Fixed costs are plotted first. They are $5,000 for all levels of volume, so the fixed cost line is horizontal.

4. Variable costs at each level of volume are *added* to the fixed cost to give total costs. At 25 hours, the variable costs are $750 so the total costs are $5,750. At 50 hours, the variable costs are $1,500 so the total costs are $6,500.

5. Sales or revenues are then plotted for each level of volume. At 25 hours, sales are $2,000; at 50 hours, sales are $4,000.

6. The point at which the sales line intersects the total cost line is the breakeven point. It is 100 hours.

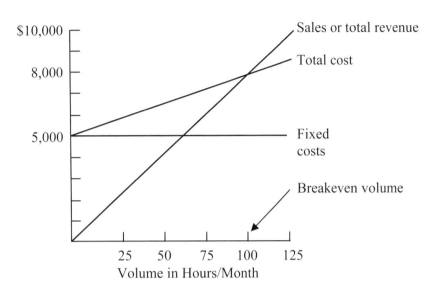

Figure 5–15: *Breakeven Analysis*

The concept of breakeven is used in many manufacturing and service industries to express the interrelationships between sales price, volume, fixed costs, and variable costs. Study these other examples:

A chain of supermarkets uses breakeven calculations to help gauge the desirability of new store locations. For example: management estimates a store's costs for lease, utilities, rent, and manager and staff salaries as $1.6 million per year. The typical customer spends $4,000 per year, and the cost of a typical customer's purchases average 80% of the selling price. Thus, the chain needs 2,000 customers to break even. (This supermarket measures volume by customers per year.)

A manufacturing company makes children's toys that sell for $4.00, and whose variable cost is $2.00 per unit. Fixed costs are $500,000 per month. Their breakeven point is 250,000 units per month.

A nursing home plans to build a new wing with 100 beds. Fixed costs, including depreciation, will be $56,000 per week. The nursing home rate per day per room is approximately $200, of which $100 goes to variable cost. Breakeven on the new facility is 80% occupancy.

Breakeven analysis can also be used to test the effect of a change in present operations. Any one or two of the variables can be increased or decreased to simulate a variety of situations. Here are five examples.

Legend:

FC: fixed cost   FC + P: fixed cost plus target profit
TR: total revenue   TC + P: total cost plus target profit
TC: total cost (fixed plus variable)

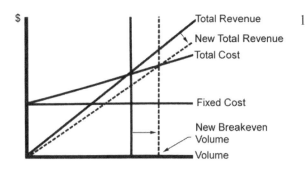

1. If we reduce our price 10%, what is our new breakeven volume? (Revenue per unit will decrease; volume is an unknown variable.) The diagonal dotted line represents the new revenue line, and where it crosses the total cost line is the new breakeven volume.

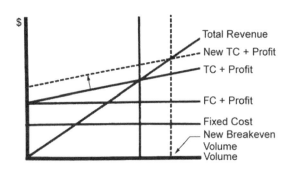

2. If we allocate another $50,000 to advertising, what increased volume must be stimulated to yield at least as much net profit as before? (Fixed costs will increase; volume is the unknown.) The new dotted total cost plus target profit line is higher than the old TC + P line by $50,000.

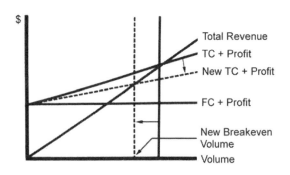

3. If we redesign the product and decrease the cost per unit, how much volume erosion can we have before profits will decrease? (Variable cost per unit decreases; volume is the unknown.)

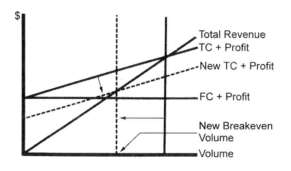

4. If a competitor enters our market and cuts our volume by 15%, what fixed cost reduction will be necessary to bring profits back to the previous level? (Volume is reduced; fixed cost is the unknown. Slope of the new TC + P line remains the same, because the unit cost is unchanged.) The required reduction in fixed costs is the amount by which the TC + P line has to be dropped so that it crosses the total revenue line at the new volume.

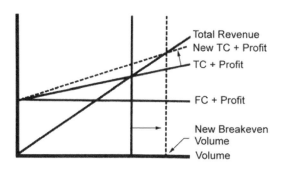

5. Though a price change is not feasible, we can increase our sales by 25% and our market share from 20% to 25% by redesigning our product to include higher cost material and quality standards. How much will be available for improved product quality if we wish to make at least our current profit? (Volume increase is given; the unknown is the increase in variable cost per unit.) The TC + P line will tilt up with higher variable cost per unit and the total amount available for redesign is the vertical distance between the new TC + P line and the old TC + P line at the new volume.

BREAKEVEN WITH MULTIPLE PRODUCTS

Those simple examples belie a more complicated situation. We can explore the problem more fully by going back to Sunshine Manufacturing Company. What is its breakeven point?

A few moments of thought produce the remarkable conclusion that there are a great many breakeven points! By using the variable margin from Figure 5–3, we see that Sunshine will break even under several conditions:

	Model	Volume	Breakeven Proof	
	A	13,939	$33 margin × 13,939 units =	$460,000
	B	0	-0-	
or if:	A	0	-0-	
	B	12,105	$38 margin × 12,105 units =	$460,000
or if:	A	10,000	$33 margin × 10,000 units =	$330,000
	B	3,421	$38 margin × 3,421 units =	130,000
				$460,000

or indeed many other combinations of volume.

Clearly, that multiplicity of answers is not what we had in mind when we tried to find the breakeven point for Sunshine. Does that mean that whenever there are multiple products or multiple services, it is not possible to find the breakeven point? Unfortunately, the answer is yes.

Companies ordinarily make a compromise, however, that allows them to calculate a single breakeven point. Study the illustration in Figure 5–16. With a projected volume of 20,000 and 5,000 units, respectively, products A and B will yield $1,325,000 in sales revenue (step 1). At that volume, gross profit will be $850,000 (step 2), or 64% of sales (step 3). Given that that analysis, in effect, says that each sales dollar provides $0.64 toward fixed costs, then the sales volume necessary to cover just the $460,000 of fixed cost is $718,750 (step 4).

	Step	*A*	*B*	*Total*
1.	Sales price/unit	$ 50	$ 65	
	Times: volume	20,000	5,000	
	Total estimated sales	$1,000,000	$325,000	$1,325,000
2.	Sales price/unit	$ 50	$ 65	
	– Variable cost	17	27	
	Gross profit/unit	33	38	
	Times: volume	20,000	5,000	
	Total gross profit	$660,000	$190,000	$ 850,000

3. $\dfrac{\$850,000}{\$1,325,000}$ = 64% contribution/sales ratio

4. $\dfrac{\$460,000}{0.64}$ = $718,750 sales volume breakeven

Figure 5–16: *Breakeven with Two Products*

Thus, the breakeven point for Sunshine Manufacturing is $718,750 of sales. Sales dollars become the units of measure for volume. The reader should be aware of the two key assumptions underlying this approach to breakeven:

1. The sales mix is always assumed to be four of A to one of B.

2. The gross profits are $33 and $38 for A and B, respectively.

If those assumptions become invalid, the breakeven point must be recalculated. Because most organizations are concerned with multiple products or services, these underlying assumptions are always present in an organization's breakeven figure.

SUMMARIZING THE TWO BREAKEVEN EQUATIONS

There are two breakeven equations available: One uses units being sold, and the other uses sales dollars as a measure of volume.

Consider this example:

Fasteners sell for	$2.00 each
Their variable cost is	<u>1.50</u> each
So contribution is	$0.50 each

and the contribution ratio is 0.50 ÷ 2.00, or 0.25
Fixed cost is $2.6 million

Equation #1:

Fixed Costs ÷ Contribution per Unit = Breakeven in Units
$2.6 Million ÷ $0.50 = 5.2 Million Units

Equation #2:

Fixed Cost ÷ Contribution Ratio = Breakeven in Sales Dollars
$2.6 Million ÷ 0.25 = $10.4 Million in Sales

The result is the same, since 5.2 million units = $10.4 million in sales. If the problem deals in units, either equation can be used, but if sales are made up of a mix of different products or services, only the second equation, using the contribution ratio, can be used.

DECISION-MAKING: THE IMPACT OF TAXES

The effect of a particular decision on income taxes is a relevant consideration, because taxes are out-of-pocket costs. Ordinarily, the taxing implications are easy to determine. If the effective total income tax rate (federal and state, where applicable) is 35%, then every $100 of additional savings or profits is worth $65, while every $100 of additional expenditures, assuming they are tax deductible, has a relevant cost of only $65. Some special tax problems related to purchase and sales of fixed assets can cause more problems. We will illustrate them with the Red Ball problem previously introduced.

Assume that Red Ball's effective tax rate is 30%. A differential cash flow analysis is shown in Figure 5–17. Look at the effect of taxes. The cost of the new diesel engine (item 1) is the same either before or after taxes—$12,000—because there are no immediate tax savings or payments when fixed assets are purchased. However, over the lifetime of the engine, $12,000 of depreciation expense will be charged to income, thus reducing taxable income by $12,000. As a result of that noncash charge to income, $12,000 × 30% or $3,600 less taxes will be paid. Though the depreciation expense is a noncash item, the taxes saved by this depreciation are cash flow items and are therefore relevant savings (item 7). Those savings explain why depreciation expense is sometimes called a tax shield, because the depreciation saves $3,600 in taxes that would otherwise have been paid in cash. Items 1 and 7 could have been combined, or netted out, leaving a net cost of the new engine of $12,000 less $3,600 or $8,400; however, it is best to separate the two items for reasons discussed later. The effect on the differential cash flow would be the same.

	Before Tax Basis	After Tax Basis
Tax rate: 30%		
Differential cash outflows:		
1. Cost of new diesel engine	$12,000	$12,000
2. Installation cost	1,000	700
3. Tax savings foregone on depreciation of gasoline engine	0	2,400
	$13,000	$15,100
Differential cash inflows:		
4. Sale of old gasoline engine	$ 1,000	$ 1,000
5. Tax savings on loss on sale of gasoline engine	0	2,100
6. Savings on fuel over lifetime of the truck	15,000	10,500
7. Tax savings on depreciation of diesel engine	0	3,600
	$16,000	$17,200
Differential cash flow	$3,000	$2,100

Figure 5–17: *Cash Flow Analysis—Red Ball Problem*

The effective after-tax cash flow cost of installation (item 2) is $700 ($1,000 × 70%). The installation expense reduces taxes by $300 ($1,000 × 30%); thus, the net cost is only $700 ($1,000 − $300). The same logic applies to the fuel savings (item 6).

Items 3, 4, and 5 are related. When the old gasoline engine is sold for $1,000, there is a book loss of $7,000 ($8,000 cost − $1,000 received). That book loss saves $2,100 ($7,000 × 30%) in taxes that would otherwise be paid (item 5). If the gasoline engine were kept, however, depreciation of $8,000 would have been taken over the lifetime of the gasoline engine. That $8,000 of depreciation would have saved $2,400 ($8,000 × 30%) in tax (item 3). The sale of the old engine yields $1,000. There is no tax penalty or savings (item 4). Taking those items together, we see that by selling the old engine, Red Ball receives $1,000 cash plus a tax savings of $2,100 on its book loss, but it gives up future depreciation on the gasoline engine that would have saved $2,400 in taxes.

DECISION-MAKING: SPECIAL CONSIDERATIONS

Semivariable Costs

Some costs are neither fixed nor variable. Sometimes, costs increase by large amounts because of only a small increase in volume, such as when a new employee is hired or production is extended to a second shift or a new machine is acquired. Sometimes costs will increase per unit because of special premiums: overtime labor or raw materials purchased at premium prices compared to the lower prices of long-term purchase contracts.

In most cases, semivariable costs can be handled by differential analysis: One looks at what the total costs will be if the action is not taken and then compares that result with the level of total costs if the action is taken. The differences can then be studied and the decision can be made. Cost analysis on a per-unit basis is generally not applicable when there are semivariable costs.

Timing

"All costs are variable in the long run and fixed in the short." That saying generalizes the behavior of costs over time. In the short run, many costs are fixed or are independent of volume, costs such as depreciation, management salaries, and certain other overheads. But, in time, even those costs change; plants can be closed or expanded, management and staff can be decreased or increased, and many overhead costs can also vary. A cost such as insurance on the plant seems fixed today, but after enough time, say three or four years, it becomes a cost that not only changes but is related to overall production capacity because it is related to plant size.

For example, if you're trying to decide whether it is worthwhile to run a particular job on the computer this afternoon, you must consider almost all the costs of the computer center as fixed, since management can do little to reduce them. On the other hand, if the job will be run each day for the next three years, then almost all the costs can be considered variable, since management can adjust the operating costs of the data center to correspond to the workload. For example, employees can be hired or fired, or equipment can be expanded or reduced.

Clearly, in making a decision, one must first determine its time frame before analyzing costs, because the same cost can be fixed today and variable tomorrow. That axiom also implies that the relevant costs of a product or service can also vary with time. Pricing a special product with a three-month life cycle is much different from pricing a similar product with a three-year lifetime.

DECISION-MAKING: OPPORTUNITY COSTS

Sometimes the relevant cost of an item has nothing at all to do with accounting costs, but is instead the value of that item if it were used in the best possible manner by the organization. For example, the copper in our warehouse may have cost $0.80 per pound, but if the current market value is now $4.00 per pound, using it today in a product deprives us of the ability to use it in some other product or to resell it for $4.00. The copper has a value of $4.00; we say that its opportunity cost is $4.00 if it is used in a product.

Another way of looking at opportunity costs is to go back to our discussion of the gasoline engine. We consider the cost of that gasoline engine to be sunk, not because the money for it has already been spent but because it has no alternative use. Its opportunity value is zero.

Sometimes the relevant cost in a particular situation is a contingency cost. Raw material may be a variable cost, such as $2.00 per pound for a particular item. But if a purchase contract specifies that we must purchase at least 100,000 pounds, then that raw material cost is not variable if we purchase less than that amount. The cost is variable only if we purchase more than 100,000 pounds. Labor in a particular skill class may cost $7.00 per hour, but if a labor contract guarantees 80% of the base rate, the incremental and variable cost for that labor is really only $1.40 per hour throughout the time of the labor contract. If production is stopped, there is still an opportunity cost of $5.60 (80% × $7.00) per hour.

Suppose that the spoilage rate for a machine is 3% and that a new machine is being considered that will reduce spoilage to 1%. The cost of the new machine is known. What is the worth or relevant value of the 2% savings? Ordinarily, the labor, material and other variable costs of the product are lost when the product is spoiled. However, if the plant expects to operate at capacity during the lifetime of the new machine, then the relevant cost is this variable cost *plus* the lost contribution that would have been earned on the items that, if not spoiled, could otherwise have been sold. In that situation, the relevant cost is the opportunity loss (lost contribution) on the unsold products plus the lost out-of-pocket costs.

Production capacity may have an opportunity cost. If a plant is operating well below capacity, any new business that will contribute to fixed costs, even though it doesn't necessarily cover full costs, would improve profits or reduce loss. However, as the organization begins to reach its operational capacity, any commitment of capacity to one project or customer means that some other project or product cannot be produced. At full capacity, the use of resources has an opportunity cost—the contribution that could be earned by the most profitable alternative. In such cases, it is important to consider each alternative and its contribution per unit of capacity. For example, if Sunshine Manufacturing's capacity is limited by assembly capacity and the labor rate in the assembly department is $6.00 per hour, we can make the following analysis of contribution shown in Figure 5–18. Contribution per assembly hour of model A Zingos is more than twice the contribution per hour of model B's.

Therefore, at capacity, Sunshine should encourage sales of model A and discourage sales of model B, because the contribution per unit of capacity made by A is more than double that of B.

		Zingos	
		A	*B*
1.	Assembly cost/unit	$ 4.50	$12.00
2.	Labor rate/hour	6.00	6.00
3.	Assembly hours (line 1/line 2)	0.75 hrs	2 hrs
4.	Sales price	$50.00	$65.00
5.	Variable costs	17.00	27.00
6.	Contribution	$33.00	$38.00
7.	Contribution/assembly hour (line 6/line 3)	$44.00 /hr	$19.00 /hr

Figure 5–18: *Contribution per Unit of Capacity*

COMMENTS ON TERMINOLOGY

Some managers use the terms *incremental*, *marginal*, *differential*, *variable*, and *direct* as if they all had the same meaning. They do not. Though different organizations may have adopted various connotations for these terms, most executives accept the following definitions.

1. *Differential costs* compare one alternative with another. That difference may be the variation in costs between one production level and another for the same product, or perhaps the cost differences between one product and another. All costs need not be considered, only those affected by the decision.

2. *Marginal costs* are the additional costs of production or service for one more unit. The level of volume must be specified. For example, one might say that the marginal cost of product 12 at 85% of capacity is $37.95.

3. *Incremental costs* are similar to marginal costs, but may be specified to cover a given number of additional units: The incremental cost of 100 gallons is $112.50 per gallon between 10,000 and 15,000 gallons of daily production.

4. *Variable costs* are those costs that vary directly with volume. They approximate, but are not always the same as out-of-pocket costs.

5. *Direct costs*, strictly speaking, are only those costs that can readily be identified or measured by product. *Allocated costs*, whether fixed or variable, are excluded. Many people confuse variable

costs and direct costs. Depreciation on a special machine may be direct to a product, but not variable.

6. *Out-of-pocket costs* are those that must be paid in cash. Excluded are noncash costs, such as depreciation and deferred taxes.

TIPS ON PROBLEM-SOLVING

Many times the analysis becomes hopelessly confused because of a failure to state the problem clearly. Another common error is to overlook the best alternative from the start. All problems involve alternatives. Neglecting to identify all feasible alternatives dooms the analysis.

It is important to segregate all cost and revenue elements of a problem according to the relative time of their occurrence. Relevant costs that occur at different times should always be separated rather than combined, because money has a time value. Techniques for analyzing present and future values are available. Those techniques require, among other things, that all cash flows be segregated by time period (month by month or year by year). Present value techniques will be discussed further in Chapter 7.

Many decisions require the evaluation of numerous alternatives. In those situations, it is generally best to select one as the base, or reference point, and then to conduct a differential analysis between that base point and each alternative. Ordinarily, one selects the status quo or "do nothing" alternative as the reference point. The differential analysis of the alternative to drop model B Zingos (Figure 5–9) is a good example. The status quo was the base point, and from that the changes in revenue and costs were measured.

Sometimes, there is no status quo alternative. For example, the decision to build a new service center in a particular location with a particular capacity may already have been made; the only remaining question is whether to lease or to buy. In that case, the cash flow costs for each alternative may be projected and evaluated. The alternative with the lowest net cost is then selected (all non-economic factors being equal).

Or a hospital may have reached capacity and must expand in order to provide continuing levels of service to its growing community. Expansion can take place in stages of varying magnitudes: the hospital may plan one large expansion that will satisfy its needs for twelve years or several smaller two-year projects that will gradually expand capacity. Incremental expansion is much more expensive, but minimizes idle capacity and has a lower initial cost. The hospital must expand and there is no status quo alternative; the remaining alternatives are mutually exclusive. Again, each alternative can be judged on the basis of total present value cost, since revenues are assumed to be the same.

A business may be trying to decide whether to prolong the life of a product via certain design changes and market promotions or to replace it with a new product. A net present value profit analysis, comparing one alternative with the other, would provide the best comparison. One might also wish to consider keeping the old product and introducing the new one as well. Thus, there are three options: Keep the old with modifications; scrap the old and introduce the new; or keep the old as is and introduce the new one. In that case, each alternative can be compared with the others, or the expected profits of each can be determined and the most profitable product selected.

SUMMARY

In this chapter, we have explored ways of measuring the costs that relate to certain types of decisions or choices. We note that when certain costs will be unaffected by a decision, they should be excluded from consideration. Those costs that are not affected by volume, commonly called fixed costs, should not be considered relevant in the analysis of decisions that change volume. Only those costs that change with a decision are relevant.

Short-term analysis of relevant costs and revenues can be done using contribution analysis (How much does each alternative contribute to fixed costs and profit?) and breakeven analysis, in which total fixed costs, variable cost per unit, or as a percentage of sales, price per unit or revenue, and desired profit can be related to compute the required breakeven volume in units or sales.

QUESTIONS AND PROBLEMS

5–1. Why might a product cost that is appropriate for one decision be wrong for a different decision? Give some examples.

5–2. What does full cost mean? What is left out if it is not a full cost?

5–3. As discussed in this chapter, what does *contribution* mean? Is it the same as profit? What is it a contribution to?

5–4. Define:

  a. Differential analysis
  b. Sunk costs
  c. Breakeven point
  d. Semivariable cost
  e. Opportunity cost
  f. Differential costs
  g. Incremental costs
  h. Out-of-pocket costs

5–5. *Keep or drop.* The Empire Company manufactures various kinds of industrial products with annual sales of $2 million. One of the company's products is the Harp-32A, which sold 10,000 units for $140,000 and had an operating profit of $18,000 in the previous year. The statement of operating income for the Harp-32A is depicted here with the controller's estimate of the variability of each cost item.

Results for Last Year

Revenue:	
Sales (10,000 units)	$140,000
Costs:	
Materials (variable)	30,000
Direct labor (variable)	20,000
Indirect labor	
(40% fixed; 60% variable)	10,000
Supplies (variable)	15,000
Depreciation–building (fixed)	20,000
Depreciation–equipment (fixed)	15,000
Utilities and all other items	
(60% fixed; 40% variable)	12,000
Total costs	122,000
Operating profit	$ 18,000

During the last weeks of the year, the market for the Harp-32A seemed to soften. As the new year began, Empire's sales manager decided that it was important to maintain his 20% share of the 50,000-unit annual market for the Harp-32A and reduced its price to $10 a unit.

Sales for the first quarter were 3,000 units, and the Harp-32A showed an operating loss of $4,290 after expenses that were about the same level as the previous year.

First Quarter Results

Revenue:		
Sales (3,000 units)		$30,000
Costs:		
Materials	9,000	
Direct labor	6,000	
Indirect labor	2,800	
Supplies	4,500	
Depreciation–building	5,000	
Depreciation–equipment	3,750	
Utilities and all other items	3,240	
Total costs		$34,290
Operating loss		$ 4,290

Upon reviewing the performance of the Harp-32A during the past quarter, Mark, Empire's president, wondered if he should consider dropping the Harp-32A. He then asked his controller to make a detailed analysis on the effect of dropping the product, assuming that the company would have sales of 9,000 units for the next three quarters and that the selling price and costs would remain the same throughout the year.

5–6.   *Subcontract.* The Industrial Chemicals Company (ICC) produces KEM, which has annual sales of 20,000 units and a unit cost of $40. The breakdown of this unit cost is as follows:

Direct materials:		
Substance A (1 kg)	$20.00	
Substance B (3 gm)	5.00	
Substance C (1gm)	2.50	$27.50
Direct labor		8.00
Manufacturing overhead		4.50
Total unit cost		$40.00

The three substances being used in the production of KEM are also produced by ICC in other sections of the production department.

One day, KEM's product manager meets with the comptroller and says that he has found a way to cut the cost of KEM. The product manager says there is a specialty chemical company to which ICC can subcontract the production of substance A for $17.50 per kilogram. He noted that his cost of KEM would thereby be reduced by $2.50.

To see if it is beneficial for ICC to subcontract substance A, the comptroller studies the composition of the production costs of this substance. He arrives at the following analysis:

	Total (20,000 units)	Per Unit	Characteristic
Direct materials	$200,000	$10.00	Variable
Direct labor	50,000	2.50	Variable
Manufacturing overhead:			
Indirect labor	20,000	1.00	Variable
Supplies	10,000	0.50	Variable
Depreciation–building	80,000	4.00	Fixed
Depreciation–equipment	20,000	1.00	Fixed
Utilities	20,000	1.00	70% fixed, 30% variable
	$400,000	$20.00	

Is the product manager right in saying that ICC can save $2.50 per unit of KEM, if it subcontracts substance A? If it is undertaken, how will the subcontracting affect KEM's product line profit? How should the controller respond to the product manager?

5–7. *Alternative leases.* Jeffrey is establishing a computer service company. He needs a van but, at the moment, he doesn't have the funds for a down payment. After shopping around a little for leasing deals, he finds two that seem better than the others. Both are net leases, which means that he would pay for insurance, repairs, and operating expenses.

> *Lease deal #1*: $200 at the beginning of each month for a five-year lease, the 60th month paid at the beginning.

> *Lease deal #2*: A five-year lease, $1,000 per year payable quarterly at the beginning of each quarter, the 20th quarter paid at the start, plus $0.10 per mile payable quarterly.

Jeffrey would like some figures to help him choose between the two lease deals.

5–8. *Breakeven.* A manufacturing company makes radios and sells them for $50 per unit. The variable cost of the product is $30 per unit, while total fixed costs are $240,000 per year.

a. What is the breakeven sales volume? If the company decides to reduce its price by 10% to $45 per unit so that its market share will increase, what then will be its breakeven sales volume? Draw a graph to illustrate the change in breakeven. [Note the graphs for questions (a) through (e) should use a vertical scale up to $1 million and a horizontal scale up to 20,000 units.]

b. Assuming that the company decides to increase its advertising expenses by $50,000 so that fixed costs increase to $290,000 instead of reducing the selling price to stimulate demand, how many will it have to sell in order to break even? Illustrate in a graph the change in breakeven.

c. If the company redesigns the product and decreases the variable cost per unit by $10 to $20 per unit, what will be its breakeven sales volume, if the selling price remains at $50 per unit and fixed costs are $240,000? Show in a graph the change in breakeven.

d. If a competitor enters the market of the company and cuts the latter's volume by 15% or to 10,200 units, how much will it have to reduce its fixed costs to in order to break even at the same selling price? Demonstrate in a graph the change in breakeven.

e. Due to competition, the company cannot increase its unit price above $50. However, it can increase its sales by 25% to 15,000 units and its market share from 20% to 25% by redesigning its products to have higher cost materials and quality standards. By how much can the company increase its variable cost per unit and still break even? Show in a graph the change in breakeven.

5–9.   *Multiple products breakeven.* The Sunshine Company has added a model C Zingo to the A and B models described in the text. In the process of expansion, its total fixed costs increased to $750,000. The selling price, variable cost, and projected volume of each model are:

	A	B	C
Selling price	$50	$65	$75
Variable cost	$17	$27	$35
Projected volume	20,000 units	10,000 units	5,000 units

1. With the projected sales mix, what is the company's breakeven in dollar sales?

2. The company's current sales mix is four, two, and one of A, B, and C, respectively. If the mix becomes two, four, and two for units of A, B, and C, respectively, what would be the breakeven in dollar sales of the company? Explain why the breakeven level is different.

3. Assuming that the projected sales mix is the same as in question (1) and the selling price of A increases by 8%, while the selling price of B remains the same, and that of C decreases by 8%, what would be the dollar sales breakeven of the company? Explain why the breakeven sales level has changed.
    Note: Use percentages rounded off to one decimal place (for example: 10.5% or 0.105).

5–10. *Opportunity cost.* The State Company manufactures three products: A, B, and C. All those products use the same equipment, which has a capacity of 95,000 hours per year. Each unit of products A, B, and C requires 1, 1.5, and 2 machine hours, respectively. This year the expected sales volume and contribution of the products are:

	A	B	C	Total
Sales volume (units)	30,000	20,000	15,000	
Contribution/unit	× $25	× $45	× $64	
	$750,000	$900,000	$960,000	$2,610,000

1. The company decides to increase sales of product C by spending $144,000 in advertising. What percentage increase in product C's sales must the company get in order to maintain its total contribution? What would be the new production level in hours for all three products?

2. Assuming that the advertising on product C will cannibalize 10% of product B's sales, what percentage increase in product C's sales should the company attain so that its total contribution will remain the same?

3. If advertising on product C will increase its sales by 35% while cannibalizing 10% of product B's sales, what should the sales mix of the company be, and how many production hours would be necessary? If more hours are needed than are available, what should be done to the sales mix?

CHAPTER 6

MANAGING COSTS

INTRODUCTION

In Chapter 2, we examined both traditional and activity-based methods of costing products and services. In Chapter 5, we analyzed the measurement of costs that are relevant to certain decisions, especially those affected by volume of activity. In this chapter, we combine the activity perspective from Chapter 2 with Chapter 5's analysis of cost behavior and consider cost management as a continuous process, using activities as the key focus.

Many businesses that have instituted cost reduction programs have discovered that simply saying they will spend 90% of what was planned, or that they will lay off 10% of the people, is rather like saying they will build a bridge 90% of the way across the river. The result is not satisfactory.

Companies have learned that rather than moving directly to cutting costs, a more fruitful approach is to follow this more logical progression: start by taking an approach to *managing costs*, which in turn means *managing the activities* that create the costs, which means *managing the drivers* that cause the activities to take place. This chapter follows that approach and focuses on *activity-based cost management*.

Imagine two companies, both making subassemblies that are sold to larger manufacturers. Both companies make a similar commodity product and had been operating with a just-in-time inventory system for several years. Last year, a large manufacturer began looking for a customized version of the product that the companies made, but not wanting to tie itself to just one supplier, signed contracts with both suppliers to produce a customized version of the product. Both suppliers made the customized version in batches whenever the customer placed an order. The customer ordered several times a year. The custom features required several parts that were not used to produce the commodity product. The following year, profits at both suppliers began to decline. Management at both suppliers engaged their organization in cost-cutting efforts.

Supplier A used a traditional cost system, allocating manufacturing overhead to the two products based on direct labor. In an effort to cut costs, Supplier A took steps to decrease direct labor usage.

Supplier B used an activity-based costing system. It utilized data from that system to pinpoint the activities that incur most of the overhead costs. It discovered that most of the costs associated with the custom product were related to receiving and material handling. They arose because the product was being made in batches. Because of the combination of the custom orders and the just-in-time system the company has been using for years, receiving and handling costs had risen out of control. Supplier B revisited its decision to use a just-in-time system for the parts required only for the custom product, decided to store those parts in inventory, and thus was able to reduce its receiving and material handling costs substantially.

It's likely that both suppliers had the same issue with receiving and material handling costs. Supplier B was able to pinpoint the issue relatively easily, because the activity-based cost system highlighted those costs. Supplier A, on the other hand, had a difficult time identifying the problem. It had no rigorous way to determine where to look. The only action suggested by the traditional cost system was to decrease direct labor. If direct labor decreased, the allocation of overhead would also decrease.

For many companies, activity-based cost management (or more simply, activity-based management) has been an outgrowth of activity-based costing (ABC). ABC shifted focus from traditional cost allocation to tracing the causes of cost incurrence. Traditional cost systems (TCS) have limited value as management tools:[1]

- Widely differentiated products utilize resources in substantially different proportions, a fact unrecognized by TCS.

- Overhead now constitutes the largest share of cost—often greater than 300%—and is typically applied to products as a percentage of the smallest cost (direct labor), which leads to serious distortion of product costs.

- Sales, distribution, and other below-the-line costs have increased dramatically and are not attached to individual products or customers at all, meaning that the system gives no information to the customer about value-chain costs.

- Improvements in data collection methodology have been used primarily to improve the precision of the numbers without addressing the accuracy of cost application.

Those shortcomings result in a system that:

- Provides virtually no meaningful analysis of the effectiveness of overhead resource utilization.

- Generates three- and four-digit overhead rates, making no attempt to trace actual resource utilization to specific products.

- Overcosts standard high-volume products and undercosts custom low-volume products, leading to incorrect pricing and product mix decisions.

- Creates a bias toward direct labor reduction as a cost reduction methodology rather than overall productivity improvement.

- Provides no information useful in either identifying productivity improvement opportunities or in determining if productivity improvement efforts have yielded significant results. Indeed, often TCS indicates higher cost in the presence of known productivity improvement and vice versa.

So instead of assigning overhead costs to products using an overhead rate such as direct labor, ABC segments the overhead cost into cost pools, which seem to be caused or driven by activities such as set-up, receiving, scheduling, materials handling, engineering, shipping, and the like. The key idea here is that those activities cause the overhead costs.

Sometimes the ABC analysis starts by defining activities, costing the activities (for example: cost per set-up), and then linking the costed activities to products, groups of products, or customers. And sometimes the analysis starts by examining output to answer questions such as how much more it costs to serve this kind of customer than that kind of customer. Either way, the analysis requires that activities be defined and costed.

---

[1] James D. Tart, *Activity-Based Management Merging Process and Measurement*, ACA Group Web site, August, 2006.

Along the way, the activity analysis for ABC merged with other approaches designed to improve the way things get done, such as process-value analysis, value-chain analysis, and total quality management. Successful ABC efforts were those that spread beyond the accountants and involved people in operations, marketing, engineering, logistics, and purchasing. How the activities were managed soon became an important concern.

Whereas ABC has been concerned primarily with what is done—for example, the activities, and how much they cost—the new focus is on why people do what they do, and that has led to activity-based management (ABM). ABC accepted activities as they were; ABM works on improving activities. Companies discovered that the payoff was often larger and quicker when they concentrated on ABM. Product costing was still important, sometimes even the main purpose, but activity-based management was being undertaken for process improvement and actually was not dependent on reasons, such as product diversity, that encouraged companies to develop an ABC system. ABM had a life of its own. The connection between ABC and ABM can be seen in the following diagram.

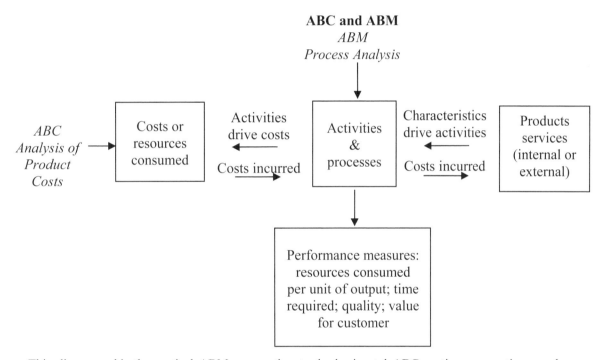

ABC and ABM

This diagram adds the vertical ABM perspective to the horizontal ABC costing perspectives we have used. The resulting diagram is similar to the two dimensional ABC model presented by Peter B.B. Turney and Norm Raffish. See *Common Cents: The ABC Performance Breakthrough* by Peter B.B. Turney, *Cost Technology* (1991): 81.

For the development of ABM, three kinds of tasks must be carried out:

1. Definition of activities;

2. Analysis of activity drivers and links to other activities and to output;

3. Costing of activities.

Those three core tasks are essentially sequential, although defining and analyzing activities overlap. Three other kinds of tasks go on throughout the ABM process:

1. *Preparation.* The whole process should be planned, staffed, and organized carefully.

   - *Planning* refers to sequencing the steps in the process;
   - *Staffing* usually requires having people who are knowledgeable in different functions not just accountants;
   - *Organizing* refers to designation of which person or group is responsible for each task.

   Studies have shown repeatedly that higher management support for an ABM project is important to the project's success, because of the scope (multiple departments) and resources required (people's time).

2. *Communication and reporting.* The objective is to inform the appropriate people outside the process. This requires documentation of the process and its results to facilitate organizational learning.

3. *Data gathering.* This is performed in the early stages to provide for defining activities, for reporting results, and for measuring and evaluating activity performance to facilitate continuous improvement. Data gathering is usually a combination of interviews, surveys, and the extraction of data from the company's existing data systems.

The output from this process of defining, analyzing, and costing activities provides input to activity management, which can include improving, combining, or eliminating the activity. This management action is where gains take place. Up to that point, the work is primarily analysis.

The overall picture looks like this:

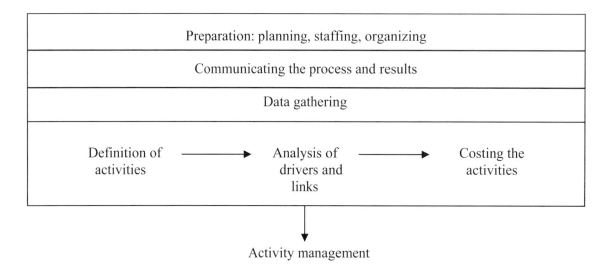

DEFINITION OF ACTIVITIES

Defining activities is often a creative process. There are a variety of methods that companies have used to identify activities. This is not a cookie-cutter process. Dozens of consultants have created their own methods, and generally all those methods can be made to work. Some consultants allow activities to emerge from the analysis of what is done and why; others find that starting with an activities "dictionary" helps, especially when interviewing people who are unfamiliar with ABM.

What is an Activity?

An activity implies action and an object to the action. "Handle mail" is an activity. An activity description usually has a verb and a noun; sometimes the noun has a modifying adjective as in "handle incoming mail."

There may be different levels of activities. For example:

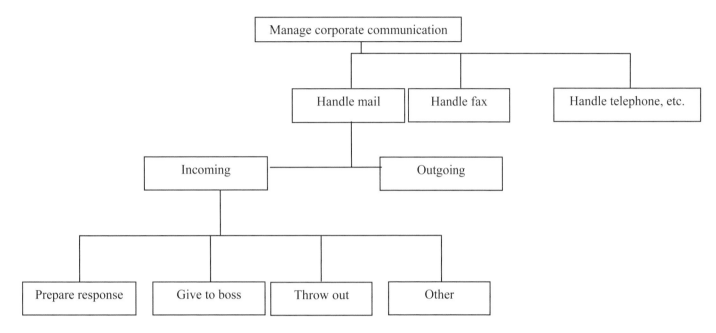

How Many Activities Should One Have?

A reasonable number of activities fall between two extremes: too small a number will fail to provide the detail needed to pick up significant differences in product costs; and with too large a number of small activities, computing their cost becomes quite arbitrary and burdensome. Activities used primarily for product costing can usually be larger than activities that are the focus of management efforts. For example, the activity "make a batch" (in contrast to "make a piece") is useful for product costing (see Chapter 2). But the batch activity includes a number of subactivities, such as setting up the machines, moving inventory, inspecting first pieces, recording labor, time, and pieces produced, and perhaps purchasing material and processing the order. All those subactivities are subject to the same activity driver (making batches), so combining them makes sense for costing output. On the other hand, efforts to improve the efficiency of the activities will work better, if focused on the subactivities. We might even find we could eliminate a subactivity.

People who have worked on ABM projects say that 100 to 200 activities for a medium-size company is normal. Larger companies would tend to have more, while smaller companies would have fewer, although the number of activities probably reflects complexity more than size.

How Do You Go about Defining Activities?

There is not a single, best way to define activities. Here are some examples:

1. Examine output and lay out the things that must be done to provide it. This works in both service and manufacturing.

2. Interview people to learn what they and their subordinates do by asking questions, such as:

   - What causes your work?

   - Who benefits from your work?

   - Whose work must precede yours?

   - How would you improve the process you are part of?

3. Work with departments or groups of people who work on a function. Get them to lay out their process. "Storyboarding" is one technique for doing that.

4. For product costing purposes, one can identify activities that are driven in different amounts by dissimilar products. Product complexity is an example. Certain activities are likely to be driven more by complex products than by simple products. Several companies have noted, for example, that the number of part numbers in an end product is an indication of product complexity.

   These companies defined an activity, handled part numbers, identified all the actions that were caused by having a variety of part numbers, and developed a cost per part number handled. In those cases, the analysis actually started from both ends: (1) knowledge that products had varying complexity, and one measure of that complexity was the number of different kinds of parts; (2) recognition that handling part numbers was an activity that used resources in several departments, and that the amount of those resources was probably large enough to be worth measuring.

ANALYSIS OF ACTIVITY DRIVERS AND LINKAGES

Activity drivers are forces that cause work to be performed in an activity. These drivers can be intentional, such as a strategy to accept small as well as large orders, or a policy, such as answering telephones before the third ring 90% of the time, or that pizzas will be delivered within 30 minutes to customers in a specified area. Or activity drivers can be unintentional, such as the need to decipher physicians' handwriting on prescriptions. Sometimes drivers are uncontrollable, such as the weather. And sometimes tradition is the driver: "We've always done it that way," may be the reason given for keeping a particular record that really is not needed anymore.

Analysis of those drivers is done to see which is a function of providing value to the customer, which is required to stay in business (for example: to satisfy safety and environmental regulations), and which does not really provide value. Managers worry about telling someone who is faithfully carrying out instructions that their work has no value. The question, however, is not one of intrinsic value, but whether it adds value for the customer and whether the customer is willing to pay for it. Indeed, the existence of valueless work is really management's fault, not the worker's.

This analysis of activity drivers naturally leads to the management of costs by managing those activity drivers. A change in the driver provides an opportunity to reduce costs. When you take away the cause of an activity, it may not change automatically, but management has an opportunity to make changes over time.

Activity costs can also be managed directly, without changing the driver. Sometimes when management realizes how much an activity costs, it is willing to make an effort and devote some resources to making the activity more efficient, or to finding alternative ways of accomplishing the same results.

> An example of what can result from this kind of analysis occurred in a yarn-spinning company with several plants. Over time, this company's customers gradually requested greater variety in the yarns they ordered. Changeovers became more frequent. Analysis showed that not only did changeovers reduce output (an opportunity cost), but they caused work for a large number of people, both on and off the production floor. Product price could not reflect the cost, because customers wanted to buy the product, not the changeover. At first, fine-tuning the scheduling was used to reduce changeover time on the floor. But that had minimal effect on the support people. In the end, an investment was made to rearrange capacity so that one plant was focused on a narrow part of the product line. That plant had very few changeovers and another plant handled the rest of the line. The first plant reduced support people by about two-thirds. The second became remarkably competent in managing the changeovers. Though improvements are still being made, the company believes it has improved its management of the changeover activity. The decision to make the switch was made when process analysis showed the large number of people off the production floor whose work was caused by changeovers. The driver (changeovers) was still there, but the company found a more efficient way to respond to it.

DEVELOPING THE COST OF ACTIVITY OUTPUT

For the product costing objective of ABC, it is necessary to link activity cost to the output of products or services. For activities management, a precise link is not necessary; however, a general link is important in order to consider the extent to which the activity provides value for the customer.

Activity cost is, of course, important for the activity management process. That cost can simply be linked to time, as it would be with a monthly budget (for example: the monthly cost of plant security or general cleaning in a hospital). But if the output can be measured in units, the cost per unit of the activity's output can be used as a basis for continuous improvement (for example: residential mortgages processed or orders handled).

The cost of an activity may be measured in terms other than dollars. Failed service or returned products represent costs that eventually will be translated into dollars, but are more easily measured in their raw state. Time is also a cost, and one that may not be automatically measured. Here is an example:

> A large urban hospital recognized that it lost money on most of its stroke patients. Medicare paid a fixed amount regardless of the length of stay, and many of the hospital's stroke patients stayed longer than the average time. At first, hospital administration thought the physicians were responsible by being slow to provide treatment. But on further analysis, aided by the physicians, the administration discovered that the problem was not with the physicians, but with CT scan testing.

The test results took a long time to reach the attending physician. More investigation uncovered a number of small reasons for the time delay (for example: poor handwriting on the orders, a cumbersome system for recording the neurologist's interpretation of the scans, an overloaded scanner). That the time delay increased the hospital's costs was generally known, but normal records showed no inefficiency in the CT scan activity. The cost per scan was recorded and was satisfactorily low. The elapsed time from order to receipt of results was not recorded until the study showed how important it was. After the study, remedial actions were taken and elapsed time performance was reported regularly.

In measuring the cost per unit of output, a question of the *activity's capacity* may arise. Should the cost of any excess capacity be charged to a product? Can the excess be eliminated or is it the result of a policy decision? Many businesses, such as hospitals and hotels, expect to have excess capacity at least some of the time, because demand varies more quickly than capacity. The process of measuring activity cost sometimes triggers an analysis of the cost of excess capacity where it may exist or may be planned.

ACTIVITY ANALYSIS: AN EXAMPLE[2]

A steel company had used a traditional cost system for many years to track product and customer profitability, but it became bogged down and increasingly unreliable as the complexity of the production process increased. Their ABC/ABM effort began as a product and customer profitability project, which eventually led to a three-dimensional activity matrix along the dimensions of product, customer, and manufacturing process by plant, business unit, and for the company as a whole. When the model was complete, they could see the impact of each activity and its cost on those three dimensions. They also found:[3]

- Sales projections could be entered into the model to determine projected profitability. Different pricing and product mixes could be tried to identify where marketing emphasis should be placed in order to maximize return.

- Because the model included capacities, it could be used to identify the volume at which a current capacity would be exceeded. Using this model in long-range planning enabled the company to adjust capacities to ensure that the business process had the capability to fulfill projected sales.

- Excess capacities can be identified and, where possible, reused or reassigned where they could be more usefully employed. If business units needed to be downsized, it could be done rationally based on resources that were identified as excess, rather than the more traditional technique of reducing everything 10% across the board.

- Productivity improvement opportunities could be analyzed based on their impact on costs in the business process. Process improvement resources could be allocated to those improvements that yielded the greatest cost reduction.

---

[2] For other examples of the installation of activity-based management systems, see: David Keys, Steve Player, ed., *Activity-Based Management: Arthur Andersen's Lessons from the ABM Battlefield*, (New York: MasterMedia Limited, 1995); and James M. Reeve, "Projects, Models, and Systems: Where Is ABM Headed?" *Journal of Cost Management* (Summer 1996): 5–16.

[3] James D. Tarr, "Activity-Based Management—Merging Process and Measurement," ACA Group Web site, August 2006.

TARGET COSTING

Imagine what happens when a company like Boeing or Caterpillar posts a request for a proposal (RFP) for a subassembly on a new product. Supplier A, with an extensive history of successful manufacturing and a wealth of detailed cost data, begins its bid preparation as it always has. Starting with an existing product in its line that is most like what's being requested, it begins assessing the differences between the two, estimating the new production steps, labor hours, and materials as well as the up-front costs for design, engineering, warranty costs, and the like. Proceeding in this fashion, supplier A assembles a projection of both the one-time costs and the fully costed product data and a standard profit mark-up. Once this work is complete, a pricing conference would typically review arguments on shaving the profit margin or granting other considerations to the customer. This process would be necessary to ensure a competitive bid.

Supplier B goes about its bid in a very different way. The first task is to decide what price will be needed in order to win the contract. This becomes the target price. Supplier B arrives at this in various ways, studying market prices and trends, consideration of how the new subassembly fits into the prime contractors' (Boeing or Caterpillar) cost plans, and a competitive analysis of what supplier A and the others are likely to bid.

Once supplier B has established the target price, it begins working backward. First comes the profit margin it will require at that price. After that comes the real work of figuring out a plan for securing the elements necessary to produce that subassembly at a cost that will meet the target price and profit margin. The elements can include design, distribution, and outsourcing—indeed, almost anything necessary to reach the target price. Supplier B practices what is called *target costing*.

Target costing is a systematic process of pricing, profit planning, and cost management. It is based on six core principles:[4]

1. *Price-led costing.* Market prices are used to determine allowable or target costs. Target costs are calculated using a formula similar to the following:

   Market Price – Required Profit Margin = Target Cost

2. *Focus on customers.* Customer requirements for quality, cost, and time are simultaneously incorporated in product and process decisions and guide cost analysis. The value (to the customer) of any features and functionality built into the product must be greater than the cost of providing those features and functionality.

3. *Focus on design.* Cost control is emphasized at the product and process design stage. Therefore, engineering changes must occur before production begins, resulting in lower costs and a reduced time-to-market for new products.

4. *Cross-functional involvement.* Cross-functional product and process teams are responsible for the entire product from initial concept through final production.

5. *Value-chain involvement.* All members of the value chain—for example: suppliers, distributors, service providers, and customers—are included in the target costing process.

---

[4] These principles are adopted from S. Ansari, J. Bell, and the CAM-I Target Cost Core Group, *Target Costing, The Next Frontier in Strategic Cost Management* (Chicago, IL: Irwin, 1997).

6. *A lifecycle orientation.* Total lifecycle costs are minimized for both the products and the customer. Lifecycle costs include purchase price, operating costs, maintenance, and distribution costs.

The primary benefits of target costing include:

- Products that better meet customer expectations, including functionality and price;
- Reduced costs, particularly indirect costs;
- Faster development;
- Better integration over the complete supply chain.

Target costing is used by many companies when launching new products. They employ a variety of marketing techniques including value engineering/analysis, which seeks to better understand the customer, what features the customer values, and why. This is often called the *voice of the customer*. The process of defining the product and its target price must also address the product's lifecycle, experience, or learning curves, and competitors' products, prices, and likely responses. Design typically involves design for manufacturing assembly, the participation of suppliers and their supply chains, cost modeling, and a design-to-cost approach.

One of the most interesting things about target costing is how it changes the way people work. It's a team-based activity integrating marketing, design, sourcing, distribution, manufacturing, engineering production, and the cost group. This activity has turned costing on its head. The question is no longer "What does it cost?" but, "What should it cost?" This is a creative process where imagination and ingenuity are prized. It broadens peoples' jobs and responsibilities. Designers, for example, must learn to understand costs and cost modeling, lean manufacturing, and value engineering as well the opportunity for collaboration with suppliers and distributors. They become part of the competitive effort.

In summary, target costing is not so much a costing process as it is a cost management and planning process whose objective is to reduce costs. It sets a target or allowable cost per unit and also sets a cost for certain functions, such as quality assurance, and then works to achieve those costs. The target cost is based on an analysis of market forces, which determines both the desired product characteristics and a planned selling price.

Though in practice the target costing process has many variations, there are several distinctive features:

1. Most of the work stimulated by target costing takes place in the design and production planning stages. But even after production begins, continuous improvement is usually sought by modification of design and production methods.
2. Plans for achieving the target cost are developed and carried out by teams of people representing a variety of functions. Target costing teams include people with diverse competencies.

Target costing and activity-based cost management are related—perhaps first cousins. In the planning process used for target costing, the production process that is being planned for a new product is laid out and costed with what appears to be a model of the drivers and required activities. The impact on those activities of cost reduction ideas is measured. For example, if the product design is changed to reduce the number of parts, the cost of activities affected will be reduced. The analysis is pro forma, that is before the activity takes place, but the concepts used for cost reduction are similar.

The target methods are most useful in industries where product lifecycles are short and hence, where continuous work on the design stages is the key to a firm's success. For example, target costing is used more in the automobile and electronics industries than in process industries.

SUMMARY

In this chapter, we have described an approach to cost management that focuses on activities. Activity-based management is related to activity-based costing described in Chapter 2 in that each focuses on activities, but ABM's purpose is to manage costs by improving the efficiency and effectiveness of activities. ABM usually requires that activities be sliced more finely than is needed for ABC, and ABM costing is done to provide a basis for continuous improvement.

Target costing is a system for managing costs that focuses on the planning process. Its objective is to manage costs before the product design and production process have been set, and it is most useful when frequent model changes or opportunities to change allow planned revisions.[5]

---

[5] Further description of target costing is contained in: Michiharu Sakurai, "Target Costing and How to Use It," *Journal of Cost Management* (Summer 1989): 39; Y. Monden and M. Sakurai, eds., *Japanese Management Accounting,* (Ronald Press/John Wiley & Sons, Inc., 1989); *Implementing Target Costing, Management Accounting Guideline #28* (CMA, IMA, and CAMI, April 1994); Germain Böer, Chee W. Chow, Yutuka Kato, "Target Costing: An Integrative Management Process," *Journal of Cost Management* (April 1995): 39–51; Joseph Fisher, "Implementing Target Costing," *Journal of Cost Management* (Summer 1995): 50–59.

QUESTIONS AND PROBLEMS

6–1.   Company A's management assigned each operating department the task of reducing costs by 10%. Company B's management sought similar reductions through an activities-based management process. Describe some of the differences between the two approaches.

6–2.   Consider a small business or a department of a larger business with which you are familiar. Make a list of the activities that take place, using a verb–noun (or verb–adjective–noun) system to define the activities.

6–3.   What is a nonvalue-added (or adding) activity? Can you think of some examples?

6–4.   Why is it usually necessary to define more focused and detailed activities when working on ABM than when working on ABC?

CHAPTER 7

EVALUATING CAPITAL EXPENDITURES

IMPORTANCE OF CAPITAL EXPENDITURES

Capital expenditure decisions are among the most important decisions an organization makes, because they tie the company to long-term commitments in equipment, plants, products, special programs, and the like. In contrast, many day-to-day operating decisions can be reversed, if future events change. For example, employment levels may be adjusted through terminations, attrition, or retirement; prices can be changed; new suppliers can be sought or old ones terminated. But plants are not so easily closed, nor are special machines and equipment sold. Thus, the results of capital expenditure quickly become permanent. Furthermore, capital expenditures typically involve relatively large sums. Consequently, such decisions are important for their magnitude as well as their permanence. Capital expenditure budgets reflect the long-range plans of an organization and are a means of implementing those plans.

FINANCIAL MEASUREMENT

The focus of this chapter is capital expenditure budgeting and project evaluation with respect to financial criteria. Financial considerations are rarely the only basis upon which investment decisions are made. Business strategy dictates most of those decisions in the modern corporation. However, financial criteria are of great importance in such planning. The reasons are obvious. Businesses invest funds to return a profit to stockholders. They may increase this pool of available funds by borrowing or by other means, but only if they are able to invest this additional amount at a profit. Governments and nonprofits operate with only limited resources, which must also be invested wisely.

While financial criteria are very important, it should be noted that not all investment decisions are made for economic reasons. Safety equipment is purchased to cut accidents and save lives. Pollution-control devices are installed to prevent contamination of air or water. Governments, nonprofits, and even businesses make investments for social rather than economic reasons. In an emergency, a company may buy a new generator, tractor, or computer in order to get a factory or office back into operation, no matter what the cost. Sometimes a decision is made on personal grounds, such as when the owner–manager of a company decides to build a new office in a particular city because that's where he or she wishes to live. Even in those cases, however, the financial implications of the decision are often assessed. In many other situations, financial matters are but one of a number of significant criteria to be considered. This chapter's primary concern, however, will be the financial considerations in capital budgeting decisions.

BASIC ELEMENTS OF CAPITAL BUDGETING

The capital budgeting process can be viewed as consisting of six parts:

1. Collecting ideas;
2. Developing alternatives;
3. Estimating results;

4. Evaluating alternatives;

5. Considering risk;

6. Relating capital budgeting and business strategy.

Each of those elements will be discussed next.

Collecting Ideas

In any large organization, ideas for change requiring capital expenditures are continually arising at all levels and for a variety of reasons including to cut costs, increase capacity, develop new products, and improve quality. New ideas are vital to any successful organization, and some procedure or mechanism must be established to collect and analyze those ideas. Some organizations are better at this than others. The key to success at this first step is the ability to encourage all types of new ideas, and thus to nurture this creative process while at the same time quickly, but carefully, screening ideas in order to select only the most promising for a detailed, thorough analysis. This balance is a delicate one, for a harsh screening process may eliminate good ideas from further consideration while a weak one allows an expensive and scarce analysis effort to be devoted to too many worthless ideas. Once a good idea has been identified, the next step is to determine how best to exploit it. Often a number of alternatives present themselves.

Developing Alternatives

Capital budgeting decisions always involve a selection among alternatives. Even if at first glance there appears to be only one option (for example, the opportunity to invest in a new labor-saving machine or to create software so as to provide new services), further analysis usually uncovers additional alternatives; if only that of maintaining the status quo, which is to do nothing. Indeed, many decisions involve comparisons against the status quo. However, if only one course of action is in fact possible, then one does not have a problem, for no decision need be made.

Discovering new ideas and developing alternative courses of action are undoubtedly the most important aspects of the capital budgeting process. It is obvious that no matter how much attention is paid to estimating cash flow, calculating paybacks, and making other evaluations, if the best alternatives are not even considered, then only a poor decision can result. Identifying additional alternatives can be quite difficult. For example, a company might come up with the idea of investing in a small computer to automate a manual payroll operation. There are apparently two alternatives: to invest in the small computer, or to continue the present operation. But further study might uncover many more alternatives including:

1. Improved manual operation;

2. Use of a computer service bureau;

3. Purchase of a large computer capable of automating other functions besides payroll, such as inventory control and production scheduling;

4. Outsourcing and/or offshoring.

In fact, the best alternative might be to abandon the payroll process altogether, to arrange for a company like ADP to do payroll accounting, and to make direct deposits into the employees' accounts. Obviously, selecting the best alternative requires a thorough analysis of each; yet without the full list of alternatives, the best choice might be overlooked. Unfortunately, many investment decisions are doomed from the start, because the best option was never even considered.

Estimating Results

An essential step in project evaluation is estimating the results of each alternative: its future profits or savings, and its future costs. Even determining the total cost of the initial investment may require an estimate; for example, the price of individual pieces of equipment, such as computers, aircraft, or vehicles may be known, but the cost of land, building construction, software development, or acquisitions of other companies requires estimates. Estimates are almost always required for future cost savings, revenue, and incremental operating costs. In preparing those estimates, one normally attempts to establish the most likely figure for profit or savings. Sometimes a separate conservative or optimistic schedule of estimates is prepared, and the results are then compared to those of the most likely estimate. In every case, however, it is important to be sure that the estimates are prepared carefully. A useful set of guidelines for making estimates consists of these rules.

1. *Be honest.* Estimating future savings or costs is not the time to bring personal preferences into the analysis.

2. *Be consistent.* Don't mix conservative estimates with the most likely or the optimistic one.

3. *Use rounded figures.* Estimates of future events normally cannot be made precisely. Figures to six decimal points or to the penny suggest a degree of precision that may be unwarranted. Rounded figures are also easier to manipulate mathematically.

4. *Collect data wisely.* Better data may enable a better decision. Sometimes an organization will spend several thousand dollars and many months of effort just to collect data for a decision. This is another tradeoff or balancing situation as collecting more data usually costs more money and takes time, thus delaying the decision, but better data may yield a better solution. The decision about when to stop collecting data and to make a decision based upon the evidence at hand is always difficult yet important.

5. *Don't estimate beyond a reasonable horizon.* Estimates should be made no further into the future than can be reasonably anticipated. For example, when a new product or service is being considered, estimates of investment, revenues, and costs beyond a limited number of years are not normally made. Some projects have lifetimes that extend 50 years or more as with investments in electrical-generating capacity, rail lines, and ports, but many projects may have lifetimes measured in months, or just a few years.

The last point is particularly important. Special attention should be given to what is called the economic life of a project, or alternative. Very few capital budgeting alternatives have unlimited lives. Often the expected life of a machine or product can be estimated and used as the economic life. Sometimes the decision is arbitrary: "We can't look beyond 60 months on this deal; the chances of keeping the product going past that time are just too low." Whatever time span is selected, the important thing is to be certain that the same span is used to evaluate each alternative. In the payroll example mentioned previously, the results of each alternative must be estimated for the same time frame. Otherwise, the alternatives are not really comparable. More will be said about that later.

In capital budgeting decisions, estimates of the total investment and its savings, costs, and profits are usually made in terms of cash flow rather than accounting income or savings. In many situations, there is little difference between income statements results and cash flow. Cash flow from sales closely follows accounting sales on the income statement. Savings in labor, materials, supplies, and so on, are frequently actual cash flow savings.

However, income statement and cash flow frequently differ regarding depreciation and book values. Depreciation is an expense item on the income statement recognizing a portion of the cost of an asset over time. But although it tends to reduce net income, depreciation is not a cash expense. Cash was spent only at the time that the asset was originally purchased. That cash outlay made sometime in the past is a sunk cost and cannot be affected by any decision made now.[1]

The book value of a machine scrapped when a new machine is purchased represents the unallocated amount of the original purchase price. But book values seldom represent market values if the asset is sold or scrapped. Since we are interested in cash flows that result from a proposed decision, it is the scrap value or resale value that is relevant, not the book value, unless they happen to be the same. However, the book value will affect taxes, and tax payments are cash flows. Generally, the write-off of book value will come either all at once, if the machine is scrapped, or over time as a depreciation charge. Thus, the difference is primarily one of timing. There will be more discussion of depreciation and book value in a later section of this chapter, which deals with taxes.

In comparing alternatives, one usually needs to specify only their differing results. For example, if we are considering the purchase of a semi-automatic or an automatic packaging machine to replace the existing manual operation, all we will be concerned with are the changes in future cash flows under each alternative. We do not need to concern ourselves with all future costs; just with those that will be affected by the investment in either machine. Also, we do not need to estimate the total plant costs five years from now; only the changes in costs. This type of estimation is usually termed a differential analysis.

Evaluating Alternatives

Several techniques exist for evaluating capital budgeting alternatives. Each method has certain advantages as well as disadvantages, and it is essential that the decision-maker be aware of each while using a particular technique. The four techniques to be discussed here are the ones most often used in business today:

1. Payback;

2. Unadjusted rate of return;

3. Net present value;

4. Internal rate of return.

Payback

The purpose of the payback method is to determine when the funds invested in a particular project will be recovered through profits or savings. The result is expressed as a period of time, such as three months or six and one-half years. The payback technique addresses the question: If we spend $10,000 on a labor-

---

[1] For a more detailed discussion of sunk costs, see Chapter 5.

saving machine, how long will it take us to recover our investment through savings?[2] If we save $2,000 per year, the payback period is five years. If we save $5,000 per year, the payback is two years.

When payback is calculated, savings or inflows are normally based on cash flows rather than on accounting or book profits. Also cash savings are calculated net of applicable income taxes. When the savings are uniform (the same each time period), payback can be calculated as:

$$\text{Payback} \quad = \quad \frac{\text{Investment}}{\text{Annual Cash Savings}}$$

For example, suppose a $10,000 machine saves $4,000 per year in labor costs and will be used for five years, the depreciation life of the machine. Suppose further that depreciation for tax purposes is to be made on a straight-line basis. What is the payback if the company expects its income taxes to be 35%? To figure the payback, we first need to determine the yearly cash flow. It is $3,300, calculated as follows:

Annual book savings	$4,000
Less: depreciation expense	(2,000)
Taxable savings	$2,000
Income taxes (35%)	700
After-tax savings	$1,300
Add: depreciation	2,000
After-tax cash savings	$3,300

In words, what we've done here is to recognize that while we expect $4,000 in yearly labor savings, we must consider depreciation expense and income taxes as well; depreciation is $10,000 ÷ 5 or $2,000 per year. Thus, taxable savings are only $2,000. After-tax savings are just $1,300. Depreciation is not a cash expense, so it must be added back to get after-tax cash savings of $3,300. Calculating cash flows is described more fully in the section discussing taxes. Using the formula, we find the payback to be three years:

$$\text{Payback} \quad = \quad \frac{\text{Investment}}{\text{Annual Cash Savings}} \quad = \quad \frac{\$10,000}{\$3,300} \quad = \quad 3 \text{ Years}$$

When the return is not the same each year, payback can only be determined by a process of counting or accumulation. For example, if our $10,000 machine is expected to yield the cash savings shown in column 1 of Figure 7–1 below, the savings accumulate as in column 2.

---

[2] Capital budgeting and investment analysis is all about projects. Most projects important enough to be subjected to formal financial evaluation have many elements including revenues and expenses, the acquisition of software, equipment, buildings, and perhaps other businesses. Many have research, development, and marketing expenditures as well. When we evaluate those opportunities, the analysis is performed on the project as a whole. In the examples, we will use greatly simplified projects—an investment and a set of cash flows. In reality, there's likely to be many elements of the investment and many elements that constitute the net cash flows.

	[1]	[2]
	Cash	Accumulated
Year	Savings	Savings
1	$ 1,000	$1,000
2	1,000	2,000
3	3,000	5,000
4	3,000	8,000
5	4,000	12,000
6	4,000	16,000
7	4,000	20,000
Total	$20,000	

Figure 7–1: *Uneven Cash Savings*

Payback is that point at which the investment is just recovered—in this case, four and one-half years. At the beginning of year 5 we would have recovered $8,000, and, assuming an equal cash flow throughout the year, we would receive the remaining $2,000 by mid-year of the fifth year.

Payback analysis has several advantages. The method is simple and the calculations are straightforward. More important, the concept of payback, the end result, is readily understood. Payback is also used by many people to deal with risk. One might ask, "How long must we count on getting these savings before we break even?" As we shall show later, however, it is a very crude and often inaccurate technique for this purpose.

Unfortunately, the payback approach has several disadvantages, the most serious of which is that it ignores any revenue or savings beyond the payback period. The following two investments both have the same payback, yet alternative B earns cash flow for several years beyond that of A and its total cash flow is much higher.

Alternative A		*Alternative B*	
Investment: $15,000		Investment: $15,000	
Cash flow:		Cash flow:	
Year	*Amount*	*Year*	*Amount*
1	$5,000	1	$6,000
2	5,000	2	5,000
3	5,000	3	4,000
		4	3,000
Payback: 3 years		5	2,000
		Payback: 3 years	

Alternatives A and B

From this example, the reader will note that payback measures return *of* investment (how long must we wait to get back what we put in?), not return *on* investment (how much do we get back compared to what we put in?) The three other techniques we'll introduce all measure return on investment.

Unadjusted Rate of Return

Investors often calculate the return on investment (ROI) of a company by dividing the profit for the year by the company's investment in land, buildings, and equipment, etc. When that approach is used to evaluate capital budgeting alternatives, it is called the unadjusted rate of return or the accountant's method.[3] The unadjusted rate of return is calculated by subtracting depreciation from the annual average savings and then dividing by the average investment outstanding. The savings or profit figures are accounting or book income rather than cash flow. Average investment is often taken to be one-half of the purchase costs.

$$\text{Unadjusted Rate of Return} = \frac{\text{Average Annual Savings}}{\text{Average Investment}}$$

For example, if a $10,000 investment is expected to yield $4,000 before depreciation each year for five years, the unadjusted rate of return is 40%.

$$\text{Return} = \frac{\$4,000 - \$2,000^*}{(\$10,000 \div 2)} = 40\%$$

* The $2,000 is the depreciation.

Savings are generally taken before taxes, although in some companies the calculation is done on an after-tax basis. Gross investment (purchase costs not halved), is sometimes used rather than average investment. The specific formula chosen makes little difference in comparing alternatives as long as a company uses the same approach to evaluate each alternative.

Unadjusted rate of return is also simple to compute, easy to understand, and widely used. Its greatest weakness is that it operates under the assumption that money received or spent today is worth the same as money received or spent in the future. For example, look at the following alternatives.

Each alternative has an unadjusted rate of return of 40%, but clearly alternative D is superior to C, for we receive our money sooner and we can then presumably invest it somewhere else. The technique has ignored the time value of money. In the previous problem, the advantages of receiving the money earlier are readily apparent through a visual inspection; no one would be foolish enough to think that the two alternatives were equal, but suppose another alternative was found. Consider alternative E.

---

[3] The term unadjusted here means the rate of return is not adjusted for the time value of money. The adjustment for the time value of money will be discussed in the next section of this chapter.

Alternative C		Alternative D		Alternative E	
Investment: $10,000		Investment: $10,000		Investment: $10,000	
Cash flow:		Cash flow:		Cash flow:	
Year	*Amount*	*Year*	*Amount*	*Year*	*Amount*
1	$2,000	1	$6,000	1	$6,000
2	3,000	2	5,000	2	6,000
3	4,000	3	4,000	3	6,000
4	5,000	4	3,000	4	500
5	6,000	5	2,000	5	500

Average annual savings:	Average annual savings:	Average annual savings:
$20,000 ÷ 5	$20,000 ÷ 5	$19,000 ÷ 5
or	or	or
$4,000	$4,000	$3,800

Unadjusted rate of return:	Unadjusted rate of return:	Unadjusted rate of return:
$4,000 – $2,000	$4,000 – $2,000	$3,800 – $2,000
$5,000	$5,000	$5,000
or 40%	or 40%	or 36%

Alternatives C, D, and E

Here the unadjusted rate of return is less than 40%. Using the unadjusted rate of return method, we would discard alternative E as being inferior to alternatives C and D, but a quick inspection shows that alternative E earns savings of $18,000 during the first three years while D yields $15,000, and C only earns $9,000. Isn't it possible that if it's worth enough to us to have our money sooner rather than later, then alternative E would be preferable to D or C? This question leads us to consider present value and its use in the time-adjusted rate of return method.

Present Value

The time value of money. As we've already noted, to us the value of money changes over time. If we are to be paid $1,000, we'd prefer to have it today rather than next year, since if we had it today we could invest it and have more than $1,000 by this time next year. Another reason for preferring to get our money sooner rather than later is that during periods of inflation the real or economic value of money declines. Thus, we'd prefer our payment to be in current dollars rather than in future, lower-valued dollars. The methods necessary to deal properly with anticipated inflation are beyond the scope of this book. In general, it is fair to say that in times of low inflation companies typically ignore it. They project future cash flows using today's dollars and they discount them with an inflationless rate, or at least that's what they should be doing. A good many organizations project cash flows on today's dollars and use a discount rate reflective of today's cost of capital, which incorporates some expected inflation. In high inflation environments, accounting is done with formal inflation adjustments as is capital budgeting. For the remainder of this chapter, we'll reflect just the cost or value of money apart from the effects of inflation.

If we were to invest $1,000 in a bank paying 5% interest, by next year we'd have $1,050. In fact, we'd only have to invest $952 today to have $1,000 next year.[4] This leads us to a very important

---

[4] 5% interest on $952 would give us $48 (0.05 × 952). This together with the return of our $952 totals $1,000.

conclusion: receiving $1,000 one year from now is not worth $1,000 to us now, it's only worth $952. Another way of viewing this is that at 5% we are indifferent as to a $952 payment now, or $1,000 received in one year. This $952 amount is called the present value of the $1,000 payment to be received in one year and this approach is called *discounting.*

Also note that present value works whether we're being paid or paying someone. At 5%, we are indifferent as to paying $952 now, or paying $1,000 a year from now. We're also indifferent as to receiving $952 now or $ 1,000 one year from now.

If we had other opportunities to invest that would yield more than 5%, the $1,000 future payment would be worth even less than $952. Thus, present value is dependent upon some interest rate (in our example: 5%). It is also clear that if the $1,000 were to be received 10 years from today, it would be worth even less than $952. Thus, present value is dependent upon some time period as well. Therefore, to be precise, we say: the present value at 5% of $1,000 received or paid one year from now is $952.

Tables exist that provide a present value factor for a large combination of interest rates and periods of time.[5] Table I in the Appendix of this chapter gives present value factors for interest rates from 2% to 30% and from 1 to 40 years. To use this table, one must first locate the present value factor corresponding to the interest rate and time period in question. The factor from the table is then multiplied by the amount to be received to yield the present value. For example, suppose a company is to receive $5,000 at the end of 12 years and money, to them, is worth 8%. What is the present value of that future payment?

Looking at Table I, we find the present value factor for 12 years at 8% to be 0.40. Multiplying this by the $5,000 yields a present value of $2,000.

In another case, suppose that we are to receive 3 equal payments of $5,000; the first at the end of year 1, the second at the end of year 2, and the last at the end of year 3. What is the present value of those payments at 8%? Figure 7–2 shows this calculation using Table I.

[1]	[2]	[3]	[4]
		Present Value	*Present Value*
End of Year	*Cash Flow*	*Factor Table 1*	*(col. 2 × 3)*
1	$5,000	0.93	$ 4,650
2	5,000	0.86	4,300
3	5,000	0.79	3,950
		Total	$12,900

The present value at 8% of $5,000 each year for three years is $12,900.

Figure 7–2: *Present Value Using Appendix Table I*

---

[5] The mathematics for determining present value are quite simple:

$$\text{Present Value} = \frac{\text{Future Payment}}{(1 + i)^n}$$

When (i) is the rate of interest and (n) is the number of years until the time of payment. In our sample problem, (i) was 0.05 (5%) and (n) was 1 (one year) so that:

$$\text{Present Value} = \frac{\$1,000}{(1.05)^1}$$

For most problems, the decision-maker has access to a table of present value factors or a computer program for those calculations.

Since we frequently find capital budgeting problems involving equal annual cash flows (Figure 7–2), tables exist to make this calculation directly. Such present value factors are shown in Table III of the Appendix. Thus, from Table III the present value factor for three equal, yearly payments at 8% is 2.58; and 2.58 × $5,000 is $12,900.[6] Table III saves a good deal of time and calculation, whenever the cash flows are equal.

In each of the above examples, the cash flow occurred as a single payment or payments made at the end of the year. What about situations where the cash flows occur more or less evenly throughout the year as would normally happen with profits from a new product or savings from a new machine? Tables II and IV may be used in such situations. Those tables assume that the annual amount is paid once in the middle of the year and although not exactly correct, this is a close approximation of continuous or monthly payments throughout the year. Table II, like Table I, applies to single payments. Table IV, as Table III does for Table I, provides cumulative figures from the single payments factors in Table II. Since it does make a difference, the decision-maker must be careful to determine the actual timing of the expected cash flows for each problem and then use the appropriate table.

Handheld calculators and computer programs have been developed to do what we do in this chapter using the tables shown. The use of such electronic assistance makes extensive computation much quicker, and enables one to check the effect of variations in inputs quite easily. It is important, however, that the calculator or computer user understand what the machine is supposed to be doing and that often means one should have a rough idea what the answer should be in order to check the calculator or computer output. Hence, we believe that learning about the use of present value analysis is best begun with the use of tables, but for those who prefer computer spreadsheets or handheld calculators, the examples throughout the remainder of this chapter are worked out in three ways.

1. With Tables I–IV;

2. With a Hewlett-Packard (HP) 12C financial calculator;

3. With Microsoft Excel spreadsheets.

How is present value used as a technique to evaluate capital budgeting alternatives? The steps are as follows:

1. *Determine* the required investment rate or hurdle rate that represents the organization's cost of funds or the earnings rate that a new investment must exceed to be approved. For some companies this rate is set at the average cost of money (both from debt and from equity) for the firm. In other organizations, the hurdle rate is set higher to eliminate all but the most profitable investment alternatives. Organizations often separate capital expenditures into one of several categories according to the riskiness of the project, establishing different hurdle rates for each category. Ordinarily, the same hurdle rate is used for all capital budgeting decisions within the same risk category, and this rate remains the same over a long period of time. Sometimes a company will set different hurdle rates for different divisions of a company reflecting its relative risk profiles. Determining this investment rate is a very important step in the net present value method, but any further discussion of it is beyond the scope of this chapter.

---

[6] The reader will note that 2.58 is simply the sum of the three present value factors: 0.93, 0.86, and 0.79. Indeed, that was how Table III was derived.

2. *Estimate* the total cash investment for each alternative. If the investment is made at the beginning of a project, no discounting is necessary, because cash is paid immediately. This investment is usually referred to as a cash flow in time period 0 (a discount or present value factor of 1).

3. *Estimate* the resulting cash savings in the future: period by period.

4. *Discount* or determine the present value of those future cash flows using present value factors for each year at the required investment rate.

5. *Add* the discounted figures together. The total is the sum of the discounted cash flows.

6. *Subtract* the original investment from the sum of the discounted cash flows. The result is the net present value (NPV). If the NPV is positive, the return provided by that alternative exceeds the investment rate, or hurdle rate. If it is negative, the alternative fails to meet the required return.

For example, using alternatives C and D shown earlier and assuming that 8% is the hurdle rate or the minimum acceptable rate of return, we perform the following calculations.

[1]	[2]	[3]	[4]	[5]
	Unadjusted	*Present*	*Discounted*	
	Cash Flow	*Value*	*Cash Flow*	*Time-*
Time	*(+ savings*	*Factor 8%*	*(col. 2*	*Adjusted*
Period	*– investment)*	*from Table I*	*× col. 3)*	*Cash Flow*
0	$(10,000)	1.00		$(10,000)
1	2,000	0.93	$ 1,860	
2	3,000	0.86	2,580	
3	4,000	0.79	3,160	
4	5,000	0.73	3,650	
5	6,000	0.68	4,080	
Sum of the discounted cash flows			$15,330	15,330
Net present value				$ 5,330

Alternative C (with Appendix tables)

	Keystrokes			Display	Comments
Numbers	White	Blue	Brown		
			REG		Clear financial registers
10,000	CHS	CFo		–10,000.00	Periodic payment (investment)
2,000		CFj		2,000.00	Periodic payment (cash flow return)
3,000		CFj		3,000.00	
4,000		CFj		4,000.00	
5,000		CFj		5,000.00	
6,000		CFj		6,000.00	
8	i			8.00	Periodic interest rate
			NPV	5,357.85	Net present value

Alternative C (with HP 12C)

Note that the difference between this $5,357.85 and the $5,330 obtained from the tables is due to rounded table values.

	A	B	C	D
			D13: =NPV(D12,D6:D10)+D5	
1				
2				
3			*End of*	*Cash*
4			*Year*	*Flow*
5			0	$(10,000)
6			1	2,000
7			2	3,000
8			3	4,000
9			4	5,000
10			5	6,000
11				
12		Present value factor		0.08
13		Net present value		$5,358

Alternative C (with Microsoft Excel)

Note the key relationship in cell D13 [= NPV (D12, D6: D10) + D5]. Excel assumes that the first item in the range is at the end of period 1, so the time period 0 cash flow in cell D5 must be added. In this example, D6 is the period 1 cash flow.

[1]	[2]	[3]	[4]	[5]
	Unadjusted		*Discounted*	
	Cash Flow	*Present Value*	*Cash Flow*	*Time-*
Time	*(+ savings*	*Factor 8%*	*(col. 2*	*Adjusted*
Period	*– investment)*	*from Table I*	*× col. 3)*	*Cash Flow*
0	$(10,000)	1.00		$(10,000)
1	6,000	0.93	$5,580	
2	5,000	0.86	4,300	
3	4,000	0.79	3,160	
4	3,000	0.73	2,190	
5	2,000	0.68	1,360	
Sum of the discounted cash flows			$16,590	16,590
Net present value				$ 6,590

Alternative D (with Appendix tables)

	Keystrokes			Display	Comments
Numbers	White	Blue	Brown		
			REG		Clear financial registers
10,000	CHS	CFo		−10,000.00	Periodic payment
6,000		CFj		6,000.00	
5,000		CFj		5,000.00	
4,000		CFj		4,000.00	
3,000		CFj		3,000.00	
2,000		CFj		2,000.00	
8	i			8.00	Periodic interest rate
			NPV	6,583.84	Net present value

Alternative D (with HP 12C)

D13: =NPV(D12,D6:D10)+D5

	A	B	C	D
1				
2				
3			*End of*	*Cash*
4			*Year*	*Flow*
5			0	$(10,000)
6			1	6,000
7			2	5,000
8			3	4,000
9			4	3,000
10			5	2,000
11				
12		Present value factor		0.08
13		Net present value		$6,584

Alternative D (with Microsoft Excel)

From those examples, we can see that since both alternatives have a positive NPV, both projects exceed the 8% investment rate requirement. We also see that at the 8% rate alternative D has a higher NPV. Other things being equal and if the alternatives are mutually exclusive (i.e., only one of the alternatives can be selected), then D is preferable.

Dealing with Taxes

Most of the discussions to date have dealt with current investments and future cash flows as if income taxes were not an issue in the decision. Indeed, many organizations that face capital budgeting decisions do not pay income taxes, including schools, municipal hospitals, governmental agencies, foundations, etc. Most business organizations, however, do pay both federal and state income taxes; and since taxes do affect investment decisions, those organizations must incorporate taxes into the analysis.

Taxes enter the evaluation of capital budgeting decisions in two ways: (1) some or all of the additional profits or savings may be subject to tax, and (2) some or all of the initial investment may be depreciated or amortized in the future, serving to reduce taxable earnings at that time. The latter consideration often causes confusion, because while depreciation reduces taxable income and thus reduces cash outflow (cash that otherwise would have gone to pay taxes), depreciation itself is not a cash expense. For example, assume that the investment in alternative E had an expected life of five years for tax purposes. Note that this time span also corresponds to the length of expected savings and is the economic life. Suppose also that the straight-line method of depreciation is to be used. We then make the following calculations, assuming a 40% tax rate:

[1] Time Period	[2] Unadjusted Cash Flow (+ savings – investment)		[3] Present Value Factor 8% from Table I	[4] Discounted Cash Flow (col. 2 × col. 3)	[5] Time- Adjusted Cash Flow
0	$(10,000)		1.00		$(10,000)
1	4,400	*	0.93	$ 4,092	
2	4,400	*	0.86	3,784	
3	4,400	*	0.79	3,476	
4	1,100	**	0.73	803	
5	1,100	**	0.68	748	
Sum of the discounted cash flows				$12,903	$12,903
Net present value					$ 2,903

Derivation of cash flows from column 2 above:

	*	**
Description	Years 1–3	Years 4–5
Total savings	$6,000	$ 500
Depreciation	(2,000)	(2,000)
Taxable savings	$4,000	$(1,500)
Taxes at 40%	1,600	(600)
Therefore:		
Total savings	6,000	500
Less: taxes	1,600	(600)
Unadjusted cash flow	$4,400	$1,100

Alternative E (with Appendix tables)

During the first three years, the $6,000 pretax savings amounts to $4,400 savings after tax. Again, this discrepancy results from two factors:

1. Taxes on $6,000 savings at 40% are $2,400, leaving $3,600 after-tax cash flow.

2. But, depreciation of $2,000/year saves $800 in taxes, leaving $4,400 ($3,600 + $800) as the total after-tax cash flow. This is sometimes called the *depreciation tax shield.*

In years 4 and 5, savings minus depreciation results in a $1,500 taxable loss. Assuming that loss can be offset against other taxable earnings, the result is a $600 tax savings.

Numbers	Keystrokes White	Blue	Brown	Display	Comments
			REG		Clear financial registers
10,000	CHS	CFo		−10,000.00	Periodic payment (investment)
4,400		CFj		4,000.00	Periodic payment
3		Nj		3.00	Number of periods
1,100		CFj		1,100.00	Periodic payment
2		Nj		2.00	Number of periods
8	i			8.00	Periodic interest rate
			NPV	2,896.40	Net present value

Alternative E (with HP 12C)

C4: =NPV(C3,D13:H13)+C13

	A	B	C	D	E	F	G	H
1								
2		Tax rate	0.40					
3		Present value factor	0.08					
4		Net present value	2,896					
5								
6			_0_	_1_	_2_	_3_	_4_	_5_
7		Initial investment	(10,000)					
8								
9		Total savings		6,000	6,000	6,000	500	500
10		Depreciation		(2,000)	(2,000)	(2,000)	(2,000)	(2,000)
11		Taxable savings (loss)		4,000	4,000	4,000	(1,500)	(1,500)
12		Taxes (taxes avoided)		1,600	1,600	1,600	(600)	(600)
13		Unadjusted cash flow	(10,000)	4,400	4,400	4,400	1,100	1,100

Alternative E (with Microsoft Excel)

An alternative form of the calculation illustrated just with present values from the tables is shown in Figure 7–3. It uses data from alternative D. Again, a tax life of five years and an income tax rate of 40% is assumed. The arrangement of this table is designed to prevent the kinds of errors in analysis that can easily occur when the tax rate is not 50%. These matters can become tricky. At a 40% tax rate, every $1 of savings before tax leaves $0.60 after tax, but every $1 of depreciation only saves $0.40 in taxes.

Description	[1] Time Period	[2] Savings	[3] Depreciation	[4] Taxable Savings	[5] Taxable Savings $[4] \times$ Tax Rate	[6] After-Tax Cash Flow $[2] - [5]$	[7] Present Value Factor 8% from Table 1	[8] Discounted Cash Flow $[6] \times [7]$	[9] Totals
Investment	0	($10,000)				($10,000)	1.00		($10,000)
	1	6,000	$2,000	$4,000	$1,600	4,400	0.93	$4,092	
	2	5,000	2,000	3,000	1,200	3,800	0.86	3,268	
	3	4,000	2,000	2,000	800	3,200	0.79	2,528	
	4	3,000	2,000	1,000	400	2,600	0.73	1,898	
	5	2,000	2,000	0	0	2,000	0.68	1,360	13,146
						Net present value			$ 3,146

Figure 7–3: *Evaluation of Alternative D*

Replacement or Scrapping. When one asset is replaced by another, the old asset is often sold for either a profit or a loss with respect to taxes. Scrapping an old asset also may yield tax advantages. Disposition of the old asset can create three basic situations:

1. Scrapping an old asset (disposing of an old asset and receiving nothing for it);

2. Loss on the sale of old asset (selling an old asset, but at some price less than book value);

3. Gain on the sale of old asset (selling an old asset at some price greater than book value).

We will illustrate each situation separately.

1. *Scrapping an old asset*:

Old asset:	Original cost–$15,000 Accumulated depreciation–$10,000 Scrap value–$0 Remaining life–5 years
New asset:	Cost–$20,000 Expected life–5 years Expected salvage at end of 5 years–$0
Savings on new asset:	$6,000/year for 5 years
Tax rate:	40%
Required investment rate:	12%

Figure 7–4 shows that the net present value at 12% is negative $720. Hence this investment does not quite meet the required investment rate of 12%.

There is an important point to observe from this example. When an asset is scrapped, but has a remaining book value (accumulated depreciation is less than the original cost), a loss equal to the book value may be reported for tax purposes—in this case, $5,000. If the tax rate is 40%, this book loss will save $2,000 in cash flow that would otherwise have been paid in taxes. This cash savings on scrapping an old asset seems like found gold; whenever we scrap an asset that has a remaining book value we get a tax savings, which reduces the total outlay for the new asset. But there is a cost to that found gold. Had we continued to use the asset, we would have eventually been able to depreciate it to 0 and thus realize the full $5,000 in depreciation (and hence save $2,000 in taxes). By scrapping the asset and taking that tax loss now, we forego taking depreciation and the resulting tax savings in the future ($400/year for 5 years or $2,000). Hence, we save $2,000 in taxes whatever we decide to do, but there is an advantage to the immediate scrapping because of the time value of money. From the above figures, we find that immediate scrapping saves $2,000 in taxes now, but we give up $400/year for five years, a sum that is worth only $1,440 at 12% now. (The present value of $400/year for five years at a 12% discount rate is $1,440.)

	[1]	[2]	[3]	[4]		[5]	[6]	[7] Present Value Factor 12% from Table III***	[8]
Description	Time Period	Savings	Depreciation	Taxable Savings		Taxes[4] × 40%	After–Tax Cash Flow [2] – [5]		Discounted Cash Flow [6] × [7]
New investment	0						$(20,000)	1.00	$(20,000)
Tax savings on scrapping	0			$(5,000)	*	$(2,000)	2,000	1.00	2,000
Future depreciation lost	1–5		$(1,000)	1,000	**	400	(400)	3.6	(1,440)
Savings	1–5	$6,000	4,000	2,000		800	5,200	3.6	18,720
							Net present value		$ (720)

* $15,000 Original cost
  10,000 Accumulated depreciation
  $ 5,000 Book value

Thus, $5,000 before tax loss on scrapping yields $2,000 tax savings at tax rate of 40%.
** Tax savings on future depreciation given up.
*** Assume year-end cash flows.

Figure 7–4: *Scrapping an Asset (with Appendix tables)*

C5: =NPV(C4,D16:H16)+C16

	A	B	C	D	E	F	G	H
1								
2		Yearly savings	6,000					
3		Tax rate	0.40					
4		Present value factor	0.12					
5		Net present value	(697)					
6								
7			0	1	2	3	4	5
8		Initial investment	(20,000)					
9								
10		Loss on scrapping asset	5,000					
11		Total savings		6,000	6,000	6,000	6,000	6,000
12		Additional depreciation		(4,000)	(4,000)	(4,000)	(4,000)	(4,000)
13		Depreciation lost		1,000	1,000	1,000	1,000	1,000
14		Taxable savings (loss)	(5,000)	3,000	3,000	3,000	3,000	3,000
15		Taxes (taxes avoided)	2,000	1,200	1,200	1,200	1,200	1,200
16		Unadjusted cash flow	(18,000)	4,800	4,800	4,800	4,800	4,800

Figure 7–4: *(continued) Scrapping an Asset (with Microsoft Excel)*

Numbers	Keystrokes White	Blue	Brown	Display	Comments
			REG		Clear financial registers
18,000	CHS	CFo		–18,000.00	Enter new investment
4,800		CFj		4,800.00	Enter net savings
5		Nj		5.00	Number of periods
12	i			12.00	Periodic interest rate
			NPV	–697.07	Net present value

Figure 7–4: *(continued) Scrapping an Asset (with HP 12C)*

In those examples, Figure 7–4 was calculated using Table III, or annual discounting in the case of Excel, as if the cash flows occurred at the end of the periods. Most likely, the savings cash flows were continuous over the years, so Table IV should have been used as shown in alternative Figure 7–4.

	[1]	[2]	[3]	[4]		[5]	[6]	[7]	[8]
								Present Value Factor 12%	
Description	Time Period	Savings	Depreciation	Taxable Savings		Taxes [4] × 40%	After-Tax Cash Flow [2] – [5]	from Table IV***	Discounted Cash Flow [6] × [7]
New investment	0						$(20,000)	1.00	$(20,000)
Tax savings on scrapping	0			$(5,000)	*	$(2,000)	2,000	1.00	2,000
Future depreciation lost	1–5		(1,000)	1,000	**	400	(400)	3.81	(1,524)
Savings	1–5	6,000	4,000	2,000		800	5,200	3.81	19,812
							Net present value		$ 288

* $15,000 Original cost
  10,000 Accumulated depreciation
  $ 5,000 Book value

Thus, $5,000 before tax loss on scrapping yields $2,000 tax savings at tax rate of 40%.
** Tax savings on future depreciation given up.
*** Assume mid-year cash flows.

Alternative Figure 7–4: *(assuming continuous savings cash flows) Scrapping an Asset (with Appendix tables)*

Numbers	Keystrokes White	Blue	Brown	Display	Comments
			REG		Clear financial registers
18,000	CHS	CFo		–18,000.00	Enter new investment
400		CFj		400.00	Enter net savings
60		Nj		60.00	Number of periods
12		12÷		1.00	Periodic interest rate
			NPV	–17.98	Net present value

Figure 7–4: *(continued: assuming continuous savings cash flows) Scrapping an Asset (with HP 12C)*

Note the relatively large difference between the two net present value figures in the alternative Figure 7–4 illustrations (i.e., $720 loss versus $288 positive NPV). This difference is due to the assumptions about the timing of the cash flows. Tables II and IV are based upon the assumption that the cash flow occurs in the middle of the period (i.e., June 30 for annual flows). The HP 12C example assumes 1/12 of the cash flows occur at the end of each month.[7]

An example was not prepared using Excel due to its size (there would have been 60 columns for the monthly cash flows), but the layout would have been similar to Figure 7–4.

Another way of explaining this so-called depreciation tax savings foregone is to consider a situation in which a new machine is to be bought and there is still a question of whether the older machine is to be kept or scrapped (Figure 7–5).

Suppose for purposes of Figure 7–5 that the old machine's depreciation is $100, while the new machine's depreciation will be $200. Clearly, if the old machine is kept when the new one is bought, then the total depreciation will be $300, or an increase of $200. But if the old asset is replaced by a new one and scrapped:

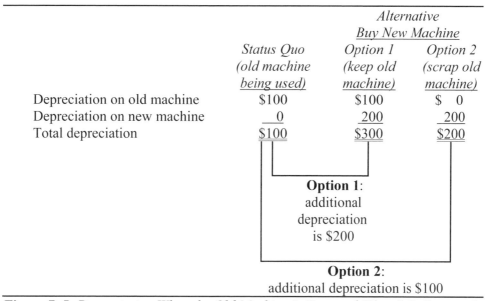

Figure 7–5: *Depreciation When the Old Machine Is Kept and When It Is Scrapped*

---

[7] There are three reasons for the difference between the NPV of $288 using the tables and $17.98 (or $18) using the financial calculator: (1) The tables use rounded figures as we've mentioned before; (2) The tables assume middle of the year flows, while the HP 12C used end of month flows; and (3) The monthly equivalent of a 12% annual discount rate is not 12% /12 or 1%. Reason number three is the most significant reason for the difference in this case. To get a monthly equivalent to an annual rate of 12%, one must use:

$$\text{Present Value} = \frac{1}{(1+i)^n} = \frac{1}{(1+i)^{12}} = \frac{1}{(1+0.1)^{12}} = \frac{1}{(1.01)^{12}}$$

which is 0.877%/month.

then the additional depreciation is only $100. Depreciation on the new asset is $200, but depreciation foregone on the scrapped machine is $100. The depreciation on the old machine is available as a tax shield whether a new machine is bought or not. But if the old machine is scrapped (and a tax loss taken at that time), then that machine's tax shield in the future is lost.

2. *Loss on the sale of old asset:*

Old asset:	Original cost–$20,000 Accumulated depreciation–$10,000 Sales value–$5,000 Remaining life–5 years
New asset:	Cost–$20,000 Expected life–5 years Expected salvage value at end of 5 years–$0
Savings on new asset:	$6,000/year for 5 years
Tax rate:	40%
Requires investment rate:	10%

Here we see that the sale of the old asset yields an immediate $5,000 in cash flow plus a $5,000 book loss (old book value was $20,000 – $10,000 or $10,000). The $5,000 loss saves $2,000 in taxes so that the cash flow effect of the sale is $7,000 ($5,000 + $2,000). Had we not sold the asset, we would continue depreciating it at $2,000 per year, thus saving $800 a year in tax. The depreciation tax savings given up is thus $800 per year for five years, which discounted at 10% is worth $3,032.

Figure 7–6 shows that the net present value at 10% is positive $3,676. Hence, this investment does meet the required investment rate of 10%.

	[1]	*[2]*	*[3]*	*[4]*		*[5]*	*[6]*	*[7]* *Present* *Value* *Factor* *10% from*	*[8]*
Description	*Time* *Period*	*Savings*	*Depreciation*	*Taxable* *Savings*		*Taxes [4]* *× 40%*	*After-Tax* *Cash Flow* *[2] – [5]*	*Table* *III******	*Discounted* *Cash Flow* *[6] × [7]*
New investment	0						$(20,000)	1.00	$(20,000)
Sale of old asset	0						5,000 *	1.00	5,000
Tax savings on loss	0			$(5,000) **		$(2,000)	2,000	1.00	2,000
Future depreciation lost	1–5		$(2,000) ***	2,000		800	(800)	3.79	(3,032)
Savings	1–5	$6,000	4,000	2,000		800	5,200	3.79	19,708
							Net present value		$ 3,676

* Sales value of old asset.
** Tax savings on loss on sale of old asset.
*** Tax savings on future depreciation given up.
**** Assume end-of-year cash flows.

Figure 7–6: *Loss on the Sale of Asset (with Appendix tables)*

Numbers	Keystrokes White	Blue	Brown	Display	Comments
			REG		Clear financial registers
13,000	CHS	CFo		−13,000.00	Enter new investment
4,400		CFj		4,400.00	Enter net savings
5		Nj		5.00	Number of periods
10		12÷		10.00	Periodic interest rate
			NPV	3,679.46	Net present value

Figure 7–6: *(continued) Loss on the Sale of Asset (with HP 12C)*

C4: =NPV(C3,D15:H15)+C15

	A	B	C	D	E	F	G	H
1								
2		Tax rate	0.40					
3		Present value factor	0.10					
4		Net present value	3,679					
5								
6			*0*	*1*	*2*	*3*	*4*	*5*
7		New investment	(20,000)					
8		Sale of old asset	5,000					
9		Tax saving on sale	2,000					
10								
11		Total savings		6,000	6,000	6,000	6,000	6,000
12		Additional depreciation		4,000	4,000	4,000	4,000	4,000
		Depreciation lost		(2,000)	(2,000)	(2,000)	(2,000)	(2,000)
13		Taxable savings (loss)		4,000	4,000	4,000	4,000	4,000
14		Taxes (taxes avoided)		1,600	1,600	1,600	1,600	1,600
15		Unadjusted cash flow	(13,000)	4,400	4,400	4,400	4,400	4,400

Figure 7–6: *(continued) Loss on the Sale of Asset (with Microsoft Excel)*

3. *Gain on the sale of old asset:*

Old asset:	Original cost–$20,000 Accumulated depreciation–$10,000 Sales value–$15,000 Remaining life–5 years
New asset:	Cost–$20,000 Expected life–5 years Expected salvage value at end of 5 years–$0
Savings on new asset:	$6,000/year for 5 years
Tax rate:	40%
Requires investment rate:	10%

Figure 7–7 shows that the net present value at 10% is positive $9,676. Hence, this investment surpasses the required investment rate of 10% by a wide margin.

	[1] Time Period	[2] Savings	[3] Depreciation		[4] Taxable Savings		[5] Taxes [4] × 40%	[6] After-Tax Cash Flow [2] − [5]		[7] Present Value Factor 10% from Table III****	[8] Discounted Cash Flow [6] × [7]
Description											
New investment	0							$(20,000)		1.00	$ (20,000)
Sale of old asset	0							15,000	*	1.00	15,000
Tax on gain	0				$5,000	**	$2,000	(2,000)		1.00	(2,000)
Future depreciation lost	1–5		$(2,000)	***	2,000		800	(800)		3.79	(3,032)
Savings	1–5	$6,000	4,000		2,000		800	5,200		3.79	19,708
								Net present value			$ 9,676

* Sales value of old asset.
** Tax on gain on sale of old asset.
*** Tax savings on future depreciation given up.
**** Assume end-of-year cash flows.

Figure 7–7: *Gain on Sale of Assets (with Appendix tables)*

	Keystrokes			Display	Comments
Numbers	White	Blue	Brown		
			REG		Clear financial registers
7,000	CHS	CFo		–7,000.00	Enter new investment
4,400		CFj		4,400.00	Enter net savings
5		Nj		5.00	Number of periods
10		12÷		10.00	Periodic interest rate
			NPV	9,679.46	Net present value

Figure 7–7: *(continued) Gain on the Sale of Asset (with HP 12C)*

```
C4:  =NPV(C3,D15:H15)+C15
```

	A	B	C	D	E	F	G	H
1								
2		Tax rate	0.40					
3		Present value factor	0.10					
4		Net present value	9,679					
5								
6			*0*	*1*	*2*	*3*	*4*	*5*
7		New investment	(20,000)					
8		Sale of old asset	15,000					
9		Tax on sale	(2,000)					
10								
11		Total savings		6,000	6,000	6,000	6,000	6,000
12		Additional depreciation		4,000	4,000	4,000	4,000	4,000
		Depreciation lost		(2,000)	(2,000)	(2,000)	(2,000)	(2,000)
13		Taxable savings (loss)		4,000	4,000	4,000	4,000	4,000
14		Taxes (taxes avoided)		1,600	1,600	1,600	1,600	1,600
15		Unadjusted cash flow	(7,000)	4,400	4,400	4,400	4,400	4,400

Figure 7–7: *(continued) Gain on the Sale of Asset (with Microsoft Excel)*

Advantages/Disadvantages of Net Present Value Method

The NPV method represents a significant improvement over the unadjusted rate of return approach in that it recognizes the time value of money and explicitly incorporates it into the calculations. However, it has several disadvantages:

1. The calculations are more difficult.

2. The meaning and importance of the time value of money must be thoroughly understood by the decision-maker.

3. The required investment rate must be known.

4. The answers are difficult to interpret.

This last item is perhaps the most serious. For example, suppose that the net present values for three mutually exclusive alternatives are as follows:

	Alternatives		
	X	*Y*	*Z*
Investment	$20,000	$20,000	$20,000
Discounted cash flow	18,000	22,000	25,000
Net present value	(2,000)	2,000	5,000

Obviously, alternative X does not meet the required investment rate, while Y and Z do. Between the two of them Z is preferable. But suppose that the alternatives were as follows:

| | Alternatives | |
	P	*Q*
Investment	$10,000	$16,000
Discounted cash flow	12,000	19,000
Net present value	2,000	3,000

Which alternative is preferable? Q has a higher net present value than P, but its required investment is also higher. If the projects are mutually exclusive, P is best if money for capital projects is scarce; Q would be the better alternative in the opposite case. But which is best financially? One approach is to calculate the profitability ratio by dividing the net present value by the initial investment.

| | Alternatives | |
	P	*Q*
Net present value	$ 2,000	$ 3,000
Investment	$10,000	$16,000
Profitability ratio	20%	18.75%

P has the highest ratio on that basis. One serious problem with this method is that the ratio itself is simply an arbitrary numerical construct; it has no economic meaning and as such is not easily explained. The internal rate of return method partly overcomes this problem.

Internal Rate of Return (adjusted rate of return)

Consider the following example:

Investment	$10,000
After-tax savings	$2,000/year for 10 years (end-of-year payments)

Now $2,000 per year for 10 years discounted at 6% is $14,720 (7.36 × $2,000). At 8%, it is $13,420 (6.71 × $2,000). As the discount rate is increased, the total discounted cash flow is reduced. Obviously, if we keep going higher we would find some rate at which the discounted cash flow is just equal to $10,000. Put another way, there is always some discount rate at which the NPV is 0. This discount rate is called the adjusted rate of return or the internal rate of return (IRR) and is shown in Figure 7–8.

The IRR for this project is thus somewhere between 14% and 16%. With a financial calculator or computer spreadsheet, the exact answer is found to be 15.10%.

Interest Rate %	*After-Tax Savings 1–10 Years*	*Table III Present Value Factors*	*Total Discounted Cash Flow*
6	$2,000	7.36	$14,720
8	2,000	6.71	13,420
10	2,000	6.14	12,280
12	2,000	5.65	11,300
14	2,000	5.22	10,440
16	2,000	4.83	9,660
18	2,000	4.49	8,980

Figure 7–8: *Internal Rate of Return*

On the HP 12C, the process is a simple one:

Numbers	Keystrokes White	Blue	Brown	Display	Comments
			REG		Clear financial registers
10,000	CHS PV			−10,000.00	Enter the investment
2,000	PMT			2,000.00	Payments are 2,000 per period
10	n			10.00	Number of periods is 10
	i			15.10	Internal rate of return

Figure 7–8: *(continued) Internal Rate of Return (with HP 12C)*

In Excel, the internal rate of return is found using the IRR function.

	B3: =IRR(C7:C17,B4)		
	A	B	C
1			
2			
3	Internal rate of return	15.10%	
4	Starting value or guess	10.00%	
5			
6		*Year*	*Amount*
7		0	(10,000)
8		1	2,000
9		2	2,000
10		3	2,000
11		4	2,000
12		5	2,000
13		6	2,000
14		7	2,000
15		8	2,000
16		9	2,000
17		10	2,000

Figure 7–8: *(continued) Internal Rate of Return (with Microsoft Excel)*

If we had, say, three alternatives, the internal rate of return could be calculated for each. If all three rates were higher than the company's required earnings rate, all three could be approved. If they were mutually exclusive, the project with the highest adjusted rate of return would be preferred.

The IRR method overcomes the problem of the NPV approach in that a definite return is calculated for each investment alternative and the rates can be compared one to another and to the organization's hurdle rate. The approach is tedious due to the complexity of the calculations, which are essentially a process of hunting for a particular discount rate. Computer programs and financial calculators make those calculations easily but, as the reader will note, this method is a long way from the simple payback calculation with respect to ease of use.[8]

---

[8] In one simple case, the internal rate of return can be calculated easily—the situation in which after-tax savings are uniform each year. The procedure is to divide the investment by the yearly after-tax savings. The results are then used to find a corresponding interest rate in Table III or IV at the end of this chapter. For example, in the previous problem: $10,000 ÷ $2,000 = 5. In Table III for 10 years, 5 falls somewhere between 14% and 16%.

Perhaps the greatest advantage of the internal rate of return method, at least as compared to net present value, is that it has a simple explanation. In fact, the internal rate of return can be explained without regard to discounting or the time value of money. Take the previous example in which a $10,000 investment yielding $2,000 cash flow for 10 years meant an internal rate of 15.10%. Exactly what does that 15.10% rate of return mean?

If a project has an internal rate of return of 15.10%, sometime over the life of the project the original investment will be repaid (return of investment). Further, for each year that some part of the original investment is not repaid (and is still at risk in the project), there will be a payment of 15.10% of the amount still at risk (return on investment).

We can prove that this explanation is accurate with the following tabulation (Figure 7–9), which is called an amortization table.

			Payment Divided between	
			15.10%	
	Investment	Total	Return on	Return of
Year	at Risk	Payment	Investment	Investment
1	$10,000	$2,000	$1,510	$ 490
2	9,510	2,000	1,436	564
3	8,946	2,000	1,351	649
.	.	.	.	.
.	.	.	.	.
.	.	.	.	.
8	4,561	2,000	689	1,311
9	3,249	2,000	491	1,509
10	1,740	2,000	263	1,737

Figure 7–9: *Amortization Table*

Thus, during the first year when $10,000 was invested (or was at risk), the return on investment is 15.10% or $1,510; this leaves $490 of the total $2,000 payment as a partial return of investment. Accordingly, during the second year, only $9,510 is at risk ($10,000 – $490), or still invested in the project, and so on. At the end of year 1, your $2,000 provided you the 15.10% return on your investment and part of that investment or principal was also returned. In the last year, the $2,000 payment is just sufficient to return 15.10% on the investment still at risk (now $1,740) and to repay the last of the investment as well ($1,737). The slight difference is because we used only four significant digits for the interest rate. If this process looks suspiciously like a mortgage table, it should, because it is. Indeed, a $10,000, 10-year, 15.10% mortgage calling for annual payments only (at year-end) would require a yearly payment of $2,000. That payment stream of $2,000/year would be divided between interest (return on investment) and principal (return of investment) just as we've done in our amortization table.

On the HP 12C amortization tables can be generated, but it requires a little practice and patience to generate amortization data for, say, year 3 in the example of Figure 7–9.

Amortization tables are easy to generate in Excel once one has mastered the "copy" command. An amortization table, using Excel, for this problem is shown in Figure 7–9.

Numbers	White	Blue	Brown	Display	Comments
	Keystrokes				
			REG		Clear financial registers
10,000	CHS PV			−10,000.00	Enter initial investment
15.10	i			15.10	Periodic interest rate
2,000	PMT			2,000.00	Enter annual payment
3			AMORT	4,296.86	Total interest paid to date
	x >< y			1,703.14	Total principal to date
	RCL PV			−8,296.86	Remaining principal (investment still at risk)

Figure 7–9: *(continued) Amortization Table (with HP 12C)*

	A	B	C	D	E	F	G	H	I
1									
2									
3									
4							*Payment Divided between*		
5							*15.10%*		
6			*Investment*		*Total*		*Return on*		*Return of*
7		*Year*	*at Risk*		*Payment*		*Investment*		*Investment*
8	1		10,000		2,000		1,510		490
9	2		9,510		2,000		1,436		564
10	3		8,946		2,000		1,351		649
11	4		8,297		2,000		1,253		747
12	5		7,550		2,000		1,140		860
13	6		6,690		2,000		1,010		990
14	7		5,700		2,000		861		1,139
15	8		4,561		2,000		689		1,311
16	9		3,249		2,000		491		1,509
17	10		1,740		2,000		263		1,737
18	End of year 10		2						

Figure 7–9: *(continued) Amortization Table (with Microsoft Excel)*

Key calculations in this spreadsheet are:

1. Return on investment—for example, the relationship in G8 is:

$$= G5 \times C8$$

2. Return of investment—for example, the relationship in I8 is:

$$= E8 - G8$$

3. Investment at risk—the beginning value is given as $10,000. The next period investment at risk, cell C9 is:

$$= C8 - I8$$

IRR is widely used in financial analysis, because it seems to yield the true rate of return on a project, while the net present value is just an absolute number. However, NPV is the preferred yardstick. A simple example shown in Figure 7–10 illustrates the problem with IRR. Two options, A and B, have the same initial investment ($10,000) and the same lifetime (six years). Option A has the higher IRR (25% versus 20%), while B has the higher NPV ($3,066 versus $2,446). Which is best? Probably B. It all depends on what will happen to the cash flows generated by the two projects. If the cash flows from A can be reinvested at 25% (the IRR), then A is more attractive than B. If the cash flows can be invested at, or are worth, only 10%, which is the hurdle rate in the example, then B is better than A. As depicted in Figure 7–11, the cash flows reinvested at 10% are worth more under B than A. For, example, under option A, at the end of year 0, or the beginning of year 1, we are out $10,000. By the end of year 1, we owe $1,000 on the initial investment, because of the 10% interest for the year, so we're out $11,000; however, we also receive $7,000 at the end of year 1 meaning we net out to −$4,000, and so forth. The accumulated reinvested value at the end of year 6 is the same as the NPV @ 10% from Figure 7–10, because $4,332 at the end of year 6 discounted at 10% is $2,446.

Look again at Figures 7–10 and 7–11 to see what is going on. Cash inflow for project A comes earlier, but over six years total cash inflow is less ($14,800 for A, $18,000 for B). We know that earlier cash inflow is worth more than later inflow. So project A is favored by early inflow, while B is favored by a greater amount over the six-year life. Reinvestment at 25% makes the early timing worth more while reinvestment at 10% means the early timing of cash inflow doesn't overcome the greater six-year amount of cash inflow.

NPV is said to be the preferred yardstick, because counting on reinvestment returns that are well above the hurdle rate is risky.[9] However, if the IRR is only slightly above the hurdle rate, then the different patterns of cash flow won't make much difference. Different signals are given when IRR is well above the NPV and when cash flow patterns differ greatly among projects.

Year	Option A	Option B
0	$(10,000)	$(10,000)
1	7,000	3,000
2	4,000	3,000
3	3,000	3,000
4	500	3,000
5	200	3,000
6	100	3,000
Totals	$ 4,800	$ 8,000
NPV at 10%	2,446	3,066
IRR	24.9%	19.9%

Figure 7–10: *Project Cash Flows*

---

[9] Just because a particular project has a high IRR doesn't mean that the cash flow from that investment can be invested somewhere else at the same high rate.

| Year | Option A | | Option B | |
	Cash Flow	Accumulated at 10%	Cash Flow	Accumulated at 10%
0	$(10,000)	$(10,000)	$(10,000)	$(10,000)
1	7,000	(4,000)	3,000	(8,000)
2	4,000	(400)	3,000	(5,800)
3	3,000	2,560	3,000	(3,380)
4	500	3,316	3,000	(718)
5	200	3,848	3,000	2,210
6	100	4,332	3,000	5,431
Totals	$ 4,800		$ 8,000	
Future value in year 6		$4,332		$5,431
Present value today at 10%		$2,446		$3,066

Figure 7–11: *Project Cash Flows Reinvested at 10%*

Considering Risk

We have mentioned risk at several points throughout this chapter and have observed several ways in which it might be handled:

1. In addition to the most likely forecast of results, a conservative or optimistic schedule may also be studied.

2. Very short payback periods may be required for risky investments. For example, some companies require a small tool-replacement investment to have a two-year payback.

3. If one of the return on investment methods is used, different risk categories may be established— each with its own hurdle rate. In one company, product enhancement investments must return 20%; new product investments, 25%; and foreign investments, 40%.

4. Short economic lives may be used to constrain the decision.

While those approaches have merit, they are not as sound as the more refined methods. When people discuss risk, what they really mean is the uncertainty of future events and the resulting difficulty in trying to predict the impact of various alternatives. Much work has been done in this area to develop practical approaches to decision-making under conditions of uncertainty. While a detailed discussion of those methods is well beyond the scope of this book, the basic approach can be summarized.

Financial theorists generally agree that the best means of dealing with uncertainty lies in trying to establish probabilities of various outcomes of a particular alternative. Instead of asking what the most likely estimate of savings is, we try to determine what the chances are of the savings being less than $2,000 (for example) per month, or $3,000, or $5,000, and so on. Of course, it is much more difficult to collect this type of information, particularly when the chances of one thing happening are related to the chances of something else. Indeed, one of the disadvantages of this approach is the cost and energy that the decision-maker must spend to gather the refined predictions. With those predictions, however, it is possible to state an answer this way—the chances of the IRR being below 12% are only 6%; below 15% the chances are 20%—instead of merely stating the single most likely answer. One can see from the following hypothetical results table that a probability answer could provide much more useful information to the decision-maker.

Hypothetical Alternative

		Probability Answer
"Most Likely" Estimate	Probability	of a Return Less than
Internal rate of	35%	6%
return 12%	40	8
	45	10
	55	12
	90	14
	95	16

Here we see that the most likely return is 12%. But the formal risk methods yield IRR probabilities showing that chances are pretty good that the return will be a lot less than 12%, while chances are slim that the return will ever be much greater than 12%.

Sensitivity

One of the most frequently used techniques for exploring risk in an investment alternative is called sensitivity analysis. The key assumptions or estimates in a project are changed in some systematic fashion and the overall effect on the net present value or internal rate of return is observed. Essentially, one is asking, "What happens if?" Excel is especially helpful in performing sensitivity analysis. For example, let's return to the sample problem in Figure 7–4. Suppose one wished to understand the impact on the net present value when the discount factor (present value factor) is something other than 12%. Figure 7–12 illustrates a one-way data table testing for the sensitivity to a changing present value factor between 9% and 14%. Note that at 12%, the NPV is ($697), which is the same as in Figure 7–4.

	A	B	C	D
1				
2	Net initial investment	$(18,000)		
3	Net yearly cash flow	$ 4,800		
4				
5				
6				Net
7		Discount		Present
8		Rate		Value
9		0.09		670
10		0.10		196
11		0.11		(260)
12		0.12		(697)
13		0.13		(1,117)
14		0.14		(1,521)

Figure 7–12: *One-Way Sensitivity Table*

Figure 7–13 illustrates a two-way sensitivity table, used to study the impact on a single variable when two separate factors are changed. In that example, we see the impact on the NPV of varying the discount factor from 9% to 14%, while at the same time varying the yearly savings (in increments of $200) from $4,400 to $5,200. Again, note in the middle of the table the original assumptions of a 12% net present value factor and $4,800 yearly savings produces a net present value of −$697. As the table illustrates, only at higher savings levels and lower discount rates is the NPV positive.

	A	B	C	D	E	F	G	H
1								
2								
3	Initial investment	(18,000)						
4								
5								
6				Table shows NPV at each discount rate and net cash flow				
7								
8		*Discount*				*Net Cash Flows*		
9		*Rate*		*4,400*	*4,600*	*4,800*	*5,000*	*5,200*
10		0.09		(886)	(108)	670	1,448	2,226
11		0.10		(1,321)	(562)	196	954	1,712
12		0.11		(1,738)	(999)	(260)	479	1,219
13		0.12		(2,139)	(1,418)	(697)	24	745
14		0.13		(2,524)	(1,821)	(1,117)	(414)	290
15		0.14		(2,894)	(2,208)	(1,521)	(835)	(148)

Figure 7–13: *Two-Way Sensitivity Table*

Sensitivity, in this example, could also be used to study the effect on the NPV of a different level of investment, an economic life of other than five years, or changes in the tax rate.

Capital Budgeting and Business Strategy

Though this chapter has focused on the financial evaluation of capital expenditures, it is important to put that analysis in a wider context, one that includes the development of business strategy. Managers should consider these ideas:

1. In the long run, the shaping of an investment project is more important than its financial evaluation. A bad or inappropriate project will not be made good by expert financial evaluation. The shaping and the evaluation of major projects should not be done by separate groups of people. There are weaknesses in the typical process by which a project is specified, then "tossed over the wall" to be evaluated and approved by a strategically oriented higher authority. The strategic perspective of the higher authority needs to be part of the process at an earlier stage, while the project is being shaped.

2. Projects are seldom discreet, independent decisions; rather, they are usually part of a strategic plan or program of activities. Unless it reviews the overall program, management runs the risk that it will combine a series of individually favorable projects into a total effort that is less than optimal. Each one of several yearly additions to a plant, for example, may have shown excellent rates of return, but in the end the plant may be producing the wrong product for the market.

3. The overall investment plan should recognize that a number of noncapital expenditures will have long-term effects, expenditures for such items as research and development (R&D), information systems, and skills training. Such expenditures are typically incorporated into an analysis of the investment project as opposed to the expenditures being evaluated separately.

SPECIAL TOPICS

Five issues arise so often in capital expenditure evaluations that special comments on each are in order.

Inflation

As mentioned earlier, present value or discounting does not explicitly incorporate any provision for anticipated price changes or inflation.[10] At times when future price levels as well as inflation are expected to change, special techniques must be employed to properly evaluate expected project returns. Such techniques involve first the projecting of cash flows based on the prices expected to be obtained during each period—what cash flows one actually expects to realize in dollars of that time period. Then an adjustment to reduce or deflate those cash flows is made, thereby expressing them all in dollars of a common purchasing power, usually the starting point or time zero of the project. After the cash flows have been deflated, they are discounted in the normal way to determine an inflation-adjusted or inflationless rate of return or net present value.

These adjustments do three important things: (1) future cash flows are projected using expected prices, which are not the same as inflation. Raw materials, labor, fuel, and so on, can all be changing at different rates; (2) deflating the net cash flow is done using a general price deflator like the consumer price index (CPI) or better still, the GNP implicit price deflator (GNPIPD); and (3) some items, such as depreciation, are unaffected by changes in price levels and inflation. As a consequence, depreciation tax savings do not increase with rising price levels and inflation, but after deflation they are worth less. This is sometimes called the inflation tax. In countries where tax authorities do not permit adjusting depreciation deductions for inflation, asset-intensive capital projects suffer from that inflation tax, because the company does not fully recover the tax savings from depreciation.

Working Capital

Should working capital (inventory and trade receivables less accounts payable) be a part of capital investment analysis? The answer is *yes* or *no*, depending upon how one has projected the cash flows. The most straightforward way to evaluate a project, such as a new product introduction or a new plant, is to schedule just the cash flow items relevant to the investment. This means considering things such as cash receipts (not sales booked or revenues) and cash disbursements (not expenses). Purchases of inventory would be one of the cash disbursements. Working just with cash flows, one does not need to schedule working capital changes explicitly into the analysis. If, however, the analysis begins by using revenues and expenses (accrual accounting concepts) as projections of inflows and outflows, then it is necessary to adjust those items into cash flows. The adjustments one usually finds necessary are changes in:

1. Trade receivables;
2. Inventory;
3. Accounts payable.

To put it another way, sometimes an investment analysis begins with a pro forma income statement (revenues, expenses, and so on). A number of adjustments—for example, depreciation and working

---

[10] There is an important distinction between changing prices and inflation. Over time, prices for some items may increase a lot, while some only increase a little, and some items such as technology actually decline in price when adjusted for functionality. These are *price level changes*. *Inflation* is a measure of the overall level of prices.

capital—are then necessary before one arrives at an appropriate cash flow projection. If the analysis considers only cash items (collections, disbursements, and so on), then working capital charges are not considered separately—in fact, they will have already been incorporated into the cash flow figures.

Economic Lives

Typically, a proposed capital expenditure represents an alternative to what will otherwise occur—the status quo. For the new project to actually be an alternative to the status quo, it is necessary for each to have the same project or economic life. Otherwise one is not the alternative to the other. Often one faces a situation like the following:

Suppose the present machine will only last for six more years, and the new, alternative machine will last ten years. This situation can be diagrammed as follows.

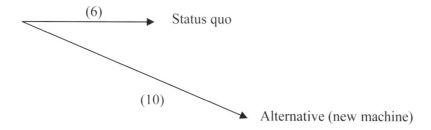

How are those two options to be compared? Actually, there are several ways of handling that. One method is to determine first what the replacement for the old machine would be in six more years, and to incorporate those costs into the cash flows. If the replacement has a life of just four years, the problem is solved because the economic lives are equal, as follows.

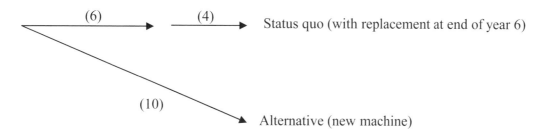

If the replacement machine envisioned in year six has an economic life, for example, of eight years, then it might be necessary to determine what the replacement in ten years would be for a new machine and continue that process until the economic lives were equal as shown next.

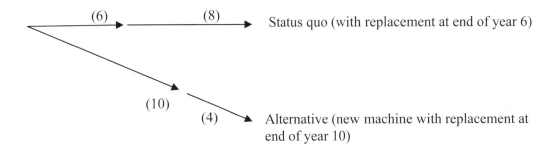

If the economic lives cannot quickly be made equal by such a process, adding replacements out into the future becomes impractical. Another means must be used to make the lives equal. Often this is to force the lives to be equal by cutting the economic life and assessing the residual value. This is diagramed next.

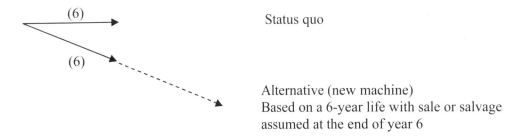

As shown, the cash flows are projected as if the new machine is kept only six years, then sold or scrapped. In effect, we're reasoning as follows: our present machine will last six more years, and the alternative is to buy a new one and run it for six years. In six years, it still has some remaining life or use, which, of course, is reflected in its sales value or residual value.

We could have forced the economic life somewhere else as shown next.

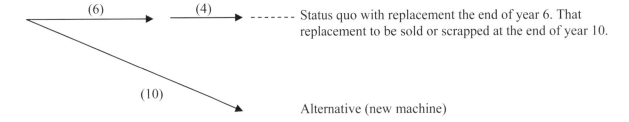

If projects are to be evaluated, they must have finite lives. If one project is really an alternative to another the economic lives must be equal. Often getting the lives equal can only be accomplished by forcing an artificial economic life, which, in turn, forces a residual value.

Residual Values

All projects have an end. At that time, assets are sold or scrapped, working capital is recovered, and other costs and revenues are realized. Assessing residual or terminal values is a vital part of the capital expenditure evaluation process. The key question is always: at the project's end, what is the cash flow? In some cases, it may be negative. For example, it is argued today that the teardown cost for a nuclear power reactor may be greater than its original construction cost. In other instances, the residual value may be the opportunity value of an established product, market, or even market potential. Often the residual value of a project is the present value of the next or follow-on effort brought about or made possible by the first project. Residual values may be decreased by technological obsolescence or increased by the effect of specific price changes or inflation. Such values, while quite difficult to assess, are crucial to sound project evaluation.[11]

Present Value Factors and Time Frames

Managers often become confused about whether to use middle-of-year or end-of-year present value factors. The answer depends upon the nature of the cash flows. If the flows occur at fixed points, such as the end of the year or end of a month, then end-of-year or end-of-month factors, respectively, should be used. If the flows occur continuously throughout a month or year, as is typical for revenue or cost savings, then factors for middle of the period are appropriate. Income taxes present special problems in that for most U.S. companies, taxes must be estimated in advance and paid quarterly. Tax savings or losses often affect the next immediate tax payment.

SUMMARY

Preparing a budget or plan for capital expenditures is an important management function, because such expenditures often involve large amounts of money and because the effect of such expenditures extends over many years. This chapter has examined a number of elements of that budgeting process: collecting ideas, developing alternatives, estimating results, evaluating alternatives, considering risk, and preparing the capital budget. Much of the chapter was spent on evaluating alternatives and particularly on the use of time-adjusted present value analysis to handle varying amounts of cash flow over different time periods. Though the numbers and projected rates of return or net present value are only part of the information managers need to consider when developing a firm's capital budget, there is no doubt that this financial analysis plays a key role in capital budgeting.

---

[11] Real options theory is an approach to valuing the opportunities (options) generated by an investment project. Investments are viewed as a stream of cash flows plus a set of options. See Martha Amram and Nalin Kulatilaka, "Real Options: Managing Strategic Investments in an Uncertain World," (Boston, MA: Harvard Business School Press, 1999).

QUESTIONS AND PROBLEMS

7–1. If you desired a 14% return on your investment, how much would you pay today for $200 received at the end of each year for the next 5 years and $100 at the end of years 6 to 10 and nothing thereafter?

7–2. If you desired a 14% return on your investment, how much would you pay today for $100 received at the end of each year for the next 5 years and $200 at the end of years 6 to 10 and nothing thereafter?

7–3. If you invested $10,000 today and received $20,000 12 years from now, what would be your return on investment?

7–4. If you invested $13,600 today and received $3,000 at the end of each year for 6 years and $10,000 at the end of the 7th year, what would be your return on investment?

7–5. You have $10,000 to invest and want a 16% rate of return. How much would you have to receive each year, in monthly payments, for eight years (nothing thereafter) to provide your desired return?

7–6. You are offered a proposal in which you invest $20,000 today in a venture that pays $4,500 at the end of each year for at least 10 years. You want a 16% return. Does the proposal meet your objective? For how many years must the venture pay $4,500 in order for you to realize your desired 16%?

7–7. *Investment is unknown.* Jane Harrison plans to enter college in eight years. Her grandparents want to set up a fund that will pay her $10,000 at the beginning of each of her 4 years in college. They estimate being able to earn an 8% return on money invested each year for the next 12 years.

  a. Ignoring taxes, how much would the grandparents have to invest as a lump sum now to provide for Jane's college education? Show your calculations.

  b. Ignoring taxes, if Jane's grandparents decided to provide for her college education by making equal payments at the beginning of each of the next eight years, how much would each payment have to be? Show your calculations.

7–8. *Revenue is unknown.* The Data Company has been asked by a prospective client to bid on a five-year data-processing service contract. In order to provide the desired services, the Data Company has determined that it would have to purchase a new computer server costing $35,000, and that it would incur annual costs of $5,000. Assume those annual costs are incurred at the end of each year. The computer server would be fully depreciated to zero over five years on a straight-line basis for tax purposes. For financial reporting, the computer server would be depreciated over six years on a straight-line basis. Salvage value is expected to be $3,000 anytime after the third year. The company's effective tax rate is 46%.

If the Data Company wants an after-tax return on its investments of 14%, how much should it charge the prospective client as an annual fee on the data-processing service contract? The fee will consist of five equal year-end payments. Show your calculations.

7–9. *Depreciable assets versus working capital.* The controller of the National Zipper Company has a project that requires a $55,000 investment in equipment that for tax purposes, he will depreciate over five years, straight line to zero, which will also be its expected salvage value. The equipment will allow National Zipper to increase its sales by $53,000 a year with additional operating costs of $33,000, not including depreciation. This sounds like a good deal to the controller, but

National Zipper has a hurdle rate of 16% and a tax rate of 46%. Explain in detail whether you think it is a good deal.

7–10. *Measures of return.* The production manager of the Solar Company has submitted a proposal to purchase a new machine that would cost $135,000. He projects that the machine will result in net annual cash savings of $30,000 for 9 years, after which the machine will be scrapped. The net annual savings include the effects of straight-line depreciation tax shield and income tax of 46%.

Compute the following measures and state the meaning and usefulness of the information provided by each one.

a. Payback period;

b. Payback period with 10% IRR, which is the point in time when the machine will have saved enough to achieve a 10% IRR;

c. NPV at a 14% hurdle rate;

d. IRR;

e. Accounting rate of return using gross fixed assets;

f. Accounting rate of return using average net fixed assets. Depreciation here is considered straight line from original cost to zero.

7–11. *Nonprofit institution.* The following two Treasury bonds, which pay interest annually, were offered in the market:

	Treasury Bond 1	*Treasury Bond 2*
Face value	$100,000	$100,000
Purchase price	$ 93,200	$ 93,200
Interest rate shown on the bond	9%	10.5%
Number of years to maturity	10	10

Questions:

a. Which bond would a nonprofit institution prefer?

b. Which bond would an individual with 50% incremental tax rate on income and 20% incremental rate on capital gains prefer?

APPENDIX

PRESENT VALUE FACTORS

Lump Sum (single investment)

End of Year	2%	4%	6%	8%	10%	12%	14%	16%	18%	20%	25%	30%
1	.98	.96	.94	.93	.91	.89	.88	.86	.85	.83	.80	.77
2	.96	.92	.89	.86	.83	.80	.77	.75	.71	.70	.64	.59
3	.94	.89	.8	.79	.75	.71	.67	.64	.61	.58	.51	.46
4	.93	.86	.79	.73	.68	.63	.59	.55	.52	.48	.41	.35
5	.90	.82	.75	.68	.62	.57	.52	.47	.44	.40	.33	.27
6	.89	.79	.71	.63	.56	.51	.46	.41	.37	.34	.26	.20
7	.87	.76	.66	.59	.51	.45	.40	.36	.31	.28	.21	.16
8	.85	.73	.63	.54	.47	.41	.35	.30	.27	.23	.17	.12
9	.84	.70	.59	.50	.42	.36	.31	.26	.22	.19	.13	.10
10	.82	.68	.56	.46	.39	.32	.27	.23	.19	.16	.11	.07
11	.81	.65	.52	.43	.35	.29	.23	.20	.16	.14	.09	.06
12	.79	.63	.50	.40	.32	.26	.21	.17	.14	.11	.07	.04
13	.77	.60	.47	.37	.29	.23	.18	.14	.12	.09	.05	.03
14	.76	.58	.4	.34	.26	.20	.16	.13	.10	.08	.04	.03
15	.74	.55	.42	.31	.24	.18	.14	.11	.08	.07	.04	.02
20	.67	.45	.31	.22	.15	.10	.07	.05	.04	.03	.01	.01
25	.61	.37	.23	15	.09	.06	.04	.03	.02	.01		
30	.55	.31	.17	.10	.06	.03	.02	.01	.01			
35	.50	.25	.13	.07	.04	.02	.01	.01				
40	.45	.21	.10	.05	.02	.01						

Table I: *Present Value of $1 Received at End of Year Indicated*

$$\text{Present Value (PV)} = \frac{1}{(1 + i)^n}$$

$PV = FV \ (TF)$

$TF = table \ factor$

Year	*2%*	*4%*	*6%*	*8%*	*10%*	*12%*	*14%*	*16%*	*18%*	*20%*	*25%*	*30%*
1	.99	.98	.97	.96	.95	.95	.94	.93	.92	.91	.89	.88
2	.97	.94	.92	.89	.87	.84	.82	.80	.78	.76	.72	.67
3	.95	.91	.86	.83	.79	.75	.72	.69	.66	.63	.57	.52
4	.93	.87	.82	.76	.72	.67	.63	.60	.56	.53	.46	.40
5	.92	.84	.77	.71	.65	.60	.55	.51	.48	.44	.37	.31
6	.90	.81	.72	.65	.59	.54	.49	.44	.40	.37	.29	.23
7	.88	.77	.69	.61	.54	.48	.43	.38	.34	.3f	.23	.18
8	.86	.75	.64	.56	.49	.43	.37	.33	.29	.25	.19	.14
9	.84	.71	.61	.52	.44	.38	.33	.28	.24	.21	.15	.11
10	.83	.69	.58	.48	.40	.34	.29	.25	.21	.18	.12	.08
11	.81	.66	.54	.45	.37	.31	.25	.21	.18	.15	.10	.07
12	.80	.64	.51	.41	.33	.27	.22	.18	.15	.12	.07	.05
13	.78	.61	.48	.38	.30	.24	.20	.15	.12	.10	.06	.04
14	.76	.59	.46	.36	.28	.22	.17	.14	.11	.09	.05	.03
15	.75	.57	.43	.33	.25	.19	.15	.11	.09	.07	.04	.02
20	.68	.47	.32	.22	.16	.11	.08	.05	.04	.03	.01	
25	.61	.38	.24	.15	.10	.06	.04	.03	.02	.02		
30	.56	.31	.18	.10	.06	.04	.02	.01	.01	.01		
35	.50	.26	.13	.07	.04	.02	.01	.01				
40	.46	.21	.10	.05	.02	.01						

Table II: *Present Value of $1 Received at Middle of Year Indicated* $PV = \dfrac{1}{(1 + i)^{n - 1/2}}$

Annuity Payments
(series of the same payment)

Period in Years	2%	4%	6%	8%	10%	12%	14%	16%	18%	20%	25%	30%
1	.98	.96	.94	.93	.91	.89	.88	.86	.85	.83	.80	.77
2	1.94	1.88	1.83	1.79	1.74	1.69	1.65	1.61	1.56	1.53	1.44	1.36
3	2.88	2.77	2.67	2.58	2.49	2.40	2.32	2.25	2.17	2.11	1.95	1.82
4	3.81	3.63	3.46	3.31	3.17	3.03	2.91	2.80	2.69	2.59	2.36	2.17
5	4.71	4.45	4.21	3.99	3.79	3.60	3.43	3.27	3.13	2.99	2.69	2.44
6	5.60	5.24	4.92	4.62	4.35	4.11	3.89	3.68	3.50	3.33	2.95	2.64
7	6.47	6.00	5.58	5.21	4.86	4.56	4.29	4.04	3.81	3.61	3.16	2.80
8	7.32	6.73	6.21	5.75	5.33	4.97	4.64	4.34	4.08	3.84	3.33	2.92
9	8.16	7.43	6.80	6.25	5.75	5.33	4.95	4.60	4.30	4.03	3.46	3.02
10	8.98	8.11	7.36	6.71	6.14	5.65	5.22	4.83	4.49	4.19	3.57	3.09
11	9.79	8.76	7.88	7.14	6.49	5.94	5.45	5.03	4.65	4.33	3.66	3.15
12	10.58	9.39	8.38	7.54	6.81	6.20	5.66	5.20	4.79	4.44	3.7	3.19
13	11.35	9.99	8.85	7.91	7.10	6.43	5.84	5.34	4.91	4.53	3.7	3.22
14	12.11	10.57	9.29	8.25	7.36	6.63	6.00	5.47	5.01	4.61	3.8	3.25
15	12.85	11.12	9.71	8.56	7.60	6.81	6.14	5.58	5.09	4.68	3.86	3.27
20	16.35	13.59	11.47	9.82	8.51	7.47	6.62	5.93	5.35	4.87	3.95	3.32
25	19.52	15.62	12.78	10.68	9.08	7.85	6.88	6.09	5.47	4.95	3.99	3.33
30	22.40	17.30	T3.76	11.26	9.43	8.06	7.01	6.18	5.52	4.98	4.00	3.33
35	25.00	18.67	14.49	11.65	9.64	8.18	7.07	6.21	5.54	4.99	4.00	3.3
40	27.36	19.80	15.04	11.92	9.78	8.25	7.11	6.23	5.55	5.00	4.00	3.3

Table III: *Present Value of $1 Received at End of Year for "N" Years*

Period in Years	2%	4%	6%	8%	10%	12%	14%	16%	18%	20%	25%	30%
1	.99	.98	.97	.96	.95	.95	.94	.93	.92	.91	.89	.88
2	1.96	1.92	1.89	1.85	1.82	1.79	1.76	1.73	1.70	1.67	1.61	1.55
3	2.91	2.83	2.75	2.68	2.61	2.54	2.48	2.42	2.36	2.30	2.18	2.07
4	3.84	3.70	3.57	3.44	3.33	3.21	3.11	3.02	2.92	2.83	2.64	2.47
5	4.76	4.54	4.34	4.15	3.98	3.81	3.66	3.53	3.40	3.27	3.01	2.78
6	5.66	5.35	5.06	4.80	4.57	4.35	4.15	3.97	3.80	3.64	3.30	3.01
7	6.54	6.12	5.75	5.41	5.11	4.83	4.58	4.35	4.14	3.95	3.53	3.19
8	7.40	6.87	6.39	5.97	5.60	5.26	4.95	4.68	4.43	4.20	3.72	3.33
9	8.24	7.58	7.00	6.49	6.04	5.64	5.28	4.96	4.67	4.41	3.87	3.44
10	9.07	8.27	7.58	6.97	6.44	5.98	5.57	5.21	4.88	4.59	3.99	3.52
11	9.88	8.93	8.12	7.42	6.81	6.29	5.82	5.42	5.06	4.74	4.09	3.59
12	10.68	9.57	8.63	7.83	7.14	6.56	6.04	5.60	5.21	4.86	4.16	3.64
13	11.46	10.18	9.11	8.21	7.44	6.80	6.24	5.75	5.33	4.96	4.22	3.68
14	12.22	10.77	9.57	8.57	7.72	7.02	6.41	5.89	5.44	5.05	4.27	3.71
15	12.97	11.34	10.00	8.90	7.97	7.21	6.56	6.00	5.53	5.12	4.31	3.73
20	16.51	13.86	11.81	10.20	8.93	7.91	7.07	4.38	5.81	5.33	4.42	3.78
25	19.72	15.93	13.16	11.09	9.52	8.30	7.34	6.56	5.94	5.42	4.45	3.80
30	22.62	17.64	14.18	11.70	9.88	8.53	7.48	6.65	5.99	5.46	4.46	3.80
35	25.25	19.04	14.93	12.11	10.11	8.66	7.55	6.69	6.02	5.47	4.46	3.80
40	27.63	20.19	15.50	12.39	10.26	8.73	7.58	6.71	6.03	5.48	4.47	3.80

Table IV: *Present Value of $ 1 Received at Middle of Each Year for "N" Years*

SECTION THREE

MANAGEMENT CONTROL SYSTEMS

CHAPTER 8

USING CONTROL SYSTEMS TO IMPROVE PERFORMANCE

Management control has many forms. Informal control is part of management by walking around; more formalized systems rely on computerized information processing. Many people perceive control systems as being necessary to averting disasters but, like the lock on your car door or the fuel gauge on your dashboard, not generally helpful in improving performance. As we shall see, such a view misses the significant positive role that control systems can play.

THREE OBJECTIVES OF CONTROL SYSTEMS

Simply put, control systems have three objectives:

1. To help keep things on track;

2. To help a company avoid bad things;

3. To encourage good things.

Those three objectives are not independent. Some kinds of information and processes serve more than one objective, but it helps to keep the three objectives in mind. In this chapter, after briefly reviewing the three objectives, we will discuss control system design, elements of a control system, control system implementation, and control system evaluation. Later chapters in this section will focus on planning and budgeting, and performance measurement and incentives.

Keeping Things on Track

Companies probably pay the most attention to keeping things on track, because that is a natural follow-through to the planning function. If you have plans laid out, you would naturally want to see if the execution is on target. The keeping-things-on-track view of control systems is essentially a feedback loop, sometimes called the thermostat model. There are three parts:

1. Defining what is to be measured and setting the desired level of achievement;

2. Measuring actual results and comparing that to the desired level;

3. Taking action when the difference exceeds a predetermined amount.

The desired level of achievement will grow out of plans and be embodied in budgets, standard costs, targets for sales or costs, or a variety of quality or time-based measures. Those targets can be dynamic (for example: a 5% reduction in cost each year) or conditional (for example: when the indirect labor target is a function of unit volume). Defining the target (the "track" on which you wish to keep) is, of course, an important and complex task—important because it says what elements of performance are significant enough to be measured, and complex because the desired level of performance almost always reflects external factors as well as different views of what is achievable.

Measuring actual results and comparing actual to expectations can be quite mechanical, such as with the computation of budget variances, where each budget line item has a predetermined range of acceptable variation. When actual costs or revenues move out of that range, the item is flagged for attention. The comparison may also rely on a manager's view of what size variance requires a response. For example, a food processing company posted pounds processed per hour for each of the five production lines. The supervisor reviewed those numbers throughout the day, and if there was a significant deviation from normal, he considered his knowledge of how the lines had been going. Most of the time, he already knew the reasons for a production shortfall, but if he did not know, he found out. In that way, he developed his own expectations or standards to compare to the actual results.

Taking action (or consciously not taking action) is a key step. If the results are off track, the person in charge is obliged to consider what measures are needed to get the results back on track. For example, when car sales dip below the factory's capacity, management of the automobile manufacturer increases its advertising budget. Within a few months, unit sales are back up to capacity. Management could have taken other actions, such as dealer incentives or rebates, but it determined that with a new brand, advertising was the best corrective action.

Corrective action requires determining not only what action is appropriate, but when to take that action. One department manager in a chemical company continually monitors many quantitative measures, such as temperature, flow rate, and acidity. She receives a weekly report on raw material consumption, but seldom takes action on the basis of variances shown in one week's report. Her decision not to act on a weekly raw material variance report is based on her experience that such variances almost always correct themselves the next week. If something were off two weeks in a row, she would investigate. Most of the weekly material variances are "noise in the system."

The three parts of keeping things on track—defining measures and setting targets; comparing actual to expectations; and taking action when appropriate—need to be as closely linked as possible. Without close linkage, the system may be useless. For example, the production manager of an industrial controls manufacturer receives a monthly report on standard cost variances that is useless to him. The numbers are too aggregated and far too much time elapses between the event and the report. To get a useful report, the manager borrows a computer and hires a person to prepare a daily report that shows unit volumes, labor used, percentage of first-pass success on circuit boards, and work in process. His bootleg report goes to only a few people, but they find it far more useful than the front office variance report.

Involving the report users as part of the team designing a control report results in the development of a more useful report. At Champion International's Mill in Hamilton, Ohio, the production people worked with the controller and the cost analysis staff to develop key success indicators for the plant and for each major product line. The indicators drew on both financial and operations data to provide what the operating people said was a useful set of performance measures.[1]

Avoiding Bad Things

Many of the control measures used to help keep things on track are also signals to help avoid bad things. In addition, companies employ many control mechanisms specifically designed to ensure the accuracy of the reporting and the handling of assets. Avoiding fraud or theft with systems of double checks is usually a central part of internal control. Detailed procedures for handling money and valuable materials are important. A separate internal control department is sometimes used to provide continual review and to

---

[1] William Rotch and Kim Constantinides, "Champion International Corporation's Hamilton Mill," (Darden Business Publishing, UVA) UVA-C-2105.

recommend any needed changes. An audit committee composed of members of the board of directors may also be used to oversee the internal control process and to provide a link with the external auditors, who periodically review the company's accounts. Those internal control systems are not very visible to an outsider, but their neglect can produce visible, unpleasant results. Large amounts of money can be dissipated, as was discovered in recent years by United Way, Tyco, and Enron, to name a few.

Measures designed specifically for internal control are an important part of a company's management control system. However, our focus here is on those elements of control systems that are designed not so much to avoid bad things, but to promote good things and to keep things on track.

Encouraging Good Things

This is perhaps the most valuable objective of management control systems, but often the one that receives the least attention. Encouraging good things involves a number of aspects of a company's overall operation. For example, it involves:

- Defining good things so they can be measured and so that those measures provide direction;

- Providing incentives and rewards that can lead to improved motivation;

- Having the right organization structure to empower people to accomplish the good things.

This is a wider, more comprehensive view of control systems. It is a view that connects goals and strategies to the actions of the people in the organization. It is, however, a complex view, and we will say more about it later in the chapter.

CONTROL SYSTEM DESIGN

The framework shown below presents a useful way to show the relationship between the control system and both organizational strategy and structure. While the central part of control systems is measuring and monitoring performance, other parts play important roles. Key elements of the control system include planning and budgeting, performance measurement, and incentives and rewards.

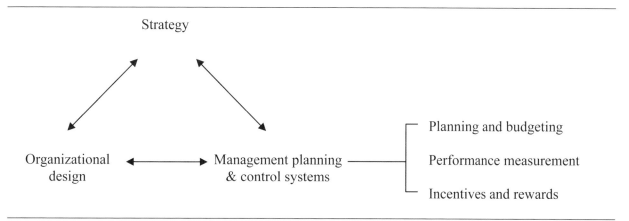

Figure 8–1: *Control System Framework*

Organizational Strategy

Management control is what happens after the vision, strategy, and goals have been shaped. Management control has to do with making the strategy happen. The process, however, is not quite as precise as the sequence of the shape-then-implement strategy implies. The way planning and control systems are designed can be part of an organization's strategy, and planning and control systems can provide information that leads to strategy reformulation or revision.

Since management control systems are used to implement strategy, the design of those systems starts with a stated strategy. The other elements, then, should help management carry out the strategy, and should be mutually supportive among themselves.

Organizational Design and Responsibility Centers

Organizational design is one of the basic building blocks of control, because it reflects the division of resources and the assignment of responsibility throughout the firm. In particular, each organizational unit headed by a manager can be considered a responsibility center. Responsibility centers vary from the simple cost centers widely used in manufacturing companies to the sophisticated profit and investment centers found in decentralized divisions of large multinational companies. Responsibility centers also may be teams that have an assigned task.

For purposes of this discussion, a responsibility center will be defined as any organizational unit headed by a person assigned a specific responsibility and where the results produced (outputs, products, services, or revenues) and/or the resources used (inputs, assets, or costs) are measured, typically in financial terms. The unit might be one of the departments of a factory, a group of departments, the whole plant, an administrative department, or perhaps the division. Responsibility centers are found in all parts of a company, from manufacturing and sales to research and administration. Whatever its size, location, or perceived importance, if the unit is a part of the organization, if it has been assigned certain responsibilities, if it is directed or managed by someone charged with those responsibilities, and if the inputs and outputs are measured, it is a responsibility center.

For control purposes, an organization's structure is best viewed as a hierarchical assembly of responsibility centers, of which there are five basic types: cost, discretionary expense, revenue, profit, and investment. A responsibility center may have a number of objectives and performance measures as depicted in Figure 8–2.

	Cost Center	Discretionary Expense Center	Revenue Center	Profit Center	Investment Center
Primary objective	Cost minimization	Spending constraints	Revenue maximization	Profit maximization	Profit optimization relative to assets employed
Primary measure	Variances or costs/unit	Expenses: actual vs. budget	Revenue: actual vs. budget	Profit: actual vs. budget	Return on investment or residual income: actual vs. budget
Information required	Cost incurred, resources used, production or service levels, standards	Expenses	Revenue	Revenue, costs, and expenses	Revenue, costs, expenses, and assets employed

Figure 8–2: *Types of Responsibility Centers*

Cost centers. Cost centers collect information on the resources used and compare those actual costs to the standards allowed for the level of goods produced or services rendered. Typical measures of performance for a cost center would be:

Example	*Typical Measure*
Factory work center	Variances such as labor efficiency, material usage, scrappage, or overhead spending
Oil refinery	Cost/barrel versus standard
Bank operations center	Cost/check handled versus standard
Trucking company	Cost/mile versus standard

A hallmark of both cost centers and expense centers is that no attempt is made to attribute revenue to them or to measure the value in financial terms of the services provided. Cost centers, however, do measure the amount of output or service produced. They either express the results in terms of cost per unit or compare actual costs with standard costs or with some other measure of what should have been spent to generate that amount of output.

The necessary ingredients for cost centers are:

1. Ability to measure the actual resources used, such as materials, labor, and overhead;

2. Ability to measure or count the output or services produced;

3. A predetermined standard cost, cost allowance, or historical base.

Not all cost centers actually use formal standard cost accounting. Instead, the actual cost per unit may be used to monitor performance by comparing actual to a projected cost, historical average, or cost in a previous period. For example, hospitals, trucking companies, airlines, food processors, and mining and manufacturing companies often calculate average cost per unit on a periodic basis and compare it to some previous period without using any formal standard cost. In recent years, some companies have moved away from standard costing systems in order to focus on continuous improvement. (A standard that has been set six months or a year earlier will be a target that may be less than optimal.) These companies still measure actual costs, but the measure of performance is not in terms of variance from standard but instead is in terms of rate of improvement.

Standard costing systems and variance analysis were discussed in detail in Chapter 3.

Discretionary expense centers. Expense centers are typically used for administrative departments. In this type of responsibility center, the control system permits or authorizes spending up to a predetermined (budget) level. Those budgets are generally established in advance and do not vary with departmental activity or output; that is, normally they do not flex. Indeed, the actual results or outputs of discretionary expense centers are not usually measured, often because of the difficulties of doing so. It is hard, for example, to measure the value or quantity of output produced by the personnel, security, or accounting departments, so in most cases actual expenses are compared to the budget or, in other words, the comparison is made between actual input of resources and planned input of resources.

There are, however, an increasing number of companies that measure activity in certain of the expense centers and compute the cost per unit of activity. This is particularly true with the increased focus on activity-based costing and activity-based management. Data processing, payroll, and even legal departments are examples. In addition to monitoring cost trends for planning and control purposes, companies have discovered that unit cost information helps them decide when they could save money by outsourcing the work to an outside specialist.

Nevertheless, the major difference between cost centers and most discretionary expense centers is the former's ability to measure results. We use cost centers when it is possible to measure the outputs produced and to prescribe what should be the costs of such output. Because this is not possible with most discretionary expense centers, their budgets cannot be considered statements of what should have been spent for the actual level of output. As a consequence, one must be cautious in interpreting a comparison of budgeted and actual expenditures as a measure of efficiency in those situations.

Revenue centers. Revenue centers are appropriate for any unit, such as marketing and sales, where the primary mission is to generate revenue. Such units always incur expenses as well (salaries, office expense, travel, advertising, and so forth), but control emphasis is not directed to cost minimization but to revenue maximization. As a general rule, all revenue centers have expense budgets as well, but those really serve as spending constraints. Revenue center control thus accomplishes two objectives: it prescribes the level of resources the manager may spend, and it directs the manager to maximize revenues subject to that constraint.

Revenue in those situations is not necessarily measured in the same way as for general accounting purposes. Orders received may be measured rather than sales billed; intercompany sales may be at some price other than market; commissions may be measured rather than sales dollars; sales or revenues might be weighted to encourage a desired sales mix. Such weights might reflect the gross margin percentage or the extent to which a company's strategy is to push some products, such as new entries into the market.

Profit centers. A profit center is any responsibility center where both expenses and revenues are attributed to the center and where the manager is expected to make tradeoffs between the two in order to increase the net difference, or profit. The chief difference between profit and revenue centers lies in the tradeoff between expense and revenue: the revenue center manager does not make those tradeoffs; the profit center manager does. Indeed, one of the key purposes of using the profit center structure is to encourage the manager to make those tradeoffs in ways that maximize profit. Decentralized divisions of large manufacturing companies might be considered profit centers; individual plants within a company might be considered profit centers; the various units of a hospital, such as intensive care or the emergency room, might be considered profit centers.

The distinction between a cost or expense center and a profit center is not whether the results or outputs of the unit *can* be measured in terms of revenue, but whether they *are* measured in terms of revenue. In a large container company, for example, all the can-and-bottle plants might be treated as cost centers, whereas at a competitor, the plants are profit centers.

Whether a center should be considered a profit center rather than a cost or expense center depends on several tests and objectives. The most obvious test concerns revenue. If revenue is not measurable or attributable to the center, the unit should not be a profit center. But suppose revenue can be attributed to the center. Whether it should then be a profit center depends on the objectives of measuring the center's results. This choice is heavily influenced by the organization's strategy. A company whose strategy is to operate as low-cost producer would be more likely to treat those plants as cost centers. With a low-cost strategy, the cost of output from the plant is perhaps the most important determinant to the success of that strategy. On the other hand, a company whose strategy is one of product differentiation might treat those plants as profit centers. With such a strategy, product quality may be of the utmost importance. Since revenue and profit are heavily influenced by the quality of the plant's output for a company with this strategy, treating the plant as a profit center highlights to plant management the impact of that feature on revenues.

Whether profit centers are compared to one another within the firm depends on the similarities between those profit centers. More often than not, profit centers are so dissimilar that they should not be compared to each another. That is why budgeting is so important. Control in a profit center is usually accomplished through an operational budget. If a plant's profit is to be compared to its budgeted profit and the manager's performance judged accordingly, the effectiveness of the control system is directly related to the quality of the budget. If the budget is a fair, meaningful target, representing real accomplishment, and if the budget is so accepted by the manager, then the control system can be a powerful instrument for directing and motivating managers. But if the budgets are arbitrary or impossible to achieve, then the profit control mechanism will be ineffective.

Investment centers. An investment center is any responsibility center whose costs and expenses, revenue, and investment in assets are all attributed to the center. All three figures are combined into a single measure of performance.

The most frequently used measure is return on investment (ROI): net income of the responsibility unit is divided by the unit's assets, which is considered to be the company's investment in that unit. In some merchandising businesses, only inventory and accounts receivable are included in the investment base; in other situations, land, buildings and equipment, and even cash are included. Current liabilities, such as accounts payable and accrued expenses, are sometimes deducted, which results in the figure known as net assets. In such instances, the ROI is often called RONA (return on net assets). ROI, RONA, ROA (return on assets), and ROCE (return on capital employed) are simply variations in terminology for the primary measure of performance (return on investment) used in an investment center. The choice of investment center measure can significantly impact the manager's motivation. We discuss alternative measures of investment center performance in Chapter 10.

Whether a center should be an investment or a profit center is a choice that is similar to the profit versus cost center choice, but the element of consideration this time is investment. To have an investment center, one must first be able to attribute a dollar amount of investment to the center. In addition, the manager is expected to make tradeoffs between additional investment and additional profit. There will be rewards for using inventory efficiently and for getting rid of unused assets. Where the center manager can influence investment and where motivation to consider tradeoffs is important, then use of the investment center system is likely to be appropriate.

Several types of centers used at once. Businesses typically employ several different types of responsibility center measures in different parts of the organization. For example, a company may treat the various manufacturing departments within its plants as cost centers, while the plants may be judged as profit centers. At the same time the company could be treating the sales regions as revenue centers, the administrative departments as expense centers, and perhaps the major product divisions of the company as investment centers.

The operations in many manufacturing and service enterprises are becoming more interdependent. An operation in such situations could not be adequately considered as an independent island of activity. For example, advanced manufacturing systems bring on a high degree of interdependence. Just-in-time (JIT) systems, for example, manage the process flow as a whole, reducing the buffer inventories that allowed independence of operation. Each step in a process is linked to and depends on the quality and timing of other steps. Each step may not be efficient by traditional measures; indeed, idle workers at a machine do not necessarily reflect inefficiency. Considering single machines or machine groups as cost centers makes less sense for control purposes in those settings,[2] even though measures like cost per machine hour may still be useful for product costing. As a result, the important performance measure becomes one that considers the whole operation.

Linking Organizational Strategy, Organizational Structure, and Control Systems

An effective management control system must carefully link the elements that make up a control system as shown in Figure 8–1.

Link between organizational strategy and organizational structure. An organization's strategy and its structure should be linked. For example, as discussed earlier, management pursuing a low-cost strategy would tend to use process-oriented cost centers, whereas with a product differentiation strategy, management is more likely to find that product-oriented profit centers work best. Sometimes a change in strategy will lead to changes in organizational structure. For example, a hospital decided to strengthen its customer service activity, and determined that both patients and physicians were customers. A special facilitation group was established with an experienced, entrepreneurial nurse as its chair. The group's members included physicians, clinic administrators, lab managers, other nurses, and financial and marketing representatives. This new structure cut across the usual functional organization, setting up a matrix design, and focused energies and attention on customer service as the new element of that hospital's strategy.

Link between organizational strategy and control systems. Management control systems are used to implement strategy. The direction signaled by the elements of the control system, such as the budget or performance measures, should be right for carrying out the desired strategy. For example, when sales volume is measured and rewarded by commissions, the sales force focuses on high sales volume. That is fine when increased sales volume is the strategic objective. But if opening new accounts is the company's strategic objective, there will be a mismatch or incongruence between the performance measures and the firm's strategy. Rewards based on sales volume will not encourage the salesperson to work on new

---

[2] C.J. McNair, "Interdependence and Control: Traditional vs. Activity-Based Responsibility Accounting," *Journal of Cost Management* (Summer 1990): 15.

accounts. The chosen performance measure should communicate the desired direction and provide the appropriate motivation, because that performance measure will determine what the manager will work to optimize. If cost variances are measured, that is what the manager will focus on. If profit is the measure, the manager will try to maximize profit. What is not measured will receive little attention. The measurement process, therefore, has two purposes: (1) to give direction about what is considered important to achieve, and (2) to monitor performance.

Control systems can be diagnostic or interactive.[3] A diagnostic system is a management-by-exception system that relies on reports to tell management when actions or outcomes are not in accordance with its intended plans. A diagnostic system suggests that management control is what happens after strategy and goals are set. However, an interactive system is one where managers use face-to-face discussion and debate to involve themselves in the decisions of subordinates. Interactive systems are more exploratory and the interaction often results in a revised strategy. The interactive process consumes more management time and energy than does the diagnostic process, but it is an effective way of giving close, continual attention to changing conditions and their strategic implications.

Link between organizational structure and control systems. The control system should relate to the organizational structure, which defines the scope of a manager's authority and responsibility. Using a profit center, for example, works best when a manager's authority enables him or her to influence both revenue and expense. A cost center works best when only cost can be influenced. The performance measure used should match the structure. Some measure of input or cost should be used to measure the performance of cost centers. Some measure of profit (revenue and expenses) should be used to measure the performance of profit centers, to reflect the tradeoffs managers of those profit centers are expected to make.

In summary, an effective control system, then, depends on having all three points of the triangle working together.

CONTROL SYSTEM ELEMENTS

Planning and Budgeting

Planning and budgeting are clearly an important element in any management control system. A budget is a quantitative statement of a firm's plans. The control system must include the planning and budgeting processes, for without them, control becomes a short-term, stick-to-the-budget effort. In our view, management control cannot be hemmed in by an existing budget, but must include the budgeting process itself. The feedback loop must be both short-term for corrections guided by the current budget, and longer term for development of the next budget. After all, it is much easier to apply direction and control before plans and budgets are set than afterward. And, of course, the planning and budgeting process must be tied in with the organizational structure and other elements of the performance measurement system.

We discuss budgeting in more detail in Chapter 9.

---

[3] Robert Simons, *Performance Measurement and Control Systems for Implementing Strategy*, (Upper Saddle River, New Jersey: Prentice Hall, 1999).

Performance Measurement

Performance measurement is at the heart of management control. How a manager is measured strongly influences that manager's decisions and how that manager spends his or her time. *What gets measured gets attention.*

Choosing the right performance measure is a challenging undertaking. One must identify the key success factors of the organization. Key success factors are those few things that an organization *must do well* to successfully implement its strategy and to achieve its objectives. We will say more about key success factors later in this chapter. Then, one must choose a performance measure that highlights the importance of the key success factors. After all, what gets measured gets attention, and we want the manager attending to those things that the organization must do well to be successful.

Various issues arise when implementing a performance measurement system and using it to evaluate the performance of managers and the responsibility centers they manage. First, one must precisely define all parts of the performance measure. Suppose we use return on sales (ROS) to evaluate a manager. Return on sales is defined as income over sales. We must decide how to measure income—operating income, net income? And we must decide how to measure sales—net sales, gross sales? Those are only some of the measurement issues that arise when trying to be precise in defining the performance measure to be used. Second, one must ensure that the performance measure used encourages the manager to act in the best interest of the company as a whole. In other words, we want the goals of the manager to be *congruent* with the goals of the organization. Third, we must decide whether to use the same performance measures to evaluate the manager that we use to evaluate the business unit he manages. Certainly, we do not want to hold managers accountable for factors beyond their control. But, at the same time, we must have a complete picture of the performance of the business unit so that we can make decisions, such as whether to keep or to sell it.

Return on investment (ROI) is perhaps the most frequent measure used to evaluate performance in investment centers. However, it does have some limitations. Several innovations in performance measurement have occurred over the past couple of decades. Economic value added (EVA), a special case of a residual income measure, and market value added (MVA) have gained momentum as measures to evaluate investment center managers. Those recent innovations are sometimes used as an alternative to ROI as a means to overcome some of its limitations. We will say more on this subject later.

Another innovation is the balanced scorecard.[4] The balanced scorecard contains measures of performance from four perspectives: financial measures, measures related to customer satisfaction, measures of internal business processes, and measures of innovation and learning in the organization. Measures from all four of those perspectives are used to evaluate performance throughout the organization. While companies have been using both financial and nonfinancial measures for some time, the introduction of and the discussion around the balanced scorecard has generated new interest and visibility. Further, the balanced scorecard has been used to do more than just measure performance. Companies have benefited from using it as a means to communicate strategy throughout the organization, encourage conversation among various groups in the organization about what is important, and facilitate the implementation of organizational change.

---

[4] Robert S. Kaplan and David P. Norton, "Balanced Scorecard–Measures that Drive Performance," *Harvard Business Review* (January–February 1992): 71.

We discuss performance measurement in more detail in Chapter 10.

Incentive and Reward Systems

Incentive and reward systems are essential to management control, because they are intended to provide motivation and to reward good performance. No doubt, though, when performance measures are tied to incentive systems, motivation is more intense. Remember—what gets measured gets attention. With incentive systems, we can extend that—what gets measured and tied to money gets *a lot* of attention.

Incentive systems have many benefits. Among those is the increased motivation for managers to perform. Oftentimes, though, incentive systems can lead to unintended consequences. It is important for management to be aware of those possibilities so that it can confront the consequences when they occur.

We discuss incentive and reward systems in more detail in Chapter 10.

CONTROL SYSTEM IMPLEMENTATION

The foregoing framework of interdependent components describes the design of a system, but the design does not tell us all that is important about a control system. Implementation of a control system is concerned with how the system is used and is essential to the part control systems play in a firm's management. For example, variances from budget are measures of performance. A supervisor may use this variance information as a blunt club or with a light touch. When used in different ways, the same measurement system is likely to have different outcomes.

Implementation concerns a cycle that runs from planning, through execution and review, and back to planning. Here are some of the management issues that arise when implementation is considered.

1. Who should be involved in planning and budgeting? What kind of participation is best? Is participatory budgeting always better?

2. What sequence in budgeting works best? Bottom up or top down? If both, where does it start?

3. How can one structure the process to minimize budget games, where slack is put in the budget in the expectation that upper management will cut the budget?

4. How should one balance the desire for budget realism (realistic projections that help overall planning) with the desire to use challenging targets to stimulate motivation?

5. What is the appropriate frequency and detail for reporting?

6. Should budget revision be allowed after the budget period has started?

7. Is the performance measure to be used to evaluate the performance of a business (a portfolio management perspective) or of the manager of business (a direction and motivation perspective)?

CONTROL SYSTEM EVALUATION

Control systems should be evaluated continually to see if changes in design or implementation are needed. For example, sometimes the need for change arises because the organization's strategy has changed or because the industry's competitive dynamics are different. There are several criteria that one should use to evaluate a proposed or existing control system. Those criteria include the following.

Focus on key success factors. Every responsibility center has a limited number of key tasks or functions critical to the organization's strategy and objectives. Those are known as *key success factors*, or *critical performance variables*. Identifying those key success factors is the most important part of control system design. Key success factors are those few things that an organization *must do well* to successfully implement its strategy and achieve its objectives.

Key success factors may not be easily measurable, but that is not critical. What is important is that the system designer understands enough about the operation of each responsibility center to be able to isolate the key success factors so that provision may be made for them in the control system design. At this step, the danger of omission is clear: a critical variable or task that is excluded from the system may be ignored by management rather than emphasized. The key success factors of a manufacturing operation may be on-time delivery, low cost, and high quality, in that order. But if a cost center control system is implemented with no provision for measuring product quality or on-time delivery, then those two key factors may be jeopardized. Indeed, a tight expense budget may motivate the plant manager to cut quality and to increase the length of production runs in spite of delays in delivery. If the key success factors are not all considered in the performance measure or measures, then managers won't be motivated to include them all as part of their decision criteria. If, as so often happens, the key success factors conflict or represent tradeoffs, and some variables are ignored by the performance system, then the decision-maker will not only ignore those variables but also may take actions directly opposed to those factors.

Goal congruence. Goal congruence means that the control system always encourages managers to take the action that is in the best interest of the organization as a whole. In other words, will managers, when acting in their own best interests by trying to maximize their performance measures, always take those actions or make those decisions that best lead to the organization achieving its objectives? This, too, is one of the most important tests of a control system. Top management might say that its division managers always recognize any conflicts or lack of goal congruence and tend to do what is best for the company as a whole. That may be true, but there is no doubt that division managers may easily take certain actions that benefit either them personally or their division, but harm the overall corporation, if the performance measures in place provide an incentive for them to do so.

Developing a performance measure congruent with the organization's goals can be very difficult. Consider the company with goals of profitability, growth, and public service, operating 27 manufacturing plants throughout the United States. Each plant is measured as a profit center, and the plant manager's bonus depends on the degree to which he or she exceeds the profit budget. One year top management installs electrostatic precipitators on the stacks of some of the plants. Senior executives, of course, expect that the precipitators will reduce air pollution. They are very upset when they discover that plant managers are turning off the precipitators to save the heavy electrical expense involved. To the plant manager, who is hard pressed to meet her budget, the large savings from shutting off the precipitators is a very real temptation. And if the manager doesn't wish to risk cutting them off during daylight hours, the precipitators can always be cut at night. Such cost cutting is clearly not what senior executives had in mind, but they encouraged those actions by evaluating the plants and their managers as profit centers. Correcting that dysfunctional motivation is no easy task. Simply decreasing each plant's profit target by the amount of the expected electrical expense is no solution—for the manager is still motivated to shut off the device. What is needed is a reliable set of measures of actual particle emissions or pollution from those stacks. Then the problem of pollution could be brought under management's control.

Feasibility. The proposed system should be practical to implement and its cost to operate should be less than the benefits it provides. Measuring the plant-generated pollution referred to above probably is feasible and cost effective, particularly in view of society's increasing concerns about the environment and the repeated suggestions that polluters be fined or forced to pay a pollution tax.

Controllability. Managers should not be held accountable for factors over which they have no control. This means that performance measures ought to include at least all the key success factors of the responsibility center, and they should not be unduly influenced by other factors beyond the manager's control. Thus, plants whose managers have no marketing or volume responsibility are usually controlled as expense centers. A profit measure might indicate performance above budget only because sales volume went up at a time when manufacturing efficiency, the only factor really under the influence of the manager, was poor. At the other extreme, profits may be down because of a sales slump, yet the manufacturing efficiency may be above standard. Obviously, the profit measure in this situation does not capture the factors under the manager's control, but the cost measure does.

Understandability. Managers cannot be motivated by measures they do not understand. By "understand," we mean that managers appreciate how each decision they make will affect the measure. Suppose that in the case of the oil company discussed earlier, both the refinery and the marketing division were measured as profit centers, and division management received a sizable bonus for performance in excess of budget. Suppose, too, that the transfer price for products between the refinery and the marketing division was to be determined at the end of each year (for that year) by taking the average wholesale price during the year for the country as a whole minus 3%. The performance measure is easily explained and its calculation readily understood, but it is not a measure that tells the managers of either division how they can improve performance. Because the refinery does not know the transfer price until the year is over, it cannot determine the optimum mix of products. Marketing has a similar problem. The system is easily explained, but not easily understood.

Fairness. Fairness is included on this list of criteria only because it is often considered important by many organizations. By itself, there is no logical reason for it. Whether a particular measure is fair or not is of little consequence to the success of a control system, other things being equal. A plant manager may be given a budget or target that he or she considers unfair. But if the performance measure is congruent with the organization's objectives, meets the other criteria, and properly motivates the manager, then the control system works whether the manager thinks it is fair or not. But if a system is so unfair that the manager loses motivation or cease to strive, then of course the system has failed. It is unlikely that any system of budgets, performance measures, and incentives will be thought fair by all parties involved. Perhaps the best way to look at it is that we do not want control systems so unfair that we impair the manager's motivation.

Long-run/short-run balance. Unless designers are careful, a control system may tend to encourage focus on current performance at the expense of future prospects. In fact, this is a continual problem faced by all organizations. Plant maintenance may be cut by managers desperately trying to meet a tight budget. Research into projects with five- and ten-year paybacks will not be undertaken by a division manager who may not keep his or her job even three months unless current profits are up.

Most criteria on this list are of a nature that one can determine whether the criteria are met or not. In other words, a control system either results in goal congruence or it does not. Unfortunately, this is not the case with the long-run/short-run balance problem. Here, there is no way to determine logically what degree or balance between short-run and long-run emphasis is correct. General Electric's former CFO

Dennis Dammerman said, "We think it is relatively easy to manage for the short term. It's relatively easy to manage for the long term. The hard job is trying to manage both."[5]

Testing and Recommending Change

Good management control systems are developed only over a period of time. Since organizational structures, relationships, and constraints are continually changing, since organizational strategy and goals may be revised, and since environmental factors often fluctuate, continuous review of management control systems is mandatory. Sometimes a new system is developed by trial and error. More often, a new system is developed when the old one is evaluated, because of some apparent weakness, or just because a review is overdue. The evaluation follows the steps outlined above. Before being implemented, the proposed system should be tested and its expected results again evaluated. By this repetitive process—evaluate, propose, evaluate, propose—a new system is eventually designed.

A word of warning: control systems cannot compensate for poor management. In this chapter, we have stressed the technical aspects of the management control system (for example: the budgets, performance measures, incentives, standards, and reports), but those are only part of the control process. The system must also be administered by competent managers. Good managers can often overcome the shortcomings of a weak control system, but the very best control methods are ineffective in the hands of incompetent management.

SUMMARY

In this chapter, we have reviewed the design, implementation, and evaluation of management control systems. Such systems can be seen as the means by which managers encourage their organization to carry out their desired strategy. Control systems, therefore, are concerned with managing the interface between strategic objectives and organizational behavior.

We noted that control systems are comprised of several elements or subsystems: planning and budgeting, and performance measurement and incentives, for example. Those elements need to support each other as well as the strategy itself. Any inconsistency or incongruence will undermine the system's effectiveness. Planning and budgeting are discussed more fully in Chapter 9. Performance measurement and incentives are discussed in Chapter 10.

We have also noted that a given system can be implemented in different ways. Process choices are separate from design choices.

Finally, we also reviewed a number of criteria that should be used to evaluate a control system's effectiveness. Focusing on key success factors and testing for goal congruence were the two most important areas to evaluate. Others include examining whether performance measures are controllable by managers whose performance is being measured, and assessing a control system's feasibility, understandability, fairness, and long-run/short-run balance.

---

[5] S.L. Mintz, "Fast Times at General Electric, A Conversation with Dennis Dammerman," *CFO Magazine* (June 1995), 34.

QUESTIONS AND PROBLEMS

8–1. Describe an example of a cost center, a discretionary expense center, and a revenue center. For each, describe what the primary measure of performance would be.

8–2. The chapter stated that the primary objective of cost centers was cost minimization, the objective of discretionary expense centers was spending constraints, and the objective of revenue centers was the maximization of revenue. Can you think of a situation for each of the three types of centers in which the primary objective would not be as stated and, in fact, would be the opposite?

8–3. The chapter said that in a profit center, "the manager is expected to make tradeoffs between" expenses and revenue. What does that mean? Give three examples.

8–4. What are key success factors and why are they important to management control systems? Give some examples.

8–5. What is meant by goal congruence? Give two examples where goal congruence exists, and two examples where goal congruence does not exist.

8–6. Do you agree that "by itself, there is no logical reason" for including fairness in the list of evaluation criteria? Why?

CHAPTER 9

PREPARING AND USING BUDGETS

Many people think of a budget as an imposed constraint on spending. "We must stick to the budget" is a frequent remark that reflects that view. When seen that way, a budget is a management tool for reducing expenditures, or at least for keeping them from rising; or to put it another way, by setting a tight budget, management can run an efficient operation.

Although that view has some truth in it, it is narrow and fails to put the budget in the context of the overall managerial process. Budgeting is part of that process, but it is certainly not the total means by which management controls or influences the behavior of an organization.

In this chapter, we will take a broader view of budgeting while we examine what budgeting is, its purpose, how it should work, and what some of the pitfalls are that may interfere with the effective process of budgeting.

WHAT IS A BUDGET?

First of all, a budget is a written plan for the operation of a business, stated in quantitative terms, for a specified future time period. The quantitative terms are usually dollars, but often other measures of physical volume or activity, such as pounds or work hours, are included as well.

As a plan, the budget represents the output or conclusion of a planning process. Hence, the preparation of a budget should be viewed not just as a compilation of numbers, but as the quantitative interpretation of action. For example, pushing numbers around might result in a budget calling for a 15% increase across the board. Such a budget might be impossible to implement, because even a small increase in production would call for a second shift or overtime, both of which might be impossible within the budget constraints of a 15% increase overall. Clearly, the budgeting process in this instance should start with a plan, which is then converted into dollars and a budget plan. A budget is also a means of communicating the agreed upon plans, and a way of encouraging adherence to those plans. More will be said on those aspects later.

TYPES OF BUDGETS

There are three basic types of budgets in business. They are:

1. Cash budgets;

2. Capital budgets;

3. Operating budgets.

Cash budgets are concerned with projecting cash inflows and outflows over some future period. Capital budgets are concerned with the allocation of resources to capital projects, such as buildings, equipment, or other programs that have benefits lasting more than one year. Capital budgeting was examined in Chapter 7 of this book. Operating budgets, which this chapter will discuss, are concerned with budgeting revenues and expenses for a business organization for a specified time period.

THE PURPOSE OF AN OPERATING BUDGET

An operating budget may include budgeted revenue and expenses, or just expenses alone. It is a statement of expected revenue and expenses for the budget period, and thus represents a plan of operation expressed in financial terms. It is important to note that the budgeting process being considered here involves the preparation of the budget as well as its use after preparation.

The value of the budgeting process arises in four ways:

1. The budgeting process enforces a discipline in planning. Operations must be examined and planned in detail, if a budget is to be constructed. Operating managers must take the time to construct plans, rather than focusing solely on day-to-day operations and meeting short-term goals.

2. The budget acts as a guide to subsequent actions and as a way of communicating operating plans in financial terms. In addition, an approved budget may grant authority to spend up to the amounts shown in the budget.

3. The adopted budget provides a benchmark against which to compare the actual results of the operation. As such, the budget is an important part of the management control process and of performance evaluation.

4. The budgeting process is essential for establishing the planned level of expenditure on which overhead rates can be based.

CONDITIONS NECESSARY FOR EFFECTIVE BUDGETING

There are several organizational and operational conditions that must be obtained in order to have effective budgeting. Some of those are:

1. Endorsement by management;

2. Involvement by participants;

3. Realism in terms of expectations;

4. Appropriate detail and time period covered by the budget;

5. Coordination of assumptions, efforts, and differences;

6. Communication to responsible managers.

Each of these conditions is discussed next.

Endorsement by Management

For a budget to serve as a meaningful plan of operations and as a vehicle for management control, it must have the endorsement of the total management structure of an organization. If top management enthusiastically provides the leadership for the use of budgets, support of the whole organization will likely follow.

Involvement by Participants

In order for the budget to be accepted as a realistic and objective plan, it is necessary for the managers responsible for operating under the budget to be involved in the preparation of the budget. An effective means of preparing the expense portion of a budget is to have each responsibility center prepare its own budget, starting with the smallest center. These expenses are then aggregated by layers of responsibility. If the people operating under the budget are involved in its preparation and accept it as being reasonable, they will be more likely to take ownership of the plan and will be more responsive to meeting the stated objectives.

Realism of Expectations

A realistic budget is an objective appraisal of the operating expectations under the conditions assumed. To be realistic, it cannot be based on hopes, which promote over-optimism, or on fears, which lead to pessimistic appraisals. If the budget is not realistic, it will not be accepted by those who must operate under it. If it is not accepted, it cannot provide an effective management planning and control system.

Appropriate Detail and Time Period

The time period for which a budget is prepared must be meaningful from an operational standpoint. The shorter the time period, the more detailed the budget. It is usually a waste of effort to prepare a three-year budget in the same detail that is appropriate for a one-year budget. Many companies will prepare detailed budgets for the next year and less detailed budgets for the following several years. Before the end of each year, the next year's rough budget is filled out in detail and adjusted for new environmental conditions and operating forecasts. At the same time, a new year is added to the rough budget extending several years out.

Coordination of Assumptions, Efforts, and Differences

One person, often called a budget director or director of planning (or one department, which is often called the budget department, or planning department), should coordinate the efforts of those persons involved in the budgetary process. At the beginning of the budget process, this individual (or department) communicates to each department or function the set of environmental or economic assumptions (often referred to as budget assumptions) on which their budgets should be based. Differences may arise between departments or functions that will have to be resolved in order to make an integrated budget. The budget coordinator can serve this role. A coordinated budget emphasizes the interrelationships that exist among the various parts of an organization and the necessity for those segments to plan for the future within the same assumed environmental framework.

Communication to Responsible Managers

After the budget has been prepared, it should receive approval from top management. This approval and the budget, or at least the relevant portions, should then be communicated to all persons responsible for operating under that budget. Effective communication involves an explanation of the budget and positive, active use of the budget for managerial planning and control.

An effective budget must:

1. Be realistic in terms of its expectations;
2. Cover a specified time period with appropriate detail;
3. Have the endorsement of or commitment by management;
4. Be prepared by those involved;
5. Be fully coordinated to assure planning under the same assumed conditions;
6. Be communicated to those responsible for planning and control.

PREPARATION OF THE BUDGET

In many organizations, the budget process will commence about six months prior to the beginning of the year being budgeted. At this time, the budget coordinator will begin developing information about the environmental framework in which the budget will be set. This framework involves the economic, social, and, in some organizations, the political conditions under which the organization expects to operate. The framework specifications and assumptions should then be communicated to those people who are responsible for preparing the various parts of the budget.

Projected Revenues

For most business organizations, the preparation of the operating budget starts with a projection of sales volume. This is often done both in terms of some measure of physical activity and in dollars. An estimate of physical activity is necessary in order for various operating departments to project expenses. A translation of the physical output into dollars is especially important in those situations where a change in prices or product mix is expected, because those changes will affect the projected sales dollars. The dual set of projections—dollars and physical activity—permits more careful evaluation of performance against plan.

With due consideration given to the environmental factors previously mentioned, revenue projections are also usually influenced by inputs from the field salesforce, market researchers, economists, and others attuned to the market environment for the particular goods or services, whose volumes are being projected. These projections may be backed up or factored by statistical or another analytical means of testing.

The revenue projection should be built up by responsibility centers, and the final plan should be agreed to by those responsible for producing the revenue. In addition to breakdowns by responsibility centers, such as product lines, divisions, and departments, revenues should be projected for useful time periods. For some businesses, this may be monthly; for others, if there are significant periodic variations in revenues, it may be useful to have daily or weekly projections. An illustrative revenue projection is presented in Figure 9–1.

Kolb Distributing Company
Projected Revenue for the Year 2006
(dollars in thousands)

Month	Product A Units	Product A Dollars	Product B Pounds	Product B Dollars	Service Department Hours	Service Department Dollars	Total Dollars
January	1,000	$ 2,000	2,000,000	$ 300	660	$ 3.30	$2,303.30
February	1,200	2,400	2,000,000	300	630	3.20	2,703.20
March	1,200	2,400	2,000,000	300	660	3.30	2,703.30
April	1,400	2,800	1,800,000	270	680	3.40	3,073.40
May	1,500	3,000	1,800,000	270	700	3.50	3,273.50
June	1,600	3,200	1,500,000	225	800	4.00	3,429.00
July	1,400	2,800	1,800,000	270	800	4.00	3,074.00
August	1,400	2,800	1,800,000	270	800	4.00	3,074.00
September	1,200	2,400	2,000,000	300	810	4.10	2,704.10
October	1,200	2,400	2,000,000	300	810	4.10	2,704.10
November	1,000	2,000	2,000,000	300	820	4.10	2,304.10
December	1,000	2,000	2,000,000	300	820	4.10	2,304.10
Total	15,100	$30,200	22,700,000	$3,405	8,990	$45.10	$33,650.10

Figure 9–1: *Revenue and Units by Month*

It should be noted that different products or services within the same business may have different seasonal or growth revenue patterns. For example, the Kolb Distributing Company in Figure 9–1 has a definite seasonal pattern for product A and a possible seasonal pattern for product B. The pattern of product B partially offsets the product A pattern. There is an apparent strong growth trend for the service department. However, the service department contributes a relatively small amount of the total revenues.

The aggregate revenue forecast for the Kolb Company should be supported by further breakdown specifying who is responsible for the origination of the revenue (for example: by field salespeople, showroom salespeople, and various sales managers).

It is critical for sales projections to be as accurate as possible. The budget for many expenses will be partially determined by expected sales volume, as each department gears up to meet expectations. If sales projections are too low, the organization may find itself short on its capacity to fill orders, as departments tailored their expense budgets, and consequently their actions, to those low projections, and thus are not equipped to meet a higher sales volume. Perhaps just as problematic is the scenario where projections are too optimistic. Excess capacity (or large unplanned inventory levels) may result, as departments tailored their actions to those optimistic sales projections.

Projected Costs and Expenses

For a manufacturing business, the amount of factory costs incurred is related to the volume of production rather than to the volume of sales. Production volume is often related directly to sales volume, but not necessarily so. Inventory could be reduced to support a high sales volume for a limited period, or production could be geared to build up the level of finished goods inventory.

Expenses for nonmanufacturing businesses or nonmanufacturing activities of a manufacturing business are based on the volume of activity, such as invoices prepared, cartons shipped, pounds processed, or on the strategic plans of management for items, such as advertising and research and development.

Manufacturing Costs

Direct manufacturing cost estimates are often based on the total projected production volume, which is related to both sales volume and projected inventory changes. Each production department can estimate the amount of material, labor, and other costs necessary to produce the projected volume of finished goods. A departmental manufacturing cost budget is illustrated in Figure 9–2.

Payne Seat Company
Sanding Department
Manufacturing Cost Budget for the Year 2006

Month	Units	Materials	Labor	Overhead	Total
January	1,000	$ 4,000	$ 2,000	$ 1,500	$ 7,500
February	1,000	4,000	2,000	1,500	7,500
March	1,000	4,000	2,000	1,500	7,500
April	1,100	4,400	2,200	1,550	8,150
May	1,100	4,400	2,200	1,550	8,150
June	1,150	4,600	2,300	1,575	8,475
July	1,200	4,800	2,400	1,600	8,800
August	1,200	4,800	2,400	1,600	8,800
September	1,150	4,600	2,300	1,575	8,475
October	1,100	4,400	2,200	1,550	8,150
November	1,050	4,200	2,100	1,525	7,825
December	1,000	4,000	2,000	1,500	7,500
Total	13,050	$52,200	$26,100	$18,525	$96,825

Figure 9–2: *Manufacturing Cost Budget*

The departmental manufacturing cost budget illustrated in Figure 9–2 is based on the production of a single product. If more than one product passes through the same department, the volume of each of the different products must be taken into consideration. Where many items are processed through the same department, it is helpful if a common unit of measurement, such as weight or length, can be used.

Direct labor costs are based on projected hours per unit (or standard hours per unit if a standard cost system is used) multiplied by the projected cost per hour. If engineered standards are not used, the projected labor costs, in effect, become a standard.

Direct material costs are computed similarly to labor costs by multiplying the projected volume of material to be used by the standard (or expected) materials price.

Overhead costs are projected based on itemizing the indirect labor, indirect materials, and nonlabor and nonmaterial costs for each department or responsibility center. Some overhead costs, such as rent, depreciation, and taxes, are relatively fixed within a given period. Others, such as power, cleaning supplies, and fringe benefits, may vary closely with units produced, direct labor hours or dollars, or some other measurable input.

Nonmanufacturing Costs

Expenses for nonmanufacturing departments or businesses are usually related to some unit of measurement other than production (for example: sales or strategic plans). An expense budget for those activities could be constructed in addition to the departmental manufacturing budget.

Projected Profit

After revenue and expense budgets have been built up by responsibility centers, they can be combined to show a projected company-level income statement for the budget period, broken down by months or quarters. For a profit-seeking enterprise, this is the objective of the budgetary process; to plan for and deliver a satisfactory profit level given the prevailing environmental conditions for the budget period. Budgeting is also essential for a nonprofit organization in order to plan requests for resource allocations and to plan and control expenses within given revenue volumes.

COMPARISON OF ACTUAL TO BUDGET

In order for the budget to serve as a control vehicle, actual performance must be measured against budget. Actual revenues and expenses should be collected by the same categories used for budgeting. For effective control, performance reports should be prepared according to the responsibility center and should show clearly those expenses that are controllable by the responsible person and those over which the manager has no control. Some reports show only the controllable expenses on the theory that if noncontrollable expenses are listed, they may cause confusion on the part of the responsible manager. A budget performance report is illustrated in Figure 9–3.

<table>
<tr><td colspan="6" align="center">**Payne Seat Company**
Sanding Department
Overhead Performance
January, 2006</td></tr>
<tr><td></td><td colspan="2">*Item*</td><td colspan="2">*Amount*</td><td colspan="2">*Over (Under)*</td></tr>
<tr><td></td><td>*No.*</td><td>*Name*</td><td>*Budget*</td><td>*Actual*</td><td>*Amount*</td><td>*Percentage*</td></tr>
<tr><td>Controllable:</td><td></td><td></td><td></td><td></td><td></td><td></td></tr>
<tr><td></td><td>1001</td><td>Indirect labor</td><td>$ 500</td><td>$ 550</td><td>$50</td><td>10.0</td></tr>
<tr><td></td><td>2001</td><td>Maintenance</td><td>200</td><td>220</td><td>20</td><td>10.0</td></tr>
<tr><td></td><td>3001</td><td>Utilities</td><td>300</td><td>330</td><td>30</td><td>10.0</td></tr>
<tr><td></td><td>4001</td><td>Supplies</td><td>300</td><td>320</td><td>20</td><td>6.7</td></tr>
<tr><td></td><td>5001</td><td>Travel</td><td>75</td><td>0</td><td>(75)</td><td>(100.0)</td></tr>
<tr><td>Noncontrollable:</td><td></td><td></td><td></td><td></td><td></td><td></td></tr>
<tr><td></td><td>6001</td><td>Taxes</td><td>25</td><td>25</td><td>0</td><td>0.0</td></tr>
<tr><td></td><td>7001</td><td>Depreciation</td><td>100</td><td>100</td><td>0</td><td>0.0</td></tr>
<tr><td></td><td></td><td>Total</td><td>$1,500</td><td>$1,545</td><td>$45</td><td>3.0</td></tr>
</table>

Figure 9–3: *Overhead Performance Report*

A complete budget performance report should include an explanation of the reason for the variances from the budget and the plans for initiating or completing corrective action, if necessary. Management should review that performance report regularly with the responsible persons involved. This review will emphasize the continued endorsement of the budget by management and will aid in communicating useful operating information up and down the management ladder.

The type of budgets discussed so far can be described as *static* budgets. Once a projected volume of activity such as revenue or production is established, variances are computed against the costs associated with this fixed projection. However, because significant environmental changes may take place within a short period, consideration should be given to periodic budget revisions. These revisions could be monthly or quarterly for the remaining months or quarters of a year.

FLEXIBLE BUDGETS

Though the purpose and function of *flexible* budgets are similar to the static (or fixed) budgets just discussed, their preparation is sufficiently different to warrant a separate discussion. Flexible budgets may be effectively used in businesses or parts of organizations in which a change in the level of activity is expected to change the level of costs. With flexible budgets, different amounts of costs are budgeted for different levels of activity.

Purpose of Flexible Budgets

A *static* or *fixed budget* is based on a single level of activity. It is often the level that, in management's judgment, is most likely to occur. In some cases, such as governmental operations, a budget is fixed as a result of fixed levels of revenue or appropriations. But it is unlikely that sales, expenses, or other measures of activity will occur exactly as planned. And if actual activity levels, such as sales volume, are different from planned levels, we would *expect* actual costs to be different from planned costs since many costs are variable costs that we expect to change as activity levels change.

The static budget provides no means of stating what costs *should* be if the level of activity is different from that which was planned originally. The use of a static budget as a control vehicle is therefore limited. A *flexible budget*, on the other hand, will indicate an estimate of what costs should be at various levels of activity. As a period of time passes, when the actual level of activity becomes known, actual costs incurred can be measured against the planned costs for that actual level of activity.

Preparation of a Flexible Budget

Historical data. The first step in preparing a flexible budget is to collect historical data which will provide a basis for determining past relationships between the volume of activity and costs. These past relationships can usually serve as a basis for projecting future cost behavior. Figure 9–4 illustrates graphically the behavior of direct labor cost in relation to pounds processed. As shown on this graph, apparently $360 of direct labor cost is incurred if the operation is open at all. No additional labor costs are required until a volume of 6,000 pounds is reached. Above a volume of 6,000 pounds, direct labor costs vary directly at $0.06 per pound with pounds processed.

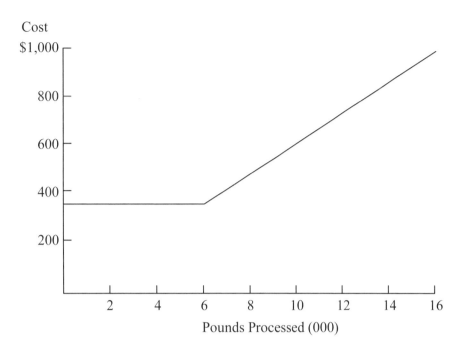

Cost

$1,000

800

600

400

200

2   4   6   8   10   12   14   16

Pounds Processed (000)

Figure 9–4: *Illustration of the Relationship between Costs and Volume of Activity*

Measure of activity. In order to measure the variability of costs, it is necessary to determine a measure of activity that has a close correlation with the work performed by the organization. The unit of measurement may be different for each department. The measurement unit can be dollars of revenue, units produced, direct labor hours, pieces, pounds, or gallons, for example. Some measures are based on inputs to a department, such as labor hours, whereas others are based on outputs, such as pounds processed. Figure 9–4 used an output measure (pounds processed) as the measure of activity.

The measure of activity should be that which has the highest degree of correlation with those costs that vary with the level of activity. It may be necessary to test the behavior of costs against several possible measures of activity to find the measure with the best correlation.

Range of activity. Normally, a flexible budget would be prepared only for those levels of activity that are probable, and not for all possible levels. The expected level of activity for the budget period should be projected. In addition, the probable range of activity should be projected. Thus, if the expected level of activity is projected as 100%, and the probable level of activity is projected at plus or minus 20%, the flexible budget would be designed for a range from 80% to 120% of the expected level.

The probable range of activity could be much wider for some organizations than for others. A power company, for example, would have a relatively narrow range. A local moving company, on the other hand, might have a relatively wide range, because of the difficulty in projecting the number of people in the community who will move during the budget period.

It is critical to specify the range of activity for which the flexible budget is prepared. Costs, which might be classified as fixed within an 80% to 120% range of expected volume, could change significantly, if volume changes more than 20%. For example, additional space may have to be rented if volume increases more than 20%. At the other end, a minimum number of employees are always retained on the payroll. In Figure 9–4, if 12,000 pounds was the expected level of activity for the organization portrayed, the range of activity might be between 9,600 pounds (80%) to 14,000 pounds (120%). However, if the range of activity was much wider, or if the expected level of activity was 4,000 pounds, the cost variability of $0.06 per pound would not hold true.

Thus, in order to determine which costs are variable and which are fixed, for the purposes of preparing a flexible budget, it is necessary to work within a meaningful range of activity. For many organizations, if volume varies more than 20% plus or minus the expected level, a new budgeting effort is necessary.

DETERMINATION OF COST BEHAVIOR

Variable Costs

Within a selected range of activity, there are many costs that will vary proportionately, or almost so, with volume. These costs are classified as variable costs. For flexible budgeting purposes, it is not necessary that a cost vary proportionately with volume at all levels—only at the levels within the selected range of activity—in order to be classified as a variable cost.

Fixed Costs

Some costs do not vary at all, or do not vary within a selected range of activity. These costs are referred to as fixed costs. Some examples of fixed costs are rent, depreciation, and property taxes.

Semivariable Costs

Some costs vary, but do not vary in proportion to volume. There are different methods that may be used to budget those costs, four of which are discussed below. They are:

1. Estimates for predetermined levels of activity;

2. Arbitrary assignment of costs as either fixed or variable, based on their most dominant behavior;

3. Breakdown by fixed and variable components;

4. Graphic analysis.

Estimates at predetermined levels of activity. Under this method, items of semivariable costs, such as maintenance costs, are projected for predetermined levels of activity within the flexible budget range. For example, predetermined ranges of 80%, 90%, 110%, and 120% of expected volume could be used. Maintenance costs would then be budgeted at each of these levels based on estimated costs at these levels. The use of this method limits the variability of the budget, because budget costs are calculated and can be compared with actual costs only at the predetermined levels. If actual volume were different from 80%, 90%, 110%, and 120% of expected volume, budgeted costs would not be known exactly, because costs at the intermediate level of activity would not necessarily follow a straight-line pattern.

Assignment by dominant behavior. Another approach is to assign semivariable costs to either the variable or the fixed category, according to its most dominant behavior. Thus, if cost varies only by a small amount and not directly with volume, it is treated as a fixed cost. If a cost varies with a relatively high degree of variability, but yet not in proportion to volume, it is treated as a variable cost.

Because that method is relatively simple and easy, it is widely used. However, it should be evident that this method is not exact and resorting to it can affect the usefulness of the flexible budget as a standard for cost behavior at various levels of activity within the range being used. The farther the results are from the expected level, the more distortion there will be.

Breakdown by fixed and variable components. This method assumes that each item classified as a semivariable cost can be broken down into variable and fixed elements. Thus, within a given range of activity, a portion of a semivariable cost would be considered fixed, while the remaining element would be assigned a proportional relationship to volume.

Under that method, an estimate is made of the level of each semivariable cost at the likely upper and lower limits of the range of activity. For example:

	Pounds Processed	Maintenance Costs
Upper limit	14,400	$2,432
Lower limit	9,600	$2,288

In this example, as the number of pounds processed changed by 4,800 pounds (lbs), the maintenance costs changed by $144. Thus, the variable element of maintenance costs would be:

$$\frac{\text{Change in Maintenance Costs}}{\text{Change in Volume}} = \frac{\$144}{4{,}800 \text{ lbs}} = \$0.03 \text{ per Pound}$$

Having determined the cost per pound that is to be considered a variable cost, we can determine the fixed cost element.

	Upper Limit	Lower Limit
Total maintenance cost	$2,432	$2,288
Variable costs:		
14,400 pounds × $0.03	432	
9,600 pounds × $0.03		288
Fixed cost	$2,000	$2,000

This method, using the upper and lower limits of the range of activity as a means of approximating the variable and fixed elements of cost items, is sometimes referred to as the *high–low method*. Though it does not give precise cost relationships, it does give approximations that can be used at any level of activity within the given range.

Graphic analysis. The high–low method of separating fixed and variable cost elements just described uses only two points or levels of activity to determine variable costs. It is sometimes advantageous to use several points. Those points can be plotted on a chart with the vertical axis representing dollar cost and the horizontal axis representing the measure of activity (pounds in the example previously used). With the points plotted on a chart, a line of best fit can be drawn by visual inspection, or by more sophisticated statistical methods, such as a regression line based on the method of least squares.[1] See Figure 9–5 for an illustration of a graphic analysis of semivariable costs.

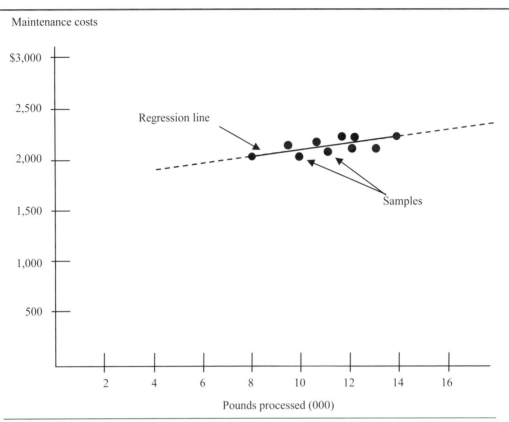

Figure 9–5: *Analysis of Semivariable Costs*

After the line of best fit has been plotted on a chart, the estimated cost can be read for any volume of activity. Thus, although a cost is not actually broken into its fixed and variable components, a total cost including both components is available for any level of activity within the range depicted. For computation without the graph, the point where the line intersects the vertical axis (here $2,000 within the range depicted) and the slope of the line (here $0.03 per pound) can be used to derive the total flexible budget. Thus, $2,000 + ($0.03 × pounds processed) would give the flexible budget for maintenance costs.

OBSERVATIONS ON COST BEHAVIOR

The following observations may be made about cost behavior:

1. Total costs for an organization do not usually vary directly with the volume of activity, because some costs are fixed, some are variable, and some are semivariable.

2. Costs may not vary with volume at a constant rate. Some costs may vary in a step fashion, that is, they may be constant for some increase in volume and then jump up with an additional increase. For example, with rising volume, the cost of supervisors will be constant until one more must be hired. Other kinds of costs may vary continuously, but at an increasing or decreasing rate. For

---

[1] This method is described in detail in most standard statistics textbooks.

instance, as working hours get longer, efficiency may go down, meaning that labor costs rise with volume, but at an increasing rate. (Most companies recognize the nonlinearity of cost changes, but in constructing flexible budgets, they conclude that a straight line is much easier to use and represents a sufficiently close fit.)

3. Costs fluctuate as a result of three basic factors: volume, spending, and efficiency in utilization. For example, labor costs will usually increase as volume increases, as wage rates increase, or as labor is used inefficiently.

4. In comparing actual costs with budgeted costs, it is helpful to isolate those changes resulting from volume changes in order to make an appraisal of relative operating efficiency. If a budget is to be used for performance evaluation as related to cost control, it must show what costs *should be* at various levels of activity. This, then, is the reason for flexible budgets.

ILLUSTRATIVE FLEXIBLE BUDGET

Figure 9–6 shows a monthly budget for the processing department of the COD Delivery Company. Note that the costs for the processing department have been broken down into their fixed and variable elements, and that controllable and noncontrollable costs are shown separately.

Cod Delivery Company
Monthly Expense Budget
Processing Department

Cost Item	*Fixed Cost per Month*	*Variable Cost per Pound*	*9,600 80%*	*10,800 90%*	*12,000 100%*	*13,200 110%*
Controllable costs:						
Direct labor	$ 0	$ 0.06	$ 576	$ 648	$ 720	$ 792
Machine rental	800	0	800	800	800	800
Supplies	0	0.02	192	216	240	264
Maintenance	2,000	0.03	2,288	2,324	2,360	2,396
Power	1,200	0.01	1,296	1,308	1,320	1,332
Total	$ 4,000	$ 0.12	$5,152	$5,296	$5,440	$5,584
Noncontrollable costs:						
Supervision	$ 700	0	$ 700	$ 700	$ 700	$ 700
Rent	300	0	300	300	300	300
Depreciation	800	0	800	800	800	800
Total	$ 1,800	0	$1,800	$1,800	$1,800	$1,800
Total costs	$ 5,800	$ 0.12	$6,952	$7,096	$7,240	$7,384

Range of Activity

Figure 9–6: *Flexible Budget*

Costs have been budgeted for selected levels of activity—80% to 110% of expected volume. With each cost item shown by fixed and variable elements, budget costs can be determined for various levels of activity between those activity levels shown in the figure. For example, if the actual level of activity for a month is 10,000 pounds, direct labor costs should be 10,000 × $0.06, or $600. If the actual activity is 13,200 pounds, direct labor costs should be 13,200 × $0.06, or $792.

Figure 9–7 shows a monthly performance report for the processing department of the COD Delivery Company for the month of March 2006. The expected level of activity was 12,000 pounds. Actual volume was 13,000 pounds. Using the budget shown in Figure 9–6, it is possible to determine the budgeted cost for each cost item at 13,000 pounds. For example, the budgeted cost for direct labor at a volume of 13,000 pounds is 13,000 × $0.06, or $780. Actual labor costs were $788, so there was an unfavorable variance of $8. Again, the budget cost for maintenance is $2,000 (fixed) + (13,000 pounds × $0.03), or $2,390. Actual costs were $2,500, so there was an unfavorable variance of $110.

Cod Delivery Company
Monthly Performance Report
Processing Department
March 2006

Measure of activity: pounds processed
Budgeted activity: 12,000
Actual activity: 13,000

Cost Item	Actual Cost	Budgeted Cost	Variance $	Variance %	Remarks
Controllable costs:					
Direct labor	$ 788	$ 780	$ 8	1.0	
Machine rental	800	800	0	0.0	
Supplies	270	260	10	3.8	
Maintenance	2,500	2,390	110	4.6	
Power	1,324	1,330	(6)	(0.5)	
Total	$5,682	$5,560	$122	2.2	
Noncontrollable costs:					
Supervision	$ 740	$ 700	$ 40	5.7	
Rent	300	300	0	0.0	
Depreciation	800	800	0	0.0	
Total	$1,840	$1,800	$ 40	2.2	
Total costs	$7,522	$7,360	$162	2.2	

Figure 9–7: *Expense Report Recognizing Variability*

With a properly constructed flexible budget, it is possible to determine what costs should be at *any* volume within the selected range of activity. Thus, poor performance cannot be blamed on changes in volume. Conversely, a department manager won't look good simply because of favorable cost variances due to a change in volume.

OTHER DRIVERS OF COST VARIABILITY

Earlier we said that there were several possible measures of activity level. We used pounds processed in the example. The implication of that analysis was that the processing of pounds influenced the level of some costs, such as maintenance costs. A higher level of pounds processed would raise the expected level of maintenance costs.

There are other drivers of cost variability; companies that establish activity-based cost systems recognize that in addition to unit-based drivers, such as pounds or direct labor hours, other drivers affect different groups of costs. (Chapter 2 describes activity-based costing.) The processing of batches, for example, is an activity that affects a certain group of costs like setup, inspection, material handling, and purchasing. Each group of costs driven by a particular driver will have its own fixed and variable components. Budgeting should reflect those differences. For example, batches may go up, while pounds processed goes down. Not only would pounds processed be a poor activity measure for all costs, but the fixed and variable split indicated by pounds processed may provide a poor flexible budget for costs driven by batches. Having recognized other drivers, a number of companies have begun to focus on activity costs as an integral part of their budgeting process.

BUDGETS AND STANDARD COSTING SYSTEMS

It is worth noting here that the budgeting process as described in this chapter relates closely to the standard costing systems discussed in Chapter 3. Budgets are planned expenditures for cost items like supplies and maintenance and are usually arranged so that an individual is responsible for managing each group of costs. Standard costs refer to the same amounts recombined to show how much a unit of output is expected to cost. Both budgeting and standard costing should show variances when actual costs differ from planned costs. Furthermore, the variances computed by standard costing systems recognize that not all costs will vary directly with units of output in the same way that flexible budgets reflect the semivariable nature of some costs. The budgeting process is, in fact, part of the planning that leads to determining standard product costs.

ISSUES IN IMPLEMENTING THE BUDGETING PROCESS

As described in the previous sections, the process of budgeting sounds quite straightforward. However, its implementation is not as easy as it sounds. There are several critical issues whose handling will determine whether the budgeting process is effective: bottom up versus top down; realism versus control; and budget revision.

Bottom-up versus Top-down Budgeting

With top-down budgeting, higher levels of management set the budget for lower levels of management. It is a way of saying, "Here's what we want you to do." With bottom-up budgeting, on the other hand, the lower levels of management say, "Here's what we think we can do." They each have advantages and disadvantages, and most budgeting systems usually end up trying to achieve a good blend of the two. Bottom-up budgeting, in which each level participates in setting its own budget goals, is most likely to generate commitment to meeting those goals. But those goals may be too easy or may not match the company's overall strategic objectives in such areas as profit level or market penetration. Top-down budgeting can insure that budgets will be acceptable to higher management and consistent with the company's strategic objectives, but the lack of commitment by those lower down, who are responsible for achieving the budget targets, may endanger the plan's success.

Clearly, a good budgeting system must have some of each. Sometimes this is done by working in stages as follows:

1. Top management assesses the market and business environment and sets a strategic framework and some general targets, including level of volume and profit for the various product lines.

2. With this strategic framework and these general targets, operating managers work on detailed plans and costs, arriving at a proposed budget.

3. Through discussion and negotiation, agreement is reached on a budget that is deemed to be both achievable and appropriate for the company's overall strategic objectives.

Realism versus Control

Budgeting is both a planning device and part of the control system. The two can work at cross purposes. For planning, one wants realistic and reliable forecasts, yet the control system may not encourage this. If the control system compares actual results with forecasted results, and penalizes managers in some way when the actual results fall short of what was forecasted, the next time around the manager whose performance is being measured will naturally try to avoid any penalty by forecasting goals that he or she is not likely to miss. These forecasts may not be the best ones for planning purposes.

There is no easy solution to this conflict. The budget certainly has a place in both the planning and control systems. But awareness of these potential unintended consequences in the budgeting system can focus management's attention on trying to deter the unwanted behavior.

The same sort of conflict also exists in the budget approval process. If one year's proposed budget is cut, the next year's proposed budget is likely to have a cushion, so that after being cut it will still be satisfactory. Recognizing that, the next cut is likely to be deeper. This game probably can never be completely eliminated, but smart budget makers and approvers will know it is there and will try to keep its distortions to a minimum.

Budget Revision

In an annual budget cycle, conditions may change, so that before the end of the budget year, the budget represents an unrealistic plan. Should the budget be revised? Some say, "Of course, it should," for an unrealistic budget does more harm than good. Others say, "No, it should not," because a budget that is changed too easily and too frequently is a confusing guide and has little discipline. And, of course, to some extent, both views are right. If a budget is revised, it should be done with the same analytical process that provided the basis for the original budget. Otherwise, budget revisions made in one department would cause that budget to wander out of coordination with other units in the company or overall company strategy. Some companies stick with the original budget but ask the department or division managers to forecast each month how they now think they will do for the rest of the year in comparison to the budget. These forecasts then become the subject of discussion and, if accepted, serve as somewhat of a revised budget for control purposes.

CONTINGENCY PLANNING

It is highly unlikely that actual revenues and expenses will agree with the amounts budgeted. Yet, many companies expect the profit as budgeted to be delivered regardless of what happens to the level of revenues. Contingency planning can be very useful in managing to achieve the desired profit level. Contingency planning is often associated with "what do we do if things go bad." It can be just as useful when things go better than expected. Thus, contingency planning, as described here, is planning the actions to be taken when actual events do not correspond with the assumptions used in preparing the budget. If sales do not materialize as budgeted, a contingency plan, prepared at the same time as the budget, would include the steps to be taken to reach the desired profit level. These steps could include more expenditures in the marketing or sales area or the reduction of managed expenses, such as research and development, training, maintenance, and travel.

One of the essential ingredients in contingency planning is identifying a "trigger point," which would signal the need to implement a contingency plan. The trigger point could be an economic indicator, the level of incoming orders, a strike at a competitor's plant, or anything different from the assumed conditions used in the budget.

The preparation of contingency plans during the budget process means that the plans can be prepared on a more rational basis than waiting until something happens during the operating period that requires fast action. Fast action, without prior planning, is often done on a more emotional basis and is less apt to be rational. Contingency plans are of little benefit unless they are executed when the trigger point is reached. Many companies prepare plans, but are hesitant to implement them until it is too late to realize the intended results.

SUMMARY

In this chapter, we have discussed budgeting. Budgeting is really the process of planning and reviewing. Six conditions were described as necessary for effective budgeting:

1. Endorsement by management;

2. Involvement by participants;

3. Realism in terms of expectations;

4. Appropriate detail and time period;

5. Coordination of assumptions, efforts, and differences;

6. Communication to responsible managers.

The process of preparing a budget, both a static budget and a flexible budget, was described and illustrated. Three issues were examined whose resolution was crucial to the effectiveness of the budgeting process:

1. The need for balance between bottom-up and top-down budgeting;

2. The conflict between the need for realistic and reliable numbers for planning and the use of budget comparisons for performance evaluation;

3. The question of when and how to revise a budget.

A final section discussed contingency planning as a means of managing when assumed conditions in the budget are changed.

QUESTIONS AND PROBLEMS

9–1.   What are the distinctive purposes of:

      a. cash budgets;

      b. capital budgets;

      c. operating budgets.

9–2.   Harry says he thinks those flexible budgets are for the birds. "A budget," he says, "should represent a solid plan; if you let it vary with every little puff of the inevitable winds of change, you'll have chaos." Do you agree? How would you respond to Harry?

9–3.   What are bottom-up and top-down budgeting? What would be the symptoms of too much of each?

9–4.   Budgeting is used for both planning and control. Describe its use for each purpose, and explain why the purposes sometimes conflict.

CHAPTER 10

MEASURING PERFORMANCE

Performance measurement is at the heart of management control. How a manager is measured strongly influences that manager's decisions and how that manager spends his or her time. Tell the manager you are going to evaluate him or her based on some performance measure. Choose the right performance measure, and you'll likely get what you want. Choose the wrong one, and you can send things into a downward spiral. *What gets measured gets attention.*

A performance measure signals what is important. Even when that measurement is not quantitatively precise, the focus of evaluation can be a powerful force. For example, Jack Welch, former CEO of General Electric, used to ask his business leaders to prepare a one-page report on questions, such as "What are your market dynamics globally today?" and "What actions have your competitors taken in the last three years to upset those global dynamics?" In effect, Welch was signaling to his leaders that those are the important questions to work on and that he would be evaluating their responses.[1]

CHOOSING THE RIGHT PERFORMANCE MEASURE

Prior to determining what performance measure to use to evaluate the performance of a manager or the business unit he manages, it is important to identify the unit's key success factors. Recall that key success factors are those few things that an organization *must do well* to successfully implement its strategy and achieve its objectives. Identifying those factors is the most important part of control system design. The implication of omitting that step or incorrectly identifying the organization's key success factors is simple; it can lead to managers ignoring rather than focusing on that factor.

Once the key success factors have been identified, the measure or measures used to evaluate managers' performance can be selected. Those performance measures should encourage managers to focus on the key success factors. If the key success factors are all considered in the performance measure or measures, then managers are motivated to consider them when making decisions. If the key success factors are not all considered in the performance measures, however, managers won't be motivated to include them all as part of their decision criteria.

Settling on the performance measure itself, though, doesn't mean the work is done. Several issues arise that warrant discussion.

Defining the Elements of the Performance Measure

Different elements of a performance measure must be precisely defined. Consider the use of ROI (return on investment) to measure the performance of an investment center. ROI (income divided by investment) is perhaps the most frequently used measure to assess the performance of investment centers. But there are numerous ways to define ROI. First, one must first decide what is meant by the term income—it could be operating income, net income, or some other measure of income. Once income is precisely defined, then one must decide what is meant by the term investment—it could be total assets, total assets minus

---

[1] Noel Tichy and Ram Charan, "Speed, Simplicity, Self-Confidence: An Interview with Jack Welch," *Harvard Business Review* (September–October 1989): 115.

working capital, or some other measure of investment. For example, in some merchandising businesses, only inventory and accounts receivable are included in the investment base; in other situations, land, buildings and equipment, and even cash are included.

Once income and investment are defined, there are more measurement issues to consider. For example, one may need to decide whether depreciation expense in computing income, and fixed assets in computing investment, should be calculated using the straight line or an accelerated method, and whether the cost of goods sold in computing income—and inventory in computing investment—should be calculated using the FIFO (first in, first out) or LIFO (last in, first out) method of inventory accounting.[2] Most companies simply choose to use the same numbers that are in the income statement produced by the financial accountants, but certainly there could be reasons to adjust some of those numbers for performance measurement purposes.

The impact that different definitions of income or investment have on the manager's motivation can easily be shown. If inventory is part of the investment base, and the manager is currently earning 10% ROI, every additional dollar of inventory must earn at least 10% plus the additional cost of handling the inventory or the manager's performance measure will decline. If inventory is not included in the investment base, then each extra dollar of inventory need only cover its carrying cost for the manager's ROI to remain at 10%. Clearly, those alternative definitions of investment can lead the manager to make different decisions about purchasing inventory.

Impact of trading between divisions. A common issue that arises when responsibility centers within an organization trade with each other is that some price must be established at which the transfer of goods occurs. That transfer price becomes very important to both responsibility centers. The buying price (cost) to one profit center is the selling price (revenue) to the other profit center. An integrated oil company might set up the oil producing properties as one profit center and the refinery and marketing divisions as two more profit centers. Clearly, a transfer price must be established for each grade of product and between each division. However, this is often difficult to do. Consider these examples. If the transfer price between the refinery and the marketing division is too low, the refinery may be encouraged to sell its product elsewhere to get a higher price or to change its production mix to yield a more profitable range of products. If the price is set too high, the refinery may switch its production the other way. Or the marketing division may be uninclined to bid on a special deal that would be beneficial to the company as a whole, because the deal would result in a loss to the marketing division.

When divisions trade with each other, they may or may not share cost information. If a division is organized as a cost center, then the sharing of cost information with other divisions is commonplace. Products or services traded among the units can be transferred at cost and costing information can be widely shared. However, when profit center divisions trade with one another, cost information often is not shared because division managers often are expected to operate each division as an independent business and to compete externally.

The transfer price at which goods are traded can take many forms, the most common of which are:

---

[2] The straight-line method and the accelerated method are alternative methods used by accountants to depreciate assets on the balance sheet, and thus to record depreciation expense on the income statement. FIFO and LIFO are alternative methods accountants utilize to value inventory on the balance sheet, and thus to record the cost of goods sold expense on the income statement.

- Variable costs (or variable costs plus a markup);

- Total or full costs (or total costs plus a markup);

- Market prices (or market price less a discount);

- Negotiated prices.

and many variations of those. The desired characteristics of transfer prices include: (1) encouraging divisions to make decisions that are in the best interests of the organization as a whole, and (2) continuing to provide an incentive for effort from both the buying and selling divisions.

Using variable costs as a basis for transfer prices highlights the behavior of costs to both the selling and buying divisions. However, it provides little incentive for the selling division to operate efficiently. Its variable costs are always covered, and it doesn't lose business from the buying division due to high fixed costs. Nor does the buying division have the incentive to apply any pressure on the selling division to control those fixed costs. Further, the selling division would prefer to sell its product elsewhere if it can get a price greater than its variable costs, even if it is in the organization's best interests to transfer internally.

Using total costs as a basis for transfer prices has the advantage of simplicity—full costs are accumulated in the accounting system for financial accounting purposes and are readily available. And it provides an incentive for the selling division to operate more efficiently. Unfortunately, it makes the fixed costs of the selling division look like variable costs to the buying division. This masking of true cost behavior can lead to decisions by the buying division that are not in the best interests of the organization as a whole.

Using market prices as a basis for transfer prices minimizes the chance of decisions by either the selling or buying division that are not in the best interests of the organization as a whole. However, market prices are often not available for products transferred from one division to another.

Many organizations have discovered that they prefer to allow divisions to negotiate their own transfer prices and to allow them to decline an inside arrangement if they prefer to deal outside.

The complexity of a transfer pricing situation depends upon the number of profit centers; the degree of trading among them; the number of different products; the frequency of changes in costs, in production volume, and in external market prices and demands; the amount of joint or byproducts; and the importance of good transfer prices. It is not unusual for an organization to commit a large group of people to the continual task of establishing and revising the transfer pricing mechanisms. And if the volume of transfers is a high percentage of a profit center's volume, it may be worth considering combining the profit center with its major partner, thereby eliminating a somewhat artificial transfer price.

Direction Implied by the Performance Measure

Besides signaling what is important, a performance measure usually implies direction, pointing out that either higher is better or lower is better. However, matching that implied direction with the company's objectives, the process of developing "goal congruence," often has complications that need to be considered. For example, here are some financial and nonfinancial measures currently in use, the direction those measures imply, and some of the issues related to that direction.

Measures	_Direction Implied_
Sales	Higher sales (revenue or unit sales) are better than lower sales. Does not consider variations in profit margins.
Contribution (revenue minus variable costs)	More contribution is better than less. Assumes that costs that are not classified as variable will remain fixed.
Net profit (revenue minus expense)	Higher is better. Managers should manage the interplay between revenue and expense to maximize the difference. Investment is not considered.
Return on investment (ROI)	Higher is better. Managers are encouraged to consider the level of investment as well as revenue and expense. Measures the rate of return, not the size of the return.
Economic value added (EVA) (net profit minus the cost of capital required to produce the profit)	Higher is better. Encourages actions to increase net profit as long as the increase more than covers the cost of capital required for the increase.
Cash flow from operations (net income plus noncash expense minus noncash income plus, or minus, changes in working capital)	Higher is better. Encourages concern for both the cash flows from adjusted income and the effect on cash flow from changes in the components of working capital.
Machine downtime	Less is better, but if it doesn't differentiate between planned and unplanned downtime, it may encourage the avoidance of preventive maintenance.
Rejects	Lower is better. However, the cost–benefit trade-off of lower rejects is hard to pin down, because costs are usually easier to measure than benefits.
Response or processing time	Faster may be better, but sometimes reliability within a range of times is more important. Also, faster than a prescribed minimum may not add value.
Customer complaints	Fewer is better, but zero complaints may reflect systems that employees use to avoid recording a complaint, thereby preventing managers from learning where improvements are needed.
Employee turnover	Lower is better, but discovering ways to improve requires careful analysis.
Write-off of uncollectible receivables	Lower is better, but a very low figure may indicate excessive rejection of credit risks and loss of business.

Evaluating the Performance of the Manager versus Evaluating the Performance of the Unit He or She Manages

Two objectives are important: (1) is to measure the performance of the center's manager in order to provide direction, motivation, and a means to evaluate the manager's performance; and (2) is to measure and evaluate the center's results as a unit of the organization, and as part of the company's overall operational strategy. Those two objectives, one focusing on the manager, the other on the center as an operating unit, usually give the same signals as to whether the unit should be a profit center or a cost/expense center. But not always.

Many companies attempt to separate the performance evaluation of an operating unit (and the measurements used to do it) from the performance evaluation of the individual managers involved. In practice, this is not easy to do, since the manager in question is responsible for the business unit. In general, it is necessary to decouple the two evaluations to allow for uncontrollable factors, such as economic conditions that bear on the results of the unit but are not controllable by the manager. This separation acknowledges in the manager's evaluation that the operating unit's original budget might not be the best set of figures for *ex post facto* managerial evaluation.

How much control or influence the center's manager has over prices or sales volume is important when deciding whether the center's profit is a good measure of the manager's performance. But suppose the manager has no control and very little influence over prices and volume. Should it then be a profit center? It would be inappropriate to use profit to measure the manager's performance, but the unit's profit may be very important for strategic decisions, such as whether to keep or to drop that segment of the business. Thus, measuring profit of a unit, when it is feasible, is often important, but the extent to which that profit reflects the performance of the center's manager must be considered in light of how much control or influence the manager has.

Sometimes if the same measure is used for both, the manager's motivation may be impaired, because he or she believes that the measure includes uncontrollable items. However, it is unwise to evaluate managers on fundamentally different measures of performance from those used for the operating unit, because the discrepancy creates conflicts in the manager's mind that weaken his or her overall motivation.

Investment Center Performance Measures

We have already indicated that ROI is perhaps the most frequent performance measure used for investment centers. ROI is not without its shortcomings, however. The following example will illustrate some of the issues.

Consider the capital budgeting process. A division earning 15% ROI can only hurt itself by proposing capital investment projects that earn 12% or 13%. What may not be so clear is that if several divisions are all earning at different rates as is usually the case, the discrepancies may have a disastrous impact on the capital budgeting system. Consider the following situation.

Division	ROI Earning Rate
A	4%
B	12
C	25

The company as a whole earns 15% ROI, but each of the three divisions has a different ROI. In this situation, where will all the capital funds go? To the C division? Not likely! In the eyes of C, good projects must earn at least 25%. Division C's managers are motivated to spurn 20% return alternatives, because division C's performance measure, ROI, will necessarily go down, even though a 20% return project will improve total company ROI. Clearly, no one wants that division to ignore 20% return projects. But, by using ROI as a performance measure, the company essentially tells the division manager to do so. At the other extreme, 5%, 6%, and 7% return projects, while falling well below the average company ROI, look very attractive to division A. Unless the capital budgeting system has been designed to thwart that tendency, division A may request funds for those projects. Since there are always many more low return ideas than high ones, division A may very well end up with the bulk of new capital funds. (Note that this is an example of a control system performance measure, ROI, failing to provide goal congruence—managers in divisions A and C are motivated to make investment decisions that are not in the best interest of the company as a whole.) As those examples indicate, the design of the investment center performance measures should be carefully related to the capital budgeting system.[3]

Residual income. An alternative approach, designed to help eliminate the problem illustrated above, measures residual income (RI), which is computed in the following manner:

$$\text{Residual Income} = \text{Income} - (\text{Capital Charge} \times \text{Investment})$$

For example, suppose that division C in the example has $100 million of investment (inventory, receivables, land, buildings, and equipment), income for the year of $25 million, and a corporate charge for assets of 15%. While ROI would be 25% ($25 million/$100 million), RI is calculated as follows:

$$\text{RI} = \$25 \text{ Million} - (0.15 \times \$100 \text{ Million}) = \$10 \text{ Million}$$

Companies that use residual income as a measure of financial performance do so partly because RI makes it easier to coordinate the capital budgeting system's required rate of return with the capital charge used for RI, thereby making the two systems more compatible. When RI is used as the performance measure, a high-earning division, such as in the previous example, is motivated to invest in projects with an ROI below 25% but above 15%. Consider a project that has an ROI of 20%. We noted above that the C division will not be motivated to invest in the project if ROI is the performance measure. However, if RI is the performance measure, division C is motivated to invest because the RI of the project is positive, so total division C RI increases:

$$\text{RI} = \$20 \text{ Million} - (0.15 \times \$100 \text{ Million}) = \$5 \text{ Million}$$

Likewise, a lower-earning division will only invest in projects expected to earn better than 15%. Consider a project that has an ROI of 7%. We noted above that the A division will be motivated to invest in the project if ROI is the performance measure. However, if RI is the performance measure, division A is not motivated to invest because the RI of the project is negative, so total division A RI decreases:

$$\text{RI} = \$7 \text{ Million} - (0.15 \times \$100 \text{ Million}) = -\$8 \text{ Million}$$

In addition to the benefits of RI just discussed, it is also possible to use different capital charge rates for different classes of assets, such as 20% for equipment or 8% for inventory.

---

[3] Relating the expected return on capital expenditures to the ROI of a responsibility center is much more complicated than is suggested by these simple examples. ROI performance for an investment center is an accounting measure often exclusive of income taxes whereas ROI as used in capital budgeting is normally either a net present value or the internal rate of return measure, derived from applying present value techniques to estimated future cash flows, almost always on an after-tax basis. Indeed, ROI as applied to historical performance of an investment center and ROI as used in capital budgeting are rarely comparable. (The only exception is when a firm uses the unadjusted rate of return method, as explained in Chapter 7, for evaluating capital expenditures. This too is often called ROI.) Because ROI is used by many executives to refer to both historical accounting results and to prospective cash flows, great care must be exercised to avoid confusion.

But one can't have one's cake and eat it too. It is important to note that even with RI, some of the measurement issues associated with ROI are also inherent in RI. Specifically, one still has to decide how to define income and how to define investment. And the measurement issues like those with inventory and fixed assets discussed above continue to be a challenge.

Economic value added. While some companies started several decades ago using RI to measure financial performance, it was not widely accepted. Operating managers complained that the number was hard to interpret. A positive RI was seen as good, but how much better for a specific operation is a positive RI of $5 million than an RI of 0?

Recently, a reincarnation of residual income has appeared under the name economic valued added (EVA), a term coined by the consulting firm Stern Stewart. EVA is essentially net operating profit minus the cost of capital used to produce the profit. Its success at companies such as Coca-Cola, Quaker Oats, and Scott Paper seems to have come from the way it has helped connect stockholder value and cash flow to operating decisions. Managers who are cognizant of EVA make operating decisions in ways that maximize EVA, not just volume, or profit. For example, EVA may influence decisions on payment terms (longer terms increase the capital used), combining production in one line or one plant, divesting profitable activities whose return is less than the cost of capital, or expanding activities that earn more than the cost of capital used. Use of EVA instead of profit obliges product managers to balance inventory levels with customer service. More inventory may improve customer service, but more inventory has a clear cost under EVA management.

This sounds very logical, but as G. Bennett Stewart says:

> You can't implement EVA overnight. Companies sometimes don't disseminate EVA knowledge widely enough through the organization. Those that understand EVA know how important it is to train everyone in the organization, because even those with the smallest jobs can help create value. This means linking EVA to key operating metrics like cycle time or inventory turns, and making sure the people involved understand how EVA fits in.[4]

The key point is that the mindset produced by knowledge of EVA can influence decisions by people throughout a company, many of whom do not themselves have direct responsibility for EVA, but whose actions and decisions can influence EVA. EVA becomes more than a financial measure; it becomes a guide to operating decisions.

Despite its attractive features, like RI, EVA does not necessarily give the same signals as ROI. EVA can go up while ROI goes down, if the capital base is expanding and producing a return higher than the cost of capital.

Market value added (MVA). This phrase, also developed by Stern Stewart, is a measure of the amount by which the market value of a firm exceeds the money investors and lenders have put into the firm. It is designed to measure how well the firm's managers have done in increasing the value of the money entrusted to their care.

As Stern Stewart computes it, investment is the sum of the amounts invested by stockholders since the firm started, amounts lent to the firm, and earnings retained by the firm. The firm also adds appropriately depreciated capitalized research and development and adds back the amortization of

---

[4] G. Bennett Stewart III, "EVA Works–But Not If You Make These Common Mistakes," *Fortune* (1 May 1995): 117–118.

goodwill if the goodwill is still valuable. In effect, it is saying that those last two should be part of retained earnings, but accounting rules prevent that. Then, the firm subtracts the figure for total investment from the total market value of debt and equity. If the result is positive, the firm's managers have added value; if it's negative, they say value has been destroyed.

Managers and investors began using MVA as an indicator of achievement. Stern Stewart sounds a note of caution, however, that the changes in MVA from one year to the next are heavily dependent on stock market fluctuations and investor preference for certain industries. It says, nevertheless, that over time its research has shown a strong relationship between MVA and EVA. Companies that have consistently shown strong EVA numbers are likely to have high MVA numbers.[5]

THE BALANCED SCORECARD

The balanced scorecard is a performance measurement system intended to provide management with a balanced look at current performance and at those factors that drive future performance. Traditionally, organizations had used financial measures, such as ROI or profit margin, to measure performance. Many recognized that financial measures, while perhaps easily understandable, have shortcomings. Previously, we discussed some of the shortcomings of investment center measures like ROI. In addition, financial measures capture the effect of past and current performance, but do not by themselves provide an indication of future performance.

Nonfinancial measures can be leading indicators of future financial performance. Consider measures of customer satisfaction, for example. Measures that indicate high customer satisfaction may suggest good future performance, but poor customer satisfaction likely suggests the opposite—they may foreshadow a future decline in financial performance. Likewise, measures of product innovation can provide an indication of future performance. Consider the pharmaceutical company with several drugs at different stages in the U.S. Food and Drug Administration's (FDA) approval process. While the effects of those drugs have not yet made their way into the financial statements, considering their stage in the approval process, as well as other data from clinical trials, can provide some indication about future performance. Clearly, continuous monitoring of some of the nonfinancial indicators can give managers insight about the future performance of the company so that they can take necessary measures to capitalize on the strengths those measures identify—or so that they can take corrective action when those measures identify issues that may show up in the financial statements at a later date if left unaddressed.

Certainly, managers were evaluating some of those factors before the balanced scorecard became popular. Can you imagine a pharmaceutical company that does not track the progress of its drugs in development and in the FDA approval process? It's not that nonfinancial measures were being ignored. But the introduction of the balanced scorecard concept by Robert S. Kaplan and David P. Norton in 1992 provided a vehicle for organizations to formalize the inclusion of both financial and nonfinancial measures in a comprehensive performance measurement system.

---

[5] Anne B. Fisher, "Creating Stockholder Wealth," *Fortune* (11 December 1995): 105.

As described by Kaplan and Norton,[6] the balanced scorecard contains measures of performance from four perspectives:

1. *Financial*: the shareholders' perspective. Measures such as return on capital employed, cash flow, EVA, sales growth, or profit forecast reliability.

2. *The customer perspective*: for example, measures of customer satisfaction, response time, delivery reliability, and quality.

3. *The internal business perspective*: for example, measures of process reliability, rework, inventory level, employee turnover.

4. *An innovation and learning perspective*: for example, measures of the percentage of revenue from new products or services, number of employee-generated new ideas, progress on process changes and improvement programs.

Again, the balanced scorecard includes financial measures as one of its perspectives. It also, though, includes three other perspectives that provide a more balanced look at a firm's performance as well as an indication of future financial performance.

A close look at how the balanced scorecard is being used shows that it is more than the identification of multiple objectives and measurements. It is really a strategic management system. Successful use in a number of companies shows the following:

1. The balanced scorecard helps clarify the links between strategy and action. For example, if the strategy is to enter new markets or design new products, each of the four perspectives will be affected—measures related to that strategy likely will be incorporated into all four of them. The scorecard provides strategic guidance to managers, letting them know what is important for them to focus on. And it encourages managers to be specific about what they want to accomplish and how to measure progress.

2. The process of identifying the measures is often more important than the scorecard data. If that process involves managers from a variety of functions, the scorecard provides a basis for examining the interdependence of the functions. Key objectives in each perspective must be identified and their interdependence with other perspectives put on the table for discussion. A target for improved customer response, for example, would have an impact on internal objectives. Innovation and learning would require management attention, time, and costs. The scorecard provides a useful template for choosing and building management initiatives.

3. The impact of using the balanced scorecard may be strongest when it is part of a process of change. It helps top management communicate a new or revised strategy to the rest of the organization. (Remember that performance measures provide guidance, and what gets measured will get attention.) It provides a discipline to help managers coordinate to bring about the desired change.

---

[6] Robert S. Kaplan and David P. Norton, "Balanced Scorecard–Measures that Drive Performance," *Harvard Business Review* (January–February 1992): 71; Robert S. Kaplan and David P. Norton, "Putting the Balanced Scorecard to Work," *Harvard Business Review* (September–October 1993): 134; and Robert S. Kaplan and David P. Norton, "Using the Balanced Scorecard as a Strategic Management System," *Harvard Business Review* (January–February 1996): 75.

INCENTIVE AND REWARD SYSTEMS

The incentive and reward systems of an organization are essential to management control, because both are intended to provide motivation. Performance measures provide motivation and guidance to managers about what they should focus on. Remember—what gets measured gets attention. Sometimes the two systems are directly related, however, as when bonuses or other incentives are tied directly to performance measures. Under those circumstances, motivation is intensified—what get measured and tied to money gets a lot of attention.

Bonus plans are common in many companies. While they have many benefits, not the least of which are the motivational benefits they provide, they pose many challenges for management to consider. First, they may result in unintended consequences. Consider the following example. Company X organizes its plants as investment centers. The company provides a bonus to all plant managers whose plants earn a profit for the year. The bonus is equal to 5% of all profits in excess of budgeted profit up to a maximum bonus of $50,000. This bonus plan is depicted in the following graph.

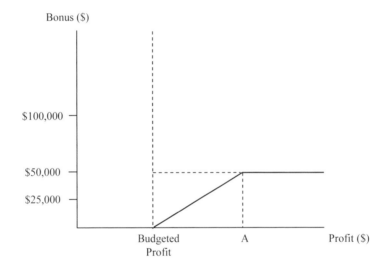

The manager begins to earn a bonus once the profit reaches the budgeted level. He continues to earn 5% of profits until profit reaches A, the point at which the manager has earned $50,000. If profit exceeds A, the manager earns no additional bonus.

At first glance, that may appear to be a good incentive plan, for it motivates plant managers to make a profit and to exceed their budgets. For the company in question, however, it has several shortcomings. First of all, the overall management control system emphasizes return on investment, not just profit, since the plants are organized as investment centers. But the bonus is paid based on profit. What results is a lack of goal congruence—managers might overinvest in assets to produce a product whose price more than covers any additional expenses incurred to make it, so they can maximize their profits. The plant's ROI decreases, which certainly wasn't what management intended when it implemented the bonus system, but profit goes up. Second, the stipulation that only those plants earning a profit were eligible meant that several plants, where even a tight budget reflected an expected loss, were ineligible—even though meeting the budget would still have represented good performance on the part of the manager. Third, placing the bonus on the difference between actual profit and budgeted profit put as much pressure on plant managers to budget low as it did to produce efficiently. Finally, limiting the bonus to $50,000 only served to dampen the managers' enthusiasm once they had approached or exceeded that $50,000 limit. In fact, they might have even been motivated to hold back and save something for next year (perhaps a cost-saving idea, a new product, or a special customer). Indeed, it is well documented that bonus plans such as those lead to some of those unintended consequences.[7]

Another thorny issue in the design of reward systems is the extent to which the reward should be based on a predetermined formula. Recently, in a company with a formula-based bonus system, top management concluded at the end of the year that one division had exceptional performance because its major competitor had been shut down for six weeks by a strike, while another division did poorly because a large customer had experienced financial difficulty. In fact, the senior vice president reviewing the performances believed that the first division could have done even better than it did and that the manager of the second division showed great skill in avoiding a major disaster. The vice president then wondered whether it was appropriate to base the bonus on the predetermined formula, thereby in this case rewarding luck more than competence, or whether some amount of *ex post* judgment should be part of the reward system. Incorporating the ability to use judgment to adjust rewards that are determined by the bonus formula allows the vice president to take out the effect of the factors that the managers can't control or influence, but it brings an element of subjectivity into the bonus system.

Finally, if you implement a performance measurement system and then tie those performance measures to the manager's wallet through an incentive system, you had better make sure you have the right measures. As we mentioned previously, what gets measured gets attention. What gets measured and compensated gets *a lot* of attention. And you want what is getting a lot of attention to be the thing the organization really needs the manager to focus on.

There is really no clear answer to those issues. Designing incentive systems is tricky. Perhaps the most important thing is for management to be aware of and understand some of the potential shortcomings of those systems, so that they can consider them in their decision-making process. Variability of the environment and the scope of the manager's assignment are important. If mixed signals are to be avoided, great care must be taken to relate rewards to strategic objectives, performance expectations, and the management control system.

SUMMARY

In this chapter, we have elaborated on the topics of performance measurement and incentive systems. We can sum up what we have said with the phrase: "What gets measured gets attention." Performance measures suggest to managers what is important to focus on and, as a result, they influence managers' decisions.

We discussed choosing the right performance measure. First, the organization must identify its key success factors. At that point, choosing the performance measures can begin. That choice, however, is not a simple one. Even once the measure is chosen, it is important to give attention to how the elements of that measure are defined, and what direction is implied by the measure.

We must decide whether to evaluate the manager and the unit he manages using the same, or different, performance measures. Here, the extent to which the manager can control the factors that affect the performance measure is important.

We discussed several alternative measures used to evaluate investment center performance: ROI, RI, EVA, and MVA. We noted that ROI is perhaps the most frequently used investment center performance

---

[7] For example, see P. Healy, "The Effect of Bonus Schemes on Accounting Decisions," *Journal of Accounting and Economics* 7 (1985): 85–107.

measure. Despite its popularity, it has several shortcomings, which we discussed. We noted how RI, EVA, and MVA can help to overcome some, but not all, of those shortcomings.

The balanced scorecard has become a popular approach to performance measurement in organizations. We discussed its four perspectives, the reasons for using the balanced scorecard, and some of the scorecard's benefits.

Finally, we discussed some aspects of incentive and reward systems. We noted that attaching incentives or rewards to performance measures substantially increases their motivational features. We noted, however, that there are many challenges in developing those systems and that there is no perfect system. Each organization must consider its specific objectives and circumstances in designing an incentive system and must be aware of any unintended consequences that may arise as a result of its implementation, so that management may manage around those consequences.

QUESTIONS AND PROBLEMS

10–1. What does residual income mean and why would a company choose to use it? What would you say to an investment center manager who was upset because his operation showed what seemed to be a good profit but a negative residual income?

10–2. *Economic value added.* The Victor Paper Company was considering the use of economic value added as a way of measuring the performance of its business. Herman Victor, the company's president, asked his controller, Carol Starkey, to develop some illustrations of how the use of EVA might affect various kinds of decisions. Starkey put together this problem, approximately based on the company's financial statements and an actual sales decision.

The sales office is asked by a large customer to accept an order for $1.11 million of paper, spread over 12 months. The cost of the specified high-rag content material would be $100,000 higher than normal for an order, but the price offered by the customer more than covered the higher material cost. The customer also asked for 4-month payment terms instead of the usual 30 days.

Analysis of the job to be done showed that although the job required higher cost material, production would involve normal conversion activities and hence the order could be expected to use capacity equivalent to an average $1 million order.

A comparison showed the following figures:

	Average Order	This Order
Sales	$1,000,000	$1,110,000
Material	350,000	450,000
Contribution	$ 650,000	$ 660,000

Approximate figures in millions of dollars for the company as a whole were:

Balance Sheet		Income Statement	
Current assets	$3.0	Sales	$10.0
Noncurrent assets	9.0		
Total assets	$12.0	Material	3.5
		Conversion	4.2
Current liabilities	$2.0	Administration*	0.8
Long-term debt	5.0	Total expense	8.5
Equity	5.0	Net before tax	1.5
Total liab. & equity	$12.0	Tax at 40%	0.6
		Net after tax	$0.9

* Administration is half interest and half other expense.

Starkey computed the firm's EVA as follows: total assets minus current liabilities (i.e., capital) = $10.0 million; cost of capital = 10%; capital charge = $1.0 million; net after tax = $0.9 million; add back after-tax cost of interest ($0.4 million × 0.6 = $0.24 million); adjusted net after tax ($1.14 million) minus the capital charge of $1.0 million leaves $0.14 million EVA.

Starkey's illustrative problem ended with this question. Would acceptance of the proposed order improve Victor's EVA?

10–3. *Economic value added.* Brad Chase is a marketing manager for Sydney Steel Company. His responsibility is to sell structural steel to building contractors. He makes daily decisions on price, terms of payment, delivery schedules, and sourcing, which could be from Sidney's two warehouses or direct from the factory. In general, he acts as an interface between the company and its customers, working to become fully knowledgeable about each potential customer as well as the market in his assigned geographical area. Brad's compensation is salary plus bonus. The bonus is a percentage of sales, modified by the amount by which each sale is below the list price. The greater the discount, the smaller the bonus.

Two weeks ago Brad's boss, the marketing vice president, told him that the president had instituted a training program on economic value added. Brad went to the day-long session, where EVA was explained. It seemed like a complicated financial formula, but he was relieved that the designated cost of capital was a nice round 10%. Nevertheless, since Brad knew he did not have direct responsibility for profit, he wasn't clear how it applied to him. Do you think EVA analysis applied to Brad's job? If so, how?

APPENDIX A

BASIC ACCOUNTING PROCESSES USED IN PREPARING FINANCIAL STATEMENTS

A firm owns things such as inventory, machines, and accounts receivable from customers. Those are called assets. Usually a firm will also owe money to people, suppliers, banks, or bondholders. As such, the firm has liabilities. If assets exceed liabilities, the difference, called *net assets*, represents the owners' equity in the business.

During the year, many transactions take place, affecting assets, liabilities, or owners' equity. We shall look at some of these in a minute, but first let us see how double-entry bookkeeping helps keep track of all these transactions.

We start with the equation reflected in the first paragraph:

$$\text{Assets} - \text{Liabilities} = \text{Owners' Equity}$$

or

$$\text{Assets} = \text{Liabilities} + \text{Owners' Equity}$$

Now try thinking of the second equation as a balance or a set of scales.

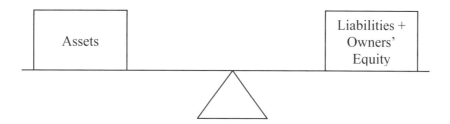

The scale must always be in balance. We can exchange one asset for another (cash for raw material) and not upset the balance. Or we can reduce an asset and a liability (cash used to pay back bank debt). Profit comes about when we have a net increase in assets. For example, we might receive $120 cash for a product with an asset value of $100. To keep in balance, owners' equity must increase $20, which is the profit on the transaction.

With thousands or millions of transactions to record, we need a system to translate what happens in each transaction into accounting terms that define the transaction's effect on assets, liabilities, or owners' equity. The system used by virtually every business, called double-entry bookkeeping, enables all transactions to be recorded in a way that keeps the books balanced. The records consist of *accounts*, with categories such as cash, accounts receivable, inventory, and trade payables. Some of those accounts are *permanent* and their balances on December 31 make up the firm's balance sheet. Other accounts are *temporary* and disappear at the end of the year. Most of those temporary accounts are expense or revenue accounts, and their balances are transferred to a profit and loss account; that in turn is closed to the retained earnings account, which is one of the owners' equity accounts. Each account has a left hand and a right hand. (A left-hand balance or entry is called a debit, while a right-hand balance or entry is called a credit, but don't worry about those labels just now.) To see how the left- and right-hand entries to the accounts work, we must expand our picture of the accounting equation (Assets = Liabilities + Owners' Equity), so that all the accounts have space for both left-hand and right-hand entries.

Asset Accounts

Left hand (Debit) Balance or increase	Right hand (Credit) Decrease

Examples:
  Cash
  Plant, equipment
  Inventory
  Accounts receivable

Liabilities Account

Left hand (Debit) Decrease	Right hand (Credit) Balance or increase

Examples:
  Trade payables
  Long-term debt
  Accrued wages

Owners' Equity Accounts

Left hand (Debit) Decrease	Right hand (Credit) Balance or increase

Examples:
  Capital stock
  Retained earnings

Every account has a left and a right. The balances shown in asset accounts are usually on the left, and balances in liability and owners' equity accounts are usually on the right. At any one time, the total of all the left-hand balances must equal the total of all the right-hand balances. Double-entry bookkeeping keeps this overall balance, because every transaction or event is translated into both left- and right-hand entries, and for each transaction the left entries must equal the right entries. Here are some examples:

Transaction	Left-Hand Entry	Right-hand Entry
Purchase of material on account	An increase in the inventory asset account is a left-hand entry	An increase in the accounts payable liability account is a right-hand entry
Payment of the bill	Accounts payable (decrease in liability account)	Cash (decrease in asset account)
Payment of employees who work on the material	Material-in-process asset account (increase – asset)	Cash (decrease – asset)
Purchase of a machine to work on the material	An increase in the machine asset by the cost of the machine (increase – asset)	An increase in the bank loan liability account used to pay for the machine (increase – liability)
Wearing out of the machine as it is used	An increase in the cost of goods produced (an inventory asset) by a portion of the machine's cost, called depreciation	A decrease in the machines asset by a portion of the machine's cost—shown as accumulated depreciation
Rent on office	Expense for period (decrease – owners' equity)	Cash (decrease – asset)
Sales – revenue part	Accounts receivable (increase – asset)	Sales (increase – owner's equity)
Sales – cost part	Cost of goods sold (decrease – owners' equity)	Finished goods (decrease – asset)

Notice that the first five of those are simply transfers among asset and liability accounts. Rent, however, decreases owners' equity. Whereas the payment to production employees was *capitalized* (i.e., added to an asset), the rent was *expensed* (i.e., considered an immediate reduction in owners' equity). The labor cost will be expensed later when the inventory asset to which it is added is sold. Until that time, it is held as an asset and does not affect owners' equity.

We can see that many of the transactions that affect owners' equity are those that recognize income and appear on the income statement. In effect, the income statement can be considered a temporary subset of accounts within the owners' equity set of accounts. The income statement account, or as it is sometimes called the *profit and loss account*, is one of the temporary accounts. At the end of the period, when financial statements are to be prepared, the balance remaining in the profit and loss account is the difference between all the expenses (debits to the P&L account) and revenues (credits to the P&L account). That is the net profit for the period and at this point, it is transferred to the retained earnings account. That closes the P&L account to zero, so it can start from scratch in the next period. The P&L account is a *temporary* account and as such does not show up among the permanent balance sheet accounts. The retained earnings account is permanent. It is increased by net income after tax and decreased by payment of dividends. The end result of posting revenue and expense accounts and then closing those balances to the P&L account (from which the income statement is prepared) and then closing that balance to the retained earnings account is illustrated as follows:

Retained Earnings

	Beginning balance
Expense transactions and other debits	Revenue transactions and other credits
Dividends paid	
	Ending balance = beginning balance for the next period

Income statement is prepared from these items ← (Expense transactions and other debits; Dividends paid)

Each year (or period if monthly or quarterly statements are being prepared), retained earnings increase by net income for the period (revenues less expenses) minus any dividends paid or promised. The ending balance in retained earnings is really the total of all net income or loss since the company began less all dividends paid out over that time. Instead of retained earnings, it should probably be called earnings retained (i.e., all profits and losses since inception less whatever has been paid out to the shareholders.) A very simple example might look like this:

Retained Earnings

		10,000	Balance 1/1/06
Cost of sales	2,700	6,500	Sales
Marketing expense	1,100	300	Interest income
Interest expense	400		
Administrative expense	800		
Income tax expense	450		
Dividends	200		
		11,150	Balance 12/31/06 and Balance 1/1/07

The income statement would be prepared from the shaded entries and would be:

Income Statement

Very Simple Example Company

Sales	$6,500
Less: cost of sales	2,700
Gross margin	$3,800
Less:	
Marketing expense	1,100
Administrative expense	800
Operating income	$1,900
Interest income	300
Interest expense	(400)
Income before income tax	$1,800
Provision for income taxes	450
Net income	$1,350

Note that net income minus dividends ($1,350 – $200) equals the change in retained earnings during the period. That is how two balance sheets (beginning and end of period) are related to the income statement for that period.

DEBITS AND CREDITS

The terms debit and credit in accounting mean nothing more or less than left-hand entry (debit) and right-hand entry (credit). A debit entry may be an increase in an asset or a decrease in a liability or the owners' equity account. A credit is just the opposite. The word *credit* sometimes carries a favorable connotation, but as one can see, a credit, such as a decrease in cash or an increase in notes payable, is not necessarily good. The term probably gets its favorable connotation by being looked at by an outsider—a customer, for example. When a customer gets credit from a store for overpayment of a bill or returned merchandise, that increases the store's liability to the customer (or decreases its receivables). This is good for the customer, but bad for the store. So remember: debit = left-hand entry; credit = right-hand entry.

COST ACCUMULATION

When costs are incurred to run a business and to produce a product or provide a service, the accountant must decide whether the costs are to be capitalized (for example: added to inventory) or expensed right away. In making that decision, the accountant has some leeway, but basically the determination rests on whether the costs are product or service costs, which are sometimes called production costs. Product or service costs, whether labor, material, or overhead, are added to the inventory cost of the product or service. That determination can affect profits, because any costs that are added to inventory—which, in turn, is not sold during the period—are not expenses of that period. And, incidentally, that shows the difference between costs and expenses. A cost is an expense only if it becomes a debit (decrease) in owners' equity, and hence shows up on the income statement. Costs that are added to unsold inventory, or a cost on a service project that is incomplete, are not expenses of the period. They become expenses when the inventory is sold or the service is delivered, and appear as cost of goods sold or cost of services provided on the income statement for that period.

BALANCE SHEET AND INCOME STATEMENTS

The balance sheet presents a picture at a point in time of the balances in the asset, liability, and owners' equity accounts. The income statement shows the change in the retained earnings account from one balance sheet date to the next. (The other accounts under owners' equity, such as capital stock, capital in excess of par value, preferred stock, and repurchased or treasury stock, do not generally change unless shares of stock are sold or repurchased, or a stock dividend is declared.) The income statement, therefore, tells how much profit the firm made, which is the same as saying how much the owners' equity increased during the period as a result of operations.

By comparing two balance sheets, such as last year's and this year's, we can tell how the composition of assets and liabilities changed during the intervening period. That is important because it reflects such things as liquidity, debt position, and so on. If assets shift from short-term receivables into long-term fixed assets, the firm's liquidity, or ability to come up with cash quickly, is diminished. If that happens while short-term debt is being increased, a dangerous condition could result from using short-term money to buy long-term assets.

Ratios are helpful in analyzing balance sheets, ratios such as the *current ratio*, which is current assets (cash, receivables, and inventory) divided by current liabilities (payables due within a year) and the *debt to equity ratio*. Often the absolute level of a ratio is less important than its trend or speed of change. A high debt to equity ratio may be good or bad depending on the type of business. A rapidly increasing ratio, however, is almost always a cause for concern and may be very difficult to reverse. Appendix B has further discussion on the use of ratios in analyzing financial statements.

CASH FLOW VERSUS NET INCOME

One might expect that the excess of revenue over expenses (which is net income) would result in an increase in the cash account by the same amount. That almost never happens because there are many factors that would cause this to not be true. The factors fall into two basic categories:

1. Some expenses recorded in the income statement may not represent cash expenditure during the period (for example: depreciation) and some revenue may not represent cash inflow (for example: amortization of customer advance payments). Additionally, many revenue and expense items in the income statement were not received or paid in cash at the same amounts. Income tax expense may have been $118 million, but taxes actually paid may have been much different.

2. Increases or decreases in assets, liabilities, and owners' equity accounts (the latter for reasons other than net income) will imply a source or application of cash. For example, if inventory rises from January 1 to December 31, that implies an application or use of cash in that the firm has apparently spent cash in buying inventory. Of course, if payables to suppliers went up at the same time, that would represent a source of cash, because in effect the firm is borrowing cash from its suppliers. From that, we can see the following:

> Uses of cash come about with increases in assets, decreases in liabilities, or decreases in owners' equity;

> Sources of cash come about with decreases in assets, increases in liabilities, or increases in owners' equity.

Companies publish a statement (along with their annual balance sheet and income statement) called the *statement of cash flows*. That statement is a listing of the sources and uses of cash for the year arranged into three general categories:

- Cash flow from operations;
- Cash flow from investing;
- Cash flow from financing.

Appendix B explains that statement and shows how it can be usefully analyzed.

APPENDIX B

UNDERSTANDING FINANCIAL STATEMENTS

The financial reports, which are issued quarterly and annually by companies, contain a wealth of information for those who know how to extract it. The purpose of this appendix is to help you discover what those reports can tell you. The first part explains the numbers contained in the reports and the second part shows how a little analysis using ratios can reveal a lot about what is going on in the company. In this appendix, we have tried to select the most important aspects of the reports. There are many other fine points in financial accounting that only a larger book could properly explore. Furthermore, since the financial accounting standards that guide the preparation of reports are continually being reviewed and are revised from time to time, a complete understanding of the accounting process that lies behind financial statements is a major undertaking. Our purpose here is to explain the basic items you will find in most statements and, without attempting to exhaust all possibilities, to show how a little analysis can greatly increase the amount you can learn from those reports. We will use the 2005 PepsiCo, Inc., Annual Report as an illustration.

THE FOUR BASIC FINANCIAL STATEMENTS

Published annual reports are now required to contain these four statements.

1. The *balance sheet* shows the firm's assets, liabilities, and shareholders' equity, for both last year and this year.

2. The *income statement* shows revenues, expenses, and net income, typically for three years. The statement also shows net income per common share figured two ways:

   - Basic earnings per share (EPS) is simply net income divided by the total number of common shares outstanding.

   - Diluted EPS adjusts for convertible preferred stock, convertible debt, and in-the-money stock options, which if changed into common stock, would be dilutive.

3. The *statement of cash flows* explains where cash came from during the year, such as from net income or borrowing, and where cash went or what it was used for, such as for capital expenditures and debt repayment. The net of those sources and applications is the year's increase or decrease in cash. The statement shows sources and uses of cash grouped according to cause: operating activities, investing activities, and financing activities. In this format, the statement tells a lot about the changes in a company's financial position. More will be said on that shortly.

4. The *statement of shareholders' equity* explains the changes in each of the shareholders' equity accounts: common stock (and perhaps capital in excess of par value, if the common stock has a par value), retained earnings, treasury stock, and an account with the ominous title of "accumulated other comprehensive gains and losses." If a company has no par value stock as many do, each time a new issue of stock is sold to the public, the common stock account is increased by the total amount of cash received from the sale less the fees paid to

the underwriters. There is no practical significance to having par or no-par stock anymore, but for a company with par stock—perhaps $0.10/share, if a new issue of stock is sold to the public—the common stock account is increased by the $0.10 times the number of shares sold. The remainder of the net proceeds increases the capital in excess of par account. We discussed retained earnings in Appendix A. Treasury stock is the company's stock that has been bought back from its owners. Companies sometimes use those shares for acquisitions, or to sell to employees, or others exercising their stock options. Sometimes a company will buy back its own shares, because it feels the stock is unrealistically low or it has excess cash or both.

Explanation of the Balance Sheet

The discussion will follow the entries shown in PepsiCo, Inc.'s 2005 statements, copies of which are at the end of this appendix. These statements serve us well, because they have been condensed to a relatively small number of entries and are clearly stated.

First, notice the overall structure of the balance sheet.

Current assets	Current liabilities
Noncurrent assets*	Noncurrent liabilities*
Total assets	Total liabilities
	Preferred stock, no par value
	Repurchased preferred stock
	Common stock, 1 2/3 cent par value
	Capital in excess of par value
	Retained earnings
	Accumulated other comprehensive loss
	Repurchased common stock
	Total common shareholders' equity
	Total liabilities and shareholders' equity

* The subtotal is not shown as a separate item.

PepsiCo puts all those items on one page and lines them up vertically. However, one can see that assets equal liabilities plus shareholders' equity. Thus, the balance sheet balances.

Items are separated into current and noncurrent categories to help analysts see the balance between current assets and current liabilities. Working capital is the amount by which current assets exceed current liabilities, or working capital. In a way, working capital says how much cash the firm would have, if it had turned all its current assets into cash and paid off its current liabilities. But, since few firms are about to do that, the liquidation view is rather artificial. However, creditors who are lending to a company do view working capital as sort of a liquidity cushion, or as a funds reservoir needed to keep the enterprise operating smoothly. Since some kinds of businesses naturally need more operating funds than others, creditors are less concerned with the level of that reservoir than with how the level changes from period to period. A sizable decrease could impair the firm's ability to operate.

A consolidated financial statement, such as PepsiCo presents, means that the statements of subsidiaries have been combined with the parent company's statements to present a consolidated picture. The process of combining is basically one of adding the assets and liabilities of subsidiaries to the assets and liabilities of the parent, eliminating receivables or payables (from the balance sheet) or transactions (from the income statement) between them. Subsidiaries that are more than 50% owned are usually consolidated. When a company owns a minority interest, it is shown as an asset labeled "investment." When others own a minority interest in a consolidated subsidiary, the consolidation process still combines 100% of the assets and liabilities, but then represents the minority interest in the equity section of the balance sheet.

Balance Sheet Items

Cash and cash equivalents. The amount shown here represents both what is in checking accounts and the ownership of temporary investments such as certificates of deposit (with original maturities not exceeding three months) as part of PepsiCo's management of day-to-day operating cash receipts and disbursements. As of December 31, 2005, those totaled $1,716 million for PepsiCo.

Short-term investments. These include all other investment portfolios of a longer term than would appear under cash, but with maturities of less than one year.

Accounts and notes receivable. These are the amounts owed by others, usually customers. One can get a rough indication of how many days net sales they represent from this formula (receivables less expected uncollectible accounts and sales in millions of dollars):

$$\frac{\text{Receivables}}{\text{Net Sales for the Year}} \times 365 \text{ Days} = \text{Days of Receivables}$$

For PepsiCo, this is:

$$\frac{\$3,261}{\$32,562} \times 365 = 0.1 \times 365 = 37$$

This says that, on the average, PepsiCo's receivables were outstanding 37 days before being paid. Some, of course, were paid earlier, while others were paid later. This calculation also builds on the assumption that sales during the last quarter (which caused the receivables) were about average for the year, since the total year's sales figure was used.

If we use the fourth quarter's sales of $10,096 (PepsiCo's fourth quarter is 17 weeks):

$$\frac{\text{Receivables}}{\text{4th Quarter Sales}} = \frac{\$3,261}{\$10,096} \times \frac{17}{52} \times 365 \text{ Days} = 0.32 \times 119 = 38 \text{ Days}$$

Inventories. The cost of raw materials, work in process, and finished goods are represented here. According to footnote 14 of it statement, PepsiCo used LIFO (last in, first out) for 17% of its inventories, so in those cases the unit costs charged against income each year were based on the latest prices. This means that the costs remaining in inventory were based on old prices, some going back to the year PepsiCo started using the LIFO method. However, PepsiCo tells us that the difference between LIFO and FIFO methods are immaterial.

Prepaid expenses and other current assets. Payments made prior to an expense being recognized in income, such as insurance, are recorded as assets on the balance sheet. Miscellaneous short-term assets (less than one year) are also included in this category.

Investments in noncontrolled affiliates. These categories include investments in companies in which PepsiCo exercises significant influence, but not control (typically between 20% and 50% ownership), which are accounted for by the equity method. Under that method, investments in noncontrolled affiliates are shown at cost plus PepsiCo's share of its net income since acquisition less cash dividends received. Other assets include prepaid pension costs and other, smaller miscellaneous assets.

Property, plant, and equipment. This represents all capital assets (i.e., those lasting over a year). Except for land, these assets will be depreciated each year. An amount representing the year's depreciation will be subtracted from the asset on the balance sheet and from revenue on the income statement. The income statement deduction will reduce net income and, in turn, reduce the retained earnings entry on the balance sheet, thereby offsetting the decrease in fixed assets and keeping the balance sheet in balance. The $8,681 million shown by PepsiCo on its balance sheet represents the net figure. In a footnote, PepsiCo tells us that the gross (original cost) figure is $17,145 million and the offsetting accumulated depreciation is $8,464 million. On average, PepsiCo's depreciable assets were about 49% depreciated.

Amortizable intangible assets net, include the cost of brands, contracts, and other investments that have limited lives. Typically, those would include brands purchased in acquisitions, which are not expected to have indefinite lives. Amortizable means that this asset is being expensed over its remaining useful life.

Goodwill is the excess of the purchase price PepsiCo paid for another company over that company's net asset value. This sort of premium is not unusual; it represents the difference between the market value of a firm (which is typically the present value of the expected future cash flows) and its net asset value. Annually PepsiCo projects future cash flows of the acquired business unit and impairs or writes down the goodwill, if that future value is below the related book value.

Other non-amortizable intangible assets include the cost of perpetual brands purchased when a business was acquired. A perpetual brand is believed to have an indefinite life, so it is not amortized; however, like goodwill, it is subject to annual impairment testing. Pepsi and Frito-Lay can be thought of as brands with an indefinite life, but they were not purchased by the company. Perpetual brands at PepsiCo today would be products like Quaker Oats, Tropicana, and Gatorade.

Short-term obligations are the amounts due within the next year on PepsiCo's long-term debt, commercial paper, and other borrowings.

Accounts payable and other current liabilities are amounts owed to suppliers, employees, and others. They also include accruals for advertising, insurance, and other expenses that have been incurred by PepsiCo, but where no invoice has been received. Since no interest is paid on those liabilities, they represent a significant, free source of funds for the company.

Income taxes payable. A company accrues taxes as it earns income. Periodic payments will reduce this accrued amount. At the end of a year, the accrued amount is really an estimate, because the financial report will probably be prepared before the company's tax return is filed.

Long-term debt obligations. These obligations include short-term borrowings that will be refinanced, notes due at dates over the next 20 years, and zero coupon notes, which pay no interest, but were sold at a discount when issued.

Other liabilities. This includes a number of long-term liabilities pertaining to financing. It also includes a portion of the present value of future pension and healthcare benefits, which PepsiCo has obligated itself to pay for certain of its retired employees.

Deferred income taxes. This liability is the accumulated difference between what PepsiCo recorded as income tax expense on its income statements and what was actually owed or paid to the Internal Revenue Service (IRS) and other governments. This difference arises because tax accounting and generally accepted accounting principles (GAAP) have different conventions, which temporarily treat some expenses and revenues differently. For example, a company may use accelerated depreciation for taxes and straight line for book accounting. On the other hand, taxing authorities typically forbid deductions for estimated bad debts and obsolete inventory, but they do recognize deductions when an account turns out to be uncollectible or when obsolete inventory is scrapped.

Preferred stock, no par value and repurchased preferred stock. PepsiCo has a small amount of preferred stock outstanding ($41 million) related to employee stock ownership in a company acquired by PepsiCo. In a footnote, the company tells us that there were 803,953 preferred shares outstanding and that by December 31, 2005, 449,100 of those shares had been repurchased. The preferred shares must have been issued at:

$$\frac{\$41,000,000}{803,953 \text{ Shares}} = \$51/\text{Share}$$

and the repurchased shares, on average, cost the company:

$$\frac{\$110,000,000}{449,100 \text{ Shares}} = \$245/\text{Share}$$

which reflects the increased value of those shares.

Common stock, par value 1 2/3 cents per share and capital in excess of par value. PepsiCo has sold new shares of its stock from time to time. Over the history of the firm, 1,782 million shares have been sold at a total net amount of $644 million ($30 million + $614 million). Thus, PepsiCo sold shares, on average, for:

$$\frac{\$644,000,000}{1,782,000,000 \text{ Shares}} = \$0.36/\text{Share}$$

For historical reasons, the company's shares had a par value of 1 2/3 cents, so:

$$1,782 \text{ Million} \times \$0.016666 = 29.7 \text{ Million}$$

This number was rounded to $30 million. The $30 million in proceeds was ascribed to common stock at par value and the remainder ($644 million − $30 million) was ascribed to capital in excess of par value. Since par value today has no practical significance, many companies with par value common stock simply combine the two items and show them as common stock and then disclose the details in a footnote.

Retained earnings. These are the total earnings of the company over time, minus the cash dividends paid. Note that most of the total shareholders' equity ($14,320 million at December 31, 2005) came from retained earnings or net profits as opposed to sales of the company's stock to its shareholders.

Accumulated other comprehensive loss. Some gains and losses, which affect assets or liabilities, are deferred as opposed to being included in the year's income statements, because it is possible that those gains and losses will reverse themselves in future periods. The largest item in this account relates to foreign-currency translation adjustments.

Repurchased common stock. As of December 31, 2005, PepsiCo had repurchased 126 million of its own shares, which had been trading in the stock markets. On average, it paid:

$$\frac{\$6,387,000,000}{126,000,000 \text{ Shares}} = \$50.69$$

Those are the same shares that were sold on average for $0.36. Those repurchased shares are actually assets of the company, but they represent ownership in the company itself. So instead of appearing on the left side of the balance sheet with all the other assets, they are shown on the right side as a deduction from owners' equity. These shares can be reissued to satisfy stock option plans or to pay for an acquisition.

Explanation of the Statement of Income

The income statement presents the revenue and expense transactions that have taken place during the year, quarter, or whatever accounting period is covered. The difference between the revenue and expense is net income.

This explanation sounds very simple, but there are many issues and decisions lying behind the determination of revenue and expense. Here are a few.

Revenue recognition. A computer company signs a $60 million three-year contract with a customer for hardware, software, and customer support. The client has agreed to make annual payments of $25 million, $20 million, and $15 million over this period. The hardware and original software suite is to be delivered and installed in the first 120 days; consulting will take place from time to time over the next three years, software upgrades will come mostly in the first year while customer support demands are likely to increase over time.

How much revenue can or should the company report in year one? It should be obvious that one can't claim the whole $60 million, nor does it make sense to treat the $25 million as sales for the year just because that's how much cash came in. Somehow, that $60 million must be unbundled and assigned to the various products and services being provided. Next, the company must have a way to determine when the product has been delivered or the service provided; then and only then can it be a sale. If the hardware and original software suite has been installed and accepted by the client, then that portion of the $60 million becomes a sale, in that year or quarter, depending upon the reporting period. The consulting and customer support revenue should be recognized over the time periods when the service is provided and in the amounts reflecting the amount of service provided.

Cost matching. Closely related to revenue recognition is cost matching. The cost of the hardware, installation, and original software suite should not be expensed as incurred, but should be inventoried or capitalized. Then when the revenue for those pieces is recognized, the cost should be expensed. The cost for consulting and customer support should probably be expensed as those costs are incurred, which should parallel the recognition of revenue for those services. Obviously, revenue recognition and cost matching are related.

Expense versus capitalized cost. In another example, a firm spends $1 million fixing its steam-generating plant, which has been operating for 10 years with only minor repairs. Is this to be considered a major repair, and therefore an expense, or an overhaul extending the generating plant's life, and therefore a capital expenditure, which adds to the value of the asset and does not affect expense, except through depreciation of the asset? The answer will have an effect on net income during the year of the expenditure. Similar questions apply to development costs on major new product lines, as with a commercial airplane, or the costs of entering a new market such as in a foreign country.

Estimates and judgment. Almost all the figures in the financial statement are based, in part, on management's estimates and judgment. We saw in the computer company example mentioned previously just how much judgment went toward assigning the $60 million revenue to the proper periods, and we saw the challenge of deciding how to account for the $ 1 million fix up to the steam plant. Such decisions are commonplace. Let's continue with the steam plant. Suppose it has been decided that this must be capitalized, then the next decision is how to determine depreciation. First, we must determine the scrap or salvage value from the million-dollar project. If $50,000 is expected to be recovered at the end of its useful life, then the total amount of depreciation is only $950,000.

Next is the question of period, or the number of years over which the asset should be depreciated; then having settled the depreciable life there is the question of a pattern. Should a straight line (the same each year) or an accelerated pattern (more in the early years) be used? The choice is frequently determined more by the tax impact than by engineering evidence but, in any case, the choice is one of timing and significantly affects net income.

In June 2005, PepsiCo reported that its most critical accounting policies, where estimates and judgements were most important, related to:

- Revenue recognition;

- Brand and goodwill evaluation;

- Income tax expense and accruals;

- Stock-based compensation expenses;

- Pension and retiree medical plans.

Taking the top one on the list in 2005, PepsiCo reported net revenues of $32.6 billion and net income of $4.1 billion. The company also reported that revenue was net of an estimated $8.9 billion in discounts and incentives that were granted to customers for volume purchases and other activities. If this $8.9 billion estimate was off just 5% either way, net income could be either $3.8 billion or $4.4 billion. You see the significance of estimates and judgment.

The use of reserves for future expenses or losses. When a product is guaranteed, there is likely to be warranty expense for subsequent repair of some of the products. At the time of sale, one can only guess at the amount. This guess, which creates a reserve, reduces revenue in the year of the sale. When claims come in later, they are not an expense of that period, but are charged to the reserve as long as it lasts. If the reserve runs out, subsequent warranty claims become an expense of the period in which the claims are paid. When those charges are more or less than the reserve, the original guess is proved wrong.

Reserves are also used to recognize that some accounts receivable will not be collected and some inventories will become obsolete. The $3,261 million of accounts and notes receivable is net of $75 million that PepsiCo expects will be uncollectible. Each year, PepsiCo computes an amount that it believes should be added to the allowance; then, as accounts are written off, their amounts are charged to the allowance. Don't be confused by the term *reserves*. No cash is involved; these are just bookkeeping entries.

The income statement format. The income statement starts with revenue or sales and then usually subtracts first those expenses that are most closely related to operations. A manufacturing firm often separates those costs that go into inventory and then the cost of goods sold from those that are administrative, selling, and other ongoing expenses. The following format can be used:

> *Sales revenue*
>   *Minus cost of goods sold*
>
> *Equals gross margin or gross profit*
>   *Minus selling, general, and administrative expenses*
>
> *Equals operating income*
>   *Minus interest and other expenses, plus interest and other income*
>
> *Equals net income before tax*
>   *Minus income tax accrued*
>
> *Equals net income*

With this format, the gross margin in total or as a percentage of sales revenue can be monitored. A change in the gross margin percentage can be caused by many factors including: a price change, a change in the cost per unit, or a change in the product mix. The implications of each of these causes are, of course, very different. If gross margin percentage narrows, because of an erosion of selling prices or a shift in the mix to lower margin products, and management incorrectly thinks it is caused instead by unit cost increases, management's corrective action would lead to unpleasant consequences. It is important, therefore, to keep accounting records in such a way that changes in price and cost can be separately computed.

In a section of its 2005 Annual Report entitled "Management's Discussion and Analysis," PepsiCo explained:

> Net revenue increased 11% reflecting, across all divisions, increased volume, favorable effective net pricing, and net favorable foreign currency movements. The volume gains contributed 3 percentage points, the effective net pricing contributed 3 percentage points, and the net favorable foreign currency movements contributed over 1 percentage point. The 53rd week contributed over 1% to revenue growth and almost 1 percentage point to volume growth.

Internally, companies do their accounting either monthly or weekly. The month-by-month firms have no trouble ending their year on December 31 or June 30; however, those whose accounting periods end on Saturday produce annual reports containing either 52 or 53 weeks.

The other categories used in the income statement format are also helpful in analyzing the data. Operating income is that income which results from the operation of the main business. Operating income is then separated from other income and expenses, which may be from financial transactions or unusual circumstances that are expected to vary greatly from year to year. These separations in the format will then help the reader analyze the different parts of the firm's activities.

PepsiCo organizes its statement of income slightly differently. It does not show a gross margin, but this can easily be determined:

	2005	2004	2003
Net revenue	$32,562	$29,261	$26,971
Cost of sales	$14,176	$12,674	$11,691
Gross margin	$18,386	$16,587	$15,280
Gross margin %	0.565	0.567	0.567

Interestingly, Coca-Cola Company does show a gross profit figure in its 2005 annual report; it is 64.5%. Not much can be concluded by just comparing those two figures, because their businesses are so different. Cost of sales includes production and distribution costs for products sold, but not marketing and other administrative expenses, which are shown separately. PepsiCo also breaks out three smaller items:

- Amortization of the intangible assets with limited lives;

- Restructuring and impairment charges;

- Merger-related costs;

in order to derive operating profit. In another part of the annual report, PepsiCo reports operating profit for each of its primary business units:

(for 2005, in millions of dollars)	Net Revenue	Amortization of Intangible Assets	Depreciation and Amortization	Operating Profit	Operating Profit to Revenue
Frito-Lay NA*	$10,322	$3	$419	$2,529	0.245
PepsiCo Beverages NA*	9,146	76	264	2,037	0.223
PepsiCo International	11,376	71	420	1,607	0.141
Quaker Foods NA*	1,718	0	34	537	0.313
Total division	$32,562	$150	$1,137	$6,710	0.206

* North America

PepsiCo International produces and distributes all Frito-Lay, Pepsi Beverages, and Quaker Foods products internationally. It is slightly larger than the North American Frito and Pepsi beverage divisions, but it's significantly less profitable.

Bottling equity income is PepsiCo's share of the net income of Pepsi Bottling Group, PepsiAmericas, and some smaller companies. As of year- end 2005, PepsiCo owned 41% and 43% respectively of these two bottlers, so they were not consolidated.

Interest expense and interest income are shown separately, because they are considered financial as opposed to operating expenses.

Income from continuing operations before income taxes does not include income taxes or any operating profit, loss, or tax expense or benefit related to discontinued operations. After those two items, the company derives net income, or the bottom line, of the financial statements.

	2005	2004	2003
Net revenue	$32,562	$29,261	$26,971
Operating profit	$5,922	$5,259	$4,781
Operating profit margin %	0.182	0.180	0.177
Net income	$4,078	$4,212	$3,568
Net income %	0.125	0.144	0.132

PepsiCo's numbers over this three-year period are interesting. While the gross margins for these three years were similar and where the operating profit margin for 2005 was higher than in 2004 or 2003, the net income/revenue percentage is considerably lower. The explanation is the income tax. Because of a tax bill approved by the U.S. congress in 2004, PepsiCo was able to repatriate cash from offshore operating companies at a significantly reduced tax rate. The untaxed earnings had been reported years earlier, but the tax—$460 million—was paid in 2005. In a footnote, PepsiCo disclosed that its 2005 net income, excluding the unusual income tax charge, the 53rd week, and its $55-million restructuring charges, was $4,536 million. This would mean a 13.9% net income percentage or return on sales—still less than 2004.

Explanation of the Statement of Cash Flows

Though this statement may be one of the more difficult to understand fully, it provides much useful information. It describes the elements of cash flow, stating both the sources of cash (positive amounts) and the uses of cash (negative amounts) during the year. As PepsiCo's annual report shows, the statement is further divided into three sections that group these cash transactions according to the type of activities involved: operating, investing, or financing.

Cash flows from operations. This section of the statement, which PepsiCo terms net cash provided by operating activities, can be derived in one of two ways. The direct method simply presents the major classes of cash receipts and cash payments in the company's operations and sums up the differences. The indirect method, on the other hand, links the income statement with the cash flow statement by providing a reconciliation of net income to operating cash flows. PepsiCo uses the indirect method in its annual report.

As shown in PepsiCo's statement, the indirect method starts by translating net income after taxes into cash flow. First, come several items that were included in the computation of net income, but which did not involve cash. For example, depreciation, usually the largest of these items, is an expense of the year and therefore reduces net income. However, it does not reflect a payment of cash during the year, so it is added back to net income. In the same way, deferred taxes and other noncash charges and credits are added or subtracted on the income statement, although they do not reflect cash transactions. They too are used to translate net income into cash flow.

Some of the changes in cash flow from operations are self-explanatory and may be summarized as decreases in current assets or increases in current liabilities if the item is a source of cash, and increases in assets or decreases in current liabilities if the item is an application of cash. PepsiCo's annual report shows that accounts payable and other current liabilities (a liability account) increased during 2005, providing a source of cash. Likewise, accounts and notes receivable (an asset account) increased, requiring PepsiCo to use cash during the year.

Some of the others require a bit more explanation. We will not attempt to explain every line item because they differ from company to company, but we'll discuss two that are typical.

In 2005, there is a $464 million addition called pension and retiree medical plan expenses. This expense reduced net income, but it was not a cash item so it was added back. The line above it, the −$877 million shows the actual cash paid to the pension trust, which is a separate organization. Also, in 2005 there is a −$411 million item called bottling equity income, net of dividends. Recall that the income statement that year reported bottling equity income as $557 million. What happened was that PepsiCo's share of the 2005 net income of the noncontrolled bottling companies was $577 million, but only $146 million was paid in the form of cash dividends. So $411 million has to be adjusted out; it was noncash income.

The sum of the items included in this section of the cash flow statement determines the company's net cash flow from operations. We can see from the PepsiCo statement that, overall, operating activities provided it with about $5.8 billion in cash during 2005. Note that the cash flow from operations for each of these three years exceeded net income, which is an advantage for PepsiCo. Indeed, an important indication of liquidity is the ratio of cash flow from operations to net income:

$$\frac{\text{Cash Flow from Operations}}{\text{Net Income}} = \frac{\$5,852}{\$4,078} = 1.44$$

which is up from 1.2 and 1.21 in 2004 and 2005, respectively.

Cash flows from investing activities. This section details the sources and applications of cash in the company's investing activities. These include capital spending on its own businesses, equity investments in other entities, and dispositions and purchases of other assets, including property, plant, and equipment. The statement shows that for each of the years 2003 through 2005, PepsiCo's investing activities required a net use of cash. In 2005, the $3.5 billion used in investing activities was fully funded by the $5.8 billion available from operations.

Cash flows from financing activities. Cash flows from financing activities reflect short- and long-term borrowings as well as payment of dividends. It also shows common or preferred stock issued or repurchased. The financing activities may suggest changes in the firm's capital structure and its strategy for providing funds in support of investing activities and operations. The statement of cash flows showed that in 2005 PepsiCo obtained about $1.85 billion in new short-term debt and $25 million in long-term debt, and repaid about $177 million for a net increase of $1.7 billion.

Conclusions from the cash flow statement. What does the cash flow statement tell us? To begin with, revenues increased 20.7% from 2003 to 2005, while net income increased only 14.3%; but cash flow from operations was up 35.2% over the same period. Cash flow generated from operations is growing faster than revenue; the company is in a strong cash position.

Capital spending exceeded depreciation each year and was increasing, which was a sign that the company was continuing to invest in new property, plant, and equipment. It also made significant acquisitions in 2005. Note that the short-term investments under investing activities are largely offset by the short-term borrowings shown under financing activities. In all three years, cash flow from operating activities was sufficient to fund all investing activities and to pay dividends. Also noteworthy were the large common stock sales related to stock options. Business people sometimes use the term free cash flow to describe cash flow from operations minus expenditures for property, plant, and equipment. For 2005,

PepsiCo's free cash flow was $4,166 million ($5,852 million − $1,736 million). This is cash that can be used to acquire other companies, pay dividends, or repurchase stock.

Another way to look at this picture is to take in the whole three years. From 2003 to 2005, PepsiCo earned $11.8 billion on $88.8 billon in revenue; generated $15.2 billion in cash flow from operations, which paid for $5.7 billion in acquisitions and new property and equipment, $4.0 billion in dividends, and $8.0 billion in common stock repurchases. This was a strong performance.

Explanation of the Statement of Common Shareholders' Equity

The purpose of this statement is to explain the changes in the shareholders' equity account from one year to the next. Note that common stock did not change; no new shares were issued. Capital in excess of par value is affected by the expense of stock options granted (a noncash expense) and stock options exercised. What happened in 2005 was that PepsiCo used repurchased common stock (treasury stock), for which the company had paid $1,523 million, to satisfy the stock options of employees and others exercised that year. Those exercised options brought in $1,099 million in cash. The ($1,523 million − $1,099 million) difference, after taxes, was charged to capital in excess of par value. Put another way, the company bought something for $1.5 billion and sold it for $1.1 billion, and that $0.4 billion didn't get treated as an expense. Who said stock options were costless?

Retained earnings increased by net income and decreased by dividends declared. If those dividends are not all paid in cash, the difference will be dividends payable, a current liability.

The items making up accumulated loss and other comprehensive loss were discussed previously. Looking over the three-year period, we see that the currency translation adjustment in 2005 was a loss, while it was a gain in the two previous years. The rest of the items are of little consequence.

Finally, in 2005 PepsiCo repurchased $2,995 million in common stock and issued $1,523 million of that same stock to satisfy stock options being exercised. The slight differences between shares repurchased in this statement and in the statement of cash flows probably represents small timing differences between the time shares that were purchased (and thus were owned by the company), and those that were paid for in cash to the brokerage firm.

ANALYZING FINANCIAL STATEMENTS USING RATIOS AND OTHER TECHNIQUES

The generally accepted purpose of financial statements is to convey financial information of interest and importance to a firm's stockholders and potential investors. With a little mathematical analysis of these statements, we can learn quite a bit about what is going on in the company.

There are, of course, some basic things that the numbers tell us, such as how big the firm is, whether it was profitable, and whether assets exceed debts. (If they did not, the firm is technically bankrupt.) In addition, a little analysis of ratios will produce more information that may not be immediately apparent. There are three general types of ratios that can be computed:

1. Ratios of liquidity and financial position;
2. Ratios of performance;
3. Ratios reflecting general strategy, such as management's dividend and capital expenditure decisions.

We will take these up in turn and give some illustrations of each.

Ratios of Liquidity and Financial Position

To illustrate the ratios discussed here, we have computed each ratio for PepsiCo, Inc., for 2005. Numbers, except per-share figures, are in millions of dollars.

Current ratio. The most frequently used ratio of liquidity is the current ratio, which is:

$$\frac{\text{Current Assets}}{\text{Current Liabilities}} = \frac{\$10,454}{\$9,406} = 1.11$$

Current assets and liabilities are those that are likely to be turned into cash within a year, such as cash, receivables, inventory, payables, and short-term debt. A ratio of more than one says that the firm has more than enough short-term assets to cover its short-term liabilities. A ratio of less than one may indicate financial weakness, although there are circumstances in which this is not so. A service firm (for example: a utility, communications company, or a leasing company), which has little or no inventory may show a current ratio of less than one while it is in normally robust financial health. A fast-food restaurant with little inventory and no receivables would be in a similar situation. PepsiCo's ratio of 1.11 reflects the high service component of its businesses, requiring relatively less inventory than a manufacturing company, as well as careful control of the receivables. Thus, one can only derive a rough indication from the level of the current ratio, and this should be taken in the context of the type of business. An average current ratio for firms in similar businesses would help show what a normal current ratio should be for the company being analyzed.

The trend or change in a current ratio over time is usually more significant than its level. A decrease in the current ratio is most often a reflection of the firm having used short-term borrowing from suppliers or a bank either to cover losses or to buy plant and equipment. Neither of those strategies can continue indefinitely. PepsiCo's current ratio decreased from 1.28 in 2004 to 1.11 in 2005, because of the significant increase in short-term debt.

Debt ratio. A commonly used ratio of financial position is the debt ratio, which shows the extent to which a company is using debt capital to finance the business. This could be shown as the ratio of debt to equity or of debt to capital, capital being equity plus long-term debt. The latter version is probably the more frequently used.

$$\text{Debt Ratio} = \frac{\text{Long-Term Debt}}{\text{Capital (Long-Term Debt + Equity)}} = \frac{\$2,456^{1}}{(\$2,456 + \$14,320)} = 14.64\%$$

as of year-end 2005, which is down from 15% as of the previous year.

Or this ratio can be expressed as the relationship between total liabilities and total liabilities plus owners' equity. This way of measuring the use of debt, or *leverage* as it is sometimes called, avoids the need to distinguish between short-term and long-term debt.

$$\text{Total Liabilities Ratio} = \frac{\text{Total Liabilities}}{\text{Total Liabilities + Owners' Equity}}$$

---

[1] Includes $143 million in current maturities of long-term debt incorporated into short-term obligations.

At the particular moment captured in the balance sheets, that distinction could well be a result of a temporary financial strategy, as would occur when a company uses short-term borrowing to support an investment until long-term financing can be arranged or assets are sold off.

The higher the debt ratio, the greater is the reliance on debt as a source of capital. It is also true that the higher the ratio the greater the risk, since debt involves fixed obligations of interest and principal repayment. With this risk comes higher leverage, which may be good or bad for the equity holders. When things go well and net income rises, the equity holders get all the benefits since interest is fixed. This effect of leverage explains how some small investors have become wealthy in highly leveraged real estate ventures. On the other hand, leverage is a two-edged sword and there are other highly leveraged investors, who have been wiped out by a relatively small decline in values and income. Among publicly held companies, one is likely to see high debt leverage in public utilities, financial companies, and companies with fixed salable assets like real estate. Those companies that show low debt leverage may be those that are subject to wide cyclical swings and high risk or those that have succeeded in paying down their debt and have not yet generated a need for further long-term investment. For comparison, this table shows other companies with total liabilities to total liabilities plus equity as follows at the end of 2005:

GE	0.84
PepsiCo	0.55
Abbott	0.5
Lowes	0.41
Johnson & Johnson	0.35
eBay	0.16

Ratios of Performance

There are many possible ratios of performance. Here are six of the most widely used performance ratios, which shed light on how a firm is doing.

Return on sales.

$$\text{Return on Sales (ROS)} = \frac{\text{Net Income}}{\text{Revenue}} = \frac{\$4,078}{\$32,562} = 12.5\%$$

This ratio tells what a company's profit is in relation to sales revenue. In some industries, such as food retailing or construction, it is likely to be a low percentage while in other industries, such as airlines, utilities, or high technology firms, it is likely to be a higher percentage.

Asset turnover.

$$\text{Asset Turnover} = \frac{\text{Revenue}}{\text{Average Total Assets}} = \frac{\$32,562}{(\$31,727 + \$27,987)/2} = 1.1$$

We typically use average assets to compute asset turnover, because revenue is for an entire year while assets are at a point in time. If assets increased over the year (or decreased), the average gives a better picture of the turnover.

If one can accept that all assets turn over in the same way that inventory turns over, this ratio tells the annual turnover of the firm's total assets. One could also say that it tells how many dollars of sales are generated by a dollar of assets. It is frequently called the *asset efficiency ratio*. As one would expect, capital-intensive businesses, such as utilities, airlines, oil production, and transport firms, are likely to have low turnover rates. Merchandising, research, and service firms are likely to have high asset turnover. One can also see that firms with low turnover are likely to have high profit margins and vice versa.

Return on assets.

$$\text{Return on Assets (ROA)} = \frac{\text{Net Income}}{\text{Average Total Assets}} = \frac{\$4,078}{\$29,857} = 13.7\%$$

This ratio closely reflects the financial objectives of a firm. It tells how well the money invested in a firm's assets is generating profit.

The first two performance ratios can be combined to produce the third ratio as follows:

$$\underbrace{\frac{\text{Net Income}}{\text{Revenue}}}_{\text{Return on Sales}} \times \underbrace{\frac{\text{Revenue}}{\text{Avg. Total Assets}}}_{\text{Asset Turnover}} = \underbrace{\frac{\text{Net income}}{\text{Avg. Total Assets}}}_{\text{Return on Assets}}$$

$$12.5\% \times 1.1 = 13.7\%$$

This is an important relationship, because it shows that there are three ways in which to improve the rate of return on assets: one is to increase the profit margin, the second is to increase the asset turnover, and of course, the third is to do both. While the former is quite obvious, the latter are less commonly recognized, but equally powerful in their effect.

Return on equity.

$$\text{Return on Equity (ROE)} = \frac{\text{Net Income}}{\text{Average Total Equity}} = \frac{\$4,078}{(\$14,320 + \$13,572)/2} = 29.2\%$$

This ratio is similar to the return on assets ratio in that it measures how well the invested funds are performing. However, this ratio focuses on that part of total capital that corresponds to stockholders' ownership. The ratio will generally be higher than return on assets, and the amount by which it is higher will depend on the amount of leverage used, or strictly speaking, the relationship between stockholders' equity and the total of equity plus all liabilities. The return on assets ratio shows the overall rate of return, while return on equity shows what that return is when modified by the effect of financial leverage.

Financial leverage. We can now state the relationship between return on assets and return on equity using the total liabilities ratio:

$$\text{Financial Leverage} = \frac{1}{1 - \text{Total Liabilities Ratio}} = \frac{\text{Average Total Assets}}{\text{Average Total Equity}}$$

This ratio is similar to the total liabilities ratio we used before only expressed in a different way.

$$\text{Financial Leverage} = \frac{\text{Average Total Assets}}{\text{Average Total Equity}} = \frac{\$29,857}{\$13,946} = 2.14$$

So we have:

Return on Assets		Financial Leverage		Return on Equity
$\dfrac{\text{Net Income}}{\text{Avg. Total Assets}}$		$\dfrac{\text{Avg. Total Assets}}{\text{Avg. Total Equity}}$		$\dfrac{\text{Net Income}}{\text{Avg. Total Equity}}$
13.7%	×	2.14	=	29.3%

The following table shows the averages of these five key profitability ratios for 18 industries for 2005. Better firms usually outperform those averages.

Industry	ROS (%)	Asset Turnover	ROA (%)	Financial Leverage	ROE (%)
Aerospace and defense	5	.8	4	3.8	15
Beverages	6	.7	4	4.5	18
Chemical	4	1.0	4	3.0	12
Commercial banks	18	0.1	1.4	11.4	16
Computer software	19	0.7	13	1.4	18
Computers and office equipment	6	0.8	5	3.0	15
Energy	3	1.0	3	3.0	9
General merchandisers	4	2.0	8	1.5	12
Homebuilders	10	1.1	11	2.4	26
Internet services and retailing	18	0.5	9	1.4	13
Mining and oil production	24	0.5	11	2.2	24
Pharmaceuticals	15	0.5	8	2.3	18
Railroads	13	0.4	5	2.8	14
Specialty retailers	4	1.8	7	1.9	13
Telecommunications	5	0.4	2	4.5	9
Tobacco	14	0.6	8	2.9	23
Trucking	5	1.2	6	2.5	15
Utilities	6	0.5	3	3.3	10

Source: *Fortune*, 17 April 2006

Price earnings ratio.

$$\text{Price Earnings Ratio (P/E)} \quad = \quad \frac{\text{Market Price per Share*}}{\text{Earnings per Share}} \quad = \quad \frac{\$59.08}{\$2.43} \quad = \quad 24.3$$

* Note: Using market closing price on 12/31/05.

The price earnings ratio (P/E) uses the price that investors are willing to pay for the company's stock, a price that will reflect their views on the company's current performance and future prospects. By relating stock price to earnings per share, we can see how much investors are paying for a dollar of current earnings. A P/E ratio of five and six is fairly low and probably means that investors believe the current earnings are not likely to grow very much. A P/E ratio of 20 or more probably means investors expect earnings (and consequently share price) to grow. Investors are willing to pay a high price for current earnings. A high P/E ratio may also be caused by a decrease in earnings, which investors expect to be temporary.

Earnings per growth share rate.

$$\text{Earnings per Share Growth Rate} = \frac{\text{EPS Increase}}{\text{EPS Last Year}} = \frac{\$(0.04)}{\$2.47} = (1.6\%)$$

Since the P/E is likely to be influenced by the rate of earnings growth, this ratio computes that directly. It ought to be computed for each year for several years to discover the compound growth rate over a period of time.

In evaluating this ratio, one should remember that any rate that is less than the prevailing inflation rate, is, in truth, no growth at all. Likewise, unless share prices increase at least with the rate of inflation, they too will not reflect any growth in real terms. For PepsiCo, even though EPS declined 1.6% in 2005, the stock market must have judged its future prospects to be strong, since the share price increased 13.7%. Remember that net income and EPS for 2005 were adversely affected by the extra tax PepsiCo chose to incur, so as to repatriate its offshore earnings.

Dividend and capital expenditure ratios. When companies pay dividends to their common stockholders, they usually pay out only a portion of the net income. Since the amount of a dividend paid is at the discretion of the firm's board of directors, it is not fixed by contract and may even reflect a longer-run strategy. A payout ratio of less than 10% usually means the firm is conserving cash, either for growth or to cover maturing debts. A payout ratio above 60% usually means the company is providing a return to stockholders more in terms of dividend income than in terms of growth and share price appreciation.

$$\frac{\text{Dividend Payout}}{\text{Ratio}} = \frac{\text{Dividends Paid per Share}}{\text{Earnings per Share for the Period}} = \frac{\$0.99}{\$2.43} = 40.7\%$$

To test this from a different viewpoint, one can relate dividends to share price to get percentage yields. If this is close to available interest rate yields on corporate bonds, the stock is probably selling on an income yield basis rather than on the basis of expected growth. PepsiCo's dividend yield was around 1.7% in 1995, too low to reflect an acceptable income yield. Thus, investors in PepsiCo expected growth in dividend and share price.

Capital expenditure ratios. A firm's capital expenditures (CAPEX) include both the costs of replacing assets as they wear out and expenditures for the firm's growth and development. Replacing an asset almost always costs more than the asset's original cost, because of the effect of inflation over the asset's life. Technological development may offset part of inflation's increase by making the same productive capacity cost less as time goes on. In a general way, therefore, there are three factors that affect the size of a firm's capital expenditures:

1. The need to replace assets when they wear out, together with their length of life;

2. The effect of inflation and technology on the cost of replacement;

3. Investment for growth.

How much of the annual capital expenditure went to finance growth rather than toward replacement is a key question in the analysis of financial statements. A review of the available information can give some idea of what the answer might be.

While it is not possible to use published financial information to separate the three factors, it is interesting to relate the cost of depreciable assets, the amount of depreciation taken during the year and the capital expenditures made during the year. The first two say something about the average depreciable life of assets, and the second and third figures tell us something about the company's expenditure toward growth. The more capital expenditures exceed depreciation, the more a company is investing for growth.

The following table gives some approximate figures from PepsiCo and six other companies. The right-hand column shows capital expenditures as a percentage of depreciation. PepsiCo's capital expenditures were 57% more than depreciation and Harley Davidson's were 4% less. There are several factors that can influence that figure. One is asset lives. Long-lived assets are likely to have been acquired further back in the past on the average, and hence at lower inflated costs. Depreciation on old assets will be lower than depreciation on recently acquired assets with similar productive capacity. Rates of growth are another factor influencing the percentage shown in the right-hand column. The figures seem to show that Lowes Companies, the home improvement chain, is spending at a much higher rate than Abbott, the pharmaceutical company; of course, they are in different industries. Lowes also has the longest depreciable lives of the group, 20 years, compared to 13 years for GE. Perhaps much of GE's depreciable assets are equipment as opposed to the stores of Lowes Companies. eBay has the shortest depreciable lives of the group, no doubt, because of its heavy investments in computer equipment and software.

Company	Depreciable Assets at Cost ($ millions)	Annual Depreciation Charge ($ millions)	Indicated Depreciable Life (years)	Capital Expenditures "CAPEX" ($ millions)	CAPEX as % of Depreciation
GE	111,733	8,538	13.1	14,441	169
PepsiCo	17,145	1,103	15.5	1,736	157
Abbott	12,760	869	14.7	895	103
Lowes	21,419	1,051	20.4	3,379	322
Harley-Davidson	2,334	206	11.3	198	96
J&J	19,716	1,500	13.1	2,632	175
eBay	1,456	159	9.2	365	230

SEGMENT REPORTING

In addition to the four financial statements described above, companies are required to provide certain information relating to segments of their business. Segments may be defined by product lines or by geographical areas. Generally, the information reported shows sales, operating profit, and assets that are identifiable with the segments. Although the necessary allocations of expenses and assets may make the segment figures less than precisely accurate, they often provide interesting information about which segments are most profitable, which are growing the fastest, and which segments receive the greatest amount of capital spending.

PepsiCo's segment reporting reflects the way it has organized its company into four business segments. (PepsiCo's disclosure of divisional information is included at the end of this appendix.) As is the case with the main financial statements, it is possible to extract some additional information by computing ratios from the figures given. The following table is an example.

	Net Revenue ($ millions)	Operating Profit ($ millions)	Operating Profit to Revenue	Total Assets ($ million)	Operating Profit to Total Assets	CAPEX ($ millions)	CAPEX to Total Assets
Frito-Lay NA*	10,322	2,529	0.245	5,948	0.43	512	0.086
PepsiCo Beverages NA*	9,146	2,037	0.223	6,316	0.32	320	0.051
PepsiCo International	11,376	1,607	0.141	9,983	0.16	667	0.067
Quaker Foods NA*	1,718	537	0.313	989	0.54	31	0.031
Division totals	32,562	6,710	0.206	23,236	0.29	1,530	0.066

* Note: North America

As we observed already, the biggest business unit, PepsiCo International, has the lowest operating profit margins, and since it also has the most total assets, the operating profit margin to total assets is even lower. Interestingly, this unit has the highest CAPEX. Quaker Foods North America, by contrast, enjoys the highest returns on revenue and total assets, and the company is making almost no investments to expand capacity here. Part of the explanation may be that the international business is profitable, but simply not as profitable as PepsiCo's North American Frito and Pepsi Beverage business; however, that still doesn't explain the lack of investment in Quaker Foods. Perhaps they're preparing to sell that unit?

THE IMPORTANCE OF TRENDS IN ANALYZING RATIOS

For most of these ratios, their change over time is as revealing as their absolute level. As noted earlier, the current ratio is a good example of this. Lenders become more worried about a company that shows a declining high current ratio than about one that shows a steady, but low, ratio. Likewise, a rising debt ratio may reveal more financial risk than one that is high, but steady. The absolute level of these ratios may be conditioned by the type of business involved whereas the trends result more from what is going on in the particular company.

SUMMARY

This discussion of ratios has covered some of the more commonly used indicators of position and performance. As you become familiar with financial statements, it is likely that others will appear useful. Each financial analyst will probably have his or her own set of ratios that he or she finds more revealing. Therefore, this discussion was more of a starting point than a comprehensive coverage of the subject.

Consolidated Statement of Income

PepsiCo, Inc. and Subsidiaries

Fiscal years ended December 31, 2005, December 25, 2004 and December 27, 2003

(in millions except per share amounts)		2005		2004		2003
Net Revenue	$	**32,562**	$	29,261	$	26,971
Cost of sales		**14,176**		12,674		11,691
Selling, general and administrative expenses		**12,314**		11,031		10,148
Amortization of intangible assets		**150**		147		145
Impairment and restructuring charges		**–**		150		147
Merger-related costs		**–**		–		59
Operating Profit		**5,922**		5,259		4,781
Bottling equity income		**557**		380		323
Interest expense		**(256)**		(167)		(163)
Interest income		**159**		74		51
Income from Continuing Operations before Income Taxes		**6,382**		5,546		4,992
Provision for Income Taxes		**2,304**		1,372		1,424
Income from Continuing Operations		**4,078**		4,174		3,568
Tax Benefit from Discontinued Operations		**–**		38		–
Net Income	$	**4,078**	$	4,212	$	3,568
Net Income per Common Share – Basic						
Continuing operations	$	**2.43**	$	2.45	$	2.07
Discontinued operations		**–**		0.02		–
Total	$	**2.43**	$	2.47	$	2.07
Net Income per Common Share – Diluted						
Continuing operations	$	**2.39**	$	2.41	$	2.05
Discontinued operations		**–**		0.02		–
Total	$	**2.39**	$	2.44 *	$	2.05

*Based on unrounded amounts.

See accompanying notes to consolidated financial statements.

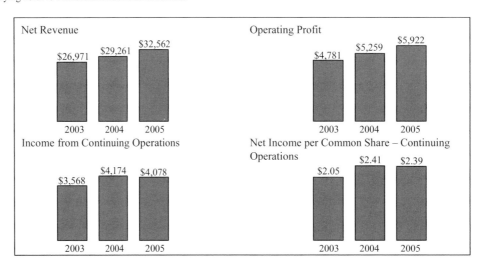

Consolidated Balance Sheet

PepsiCo, Inc. and Subsidiaries
December 31, 2005 and December 25, 2004

(in millions except per share amounts)		2005		2004
ASSETS				
Current Assets				
Cash and cash equivalents	$	1,716	$	1,280
Short-term investments		3,166		2,165
		4,882		3,445
Accounts and notes receivable, net		3,261		2,999
Inventories		1,693		1,541
Prepaid expenses and other current assets		618		654
Total Current Assets		10,454		8,639
Property, Plant and Equipment, net		8,681		8,149
Amortizable Intangible Assets, net		530		598
Goodwill		4,088		3,909
Other nonamortizable intangible assets		1,086		933
Nonamortizable Intangible Assets		5,174		4,842
Investments in Noncontrolled Affiliates		3,485		3,284
Other Assets		3,403		2,475
Total Assets	$	31,727	$	27,987
LIABILITIES AND SHAREHOLDERS' EQUITY				
Current Liabilities				
Short-term obligations	$	2,889	$	1,054
Accounts payable and other current liabilities		5,971		5,599
Income taxes payable		546		99
Total Current Liabilities		9,406		6,752
Long-Term Debt Obligations		2,313		2,397
Other Liabilities		4,323		4,099
Deferred Income Taxes		1,434		1,216
Total Liabilities		17,476		14,464
Commitments and Contingencies				
Preferred Stock, no par value		41		41
Repurchased Preferred Stock		(110)		(90)
Common Shareholders' Equity				
Common stock, par value 1 2/3¢ per share (issued 1,782 shares)		30		30
Capital in excess of par value		614		618
Retained earnings		21,116		18,730
Accumulated other comprehensive loss		(1,053)		(886)
		20,707		18,492
Less: repurchased common stock, at cost (126 and 103 shares, res		(6,387)		(4,920)
Total Common Shareholders' Equity		14,320		13,572
Total Liabilities and Shareholders' Equity	$	31,727	$	27,987

See accompanying notes to consolidated financial statements.

Consolidated Statement of Cash Flows

PepsiCo, Inc. and Subsidiaries
Fiscal years ended December 31, 2005, December 25, 2004 and December 27, 2003

(in millions)	2005	2004	2003
Operating Activities			
Net income	$ 4,078	$ 4,212	$ 3,568
Adjustments to reconcile net income to net cash provided by operating activities			
Depreciation and amortization	1,308	1,264	1,221
Stock-based compensation expense	311	368	407
Restructuring and impairment charges	–	150	147
Cash payments for merger-related costs and restructuring charges	(22)	(92)	(109)
Tax benefit from discontinued operations	–	(38)	–
Pension and retiree medical plan contributions	(877)	(534)	(605)
Pension and retiree medical plan expenses	464	395	277
Bottling equity income, net of dividends	(411)	(297)	(276)
Deferred income taxes and other tax charges and credits	440	(203)	(286)
Merger-related costs	–	–	59
Other non-cash charges and credits, net	145	166	101
Changes in operating working capital, excluding effects of acquisitions and divestitures			
Accounts and notes receivable	(272)	(130)	(220)
Inventories	(132)	(100)	(49)
Prepaid expenses and other current assets	(56)	(31)	23
Accounts payable and other current liabilities	188	216	(11)
Income taxes payable	609	(268)	182
Net change in operating working capital	337	(313)	(75)
Other	79	(24)	(101)
Net Cash Provided by Operating Activities	5,852	5,054	4,328
Investing Activities			
Snack Ventures Europe (SVE) minority interest acquisition	(750)	–	–
Capital spending	(1,736)	(1,387)	(1,345)
Sales of property, plant and equipment	88	38	49
Other acquisitions and investments in noncontrolled affiliates	(345)	(64)	(71)
Cash proceeds from sale of PBG stock	214		
Divestitures	3	52	46
Short-term investments, by original maturity			
More than three months–purchases	(83)	(44)	(38)
More than three months–maturities	84	38	28
Three months or less, net	(992)	(963)	(940)
Net Cash Used for Investing Activities	(3,517)	(2,330)	(2,271)
Financing Activities			
Proceeds from issuances of long-term debt	25	504	52
Payments of long-term debt	(177)	(512)	(641)
Short-term borrowings, by original maturity			
More than three months–proceeds	332	153	88
More than three months–payments	(85)	(160)	(115)
Three months or less, net	1,601	1,119	40
Cash dividends paid	(1,642)	(1,329)	(1,070)
Share repurchases–common	(3,012)	(3,028)	(1,929)
Share repurchases–preferred	(19)	(27)	(16)
Proceeds from exercises of stock options	1,099	965	689
Net Cash Used for Financing Activities	(1,878)	(2,315)	(2,902)
Effect of exchange rate changes on cash and cash equivalents	(21)	51	27
Net Increase/(Decrease) in Cash and Cash Equivalents	436	460	(818)
Cash and Cash Equivalents, Beginning of Year	1,280	820	1,638
Cash and Cash Equivalents, End of Year	$ 1,716	$ 1,280	$ 820

See accompanying notes to consolidated financial statements.

Consolidated Statement of Common Shareholders' Equity

PepsiCo, Inc. and Subsidiaries
Fiscal years ended December 31, 2005, December 25, 2004 and December 27, 2003

(in millions)		2005		2004		2003
	Shares	Amount	Shares	Amount	Shares	Amount
Common Stock	**1,782**	**$30**	1,782	$30	1,782	$30
Capital in Excess of Par Value						
Balance, beginning of year		**618**		548		207
Stock-based compensation expense		**311**		368		407
Stock-based exercises[a]		**(315)**		(298)		(66)
Balance, end of year		**614**		618		548
Retained Earnings						
Balance, beginning of year		**18,730**		15,961		13,489
Net Income		**4,078**		4,212		3,568
Cash dividends declared --- common		**(1,684)**		(1,438)		(1,082)
Cash dividends declared --- preferred		**(3)**		(3)		(3)
Cash dividends declared --- RSUs		**(5)**		(2)		
Other		**--**		--		(11)
Balance, end of year		**21,116**		18,730		15,961
Accumulated Other Comprehensive Loss						
Balance, beginning of year		**(886)**		(1,267)		(1,672)
Currency translation adjustment		**(251)**		401		410
Cash flow hedges, net of tax:						
Net derivative gains/(losses)		**54**		(16)		(11)
Reclassification of (gains)/losses to net income		**(8)**		9		(1)
Minimum pension liability adjustment, net of tax		**16**		(19)		7
Unrealized gain on securities, net of tax		**24**		6		1
Other		**(2)**		--		(1)
Balance, beginning of year		**(1,053)**		(886)		(1,267)
Repurchased Common Stock						
Balance, beginning of year	(103)	**(4,920)**	(77)	(3,376)	(60)	(2,524)
Share repurchases	(54)	**(2,995)**	(58)	(2,994)	(43)	(1,946)
Stock option exercises	31	**1,523**	32	1,434	26	1,096
Other	--	**5**		16	--	(2)
Balance, end of year	(126)	**(6,387)**	(103)	(4,920)	(77)	(3,376)
Total Common Shareholders' Equity		**$14,320**		$13,572		$11,896

	2005	2004	2003
Comprehensive Income			
Net income	**$4,078**	$4,212	$3,568
Currency translation adjustment	**(251)**	401	410
Cash flow hedges, net of tax	**46**	(7)	(12)
Minimum pension liability adjustment, net of tax	**16**	(19)	7
Unrealized gain on securities, net of tax	**24**	6	1
Other	**(2)**	--	(1)
Total Comprehensive Income	**$3,911**	$4,593	$3,973

(a) Includes total tax benefit of $125 million in 2005, $183 million in 2004 and $340 million in 2003.

See accompanying notes to consolidated financial statements.

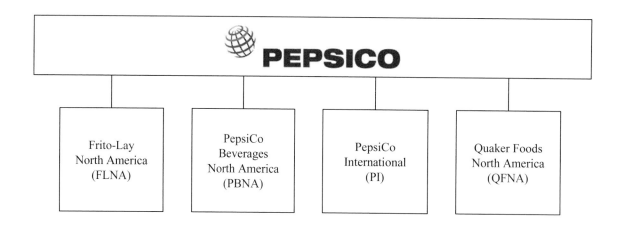

	2005	2004	2003	2005	2004	2003
		Net Revenue			Operating Profit	
FLNA	$ 10,322	$ 9,560	$ 9,091	$ 2,529	$ 2,389	$ 2,242
PBNA	9,146	8,313	7,733	2,037	1,911	1,690
PI	11,376	9,862	8,678	1,607	1,323	1,061
QFNA	1,718	1,526	1,467	537	475	470
Total division	32,562	29,261	26,969	6,710	6,098	5,463
Divested businesses	-	-	2	-	-	26
Corporate	-	-	-	(788)	(689)	(502)
	32,562	29,261	26,971	5,922	5,409	4,987
Restructuring and impairment charges	-	-	-	-	(150)	(147)
Merger-related costs	-	-	-	-	-	(59)
Total	$ 32,562	$ 29,261	$ 26,971	$ 5,922	$ 5,259	$ 4,781

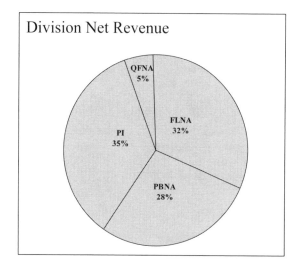

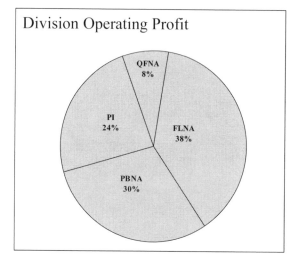

Divested Businesses

During 2003, we sold our Quaker Foods North America Mission pasta business. The results of this business are reported as divested businesses.

Corporate

Corporate includes costs of our corporate headquarters, centrally managed initiatives, such as our BPT initiative, unallocated insurance and benefit programs, foreign exchange transaction gains and losses, and certain commodity derivative gains and losses, as well as profit-in-inventory elimination adjustments for our non-controlled bottling affiliates and certain other items.

Other Division Information

		2005		2004		2003		2005		2004		2003
			Total Assets						Capital Spending			
FLNA	$	5,948	$	5,476	$	5,332	$	512	$	469	$	426
PBNA		6,316		6,048		5,856		320		265		332
PI		9,983		8,921		8,109		667		537		521
QFNA		989		978		995		31		33		32
Total division		23,236		21,423		20,292		1,530		1,304		1,311
Corporate(a)		5,331		3,569		2,384		206		83		34
Investments in bottling affiliates		3,160		2,995		2,651						
	$	31,727	$	27,987	$	25,327	$	1,736	$	1,387	$	1,345

(a)Corporate assets consist principally of cash and cash equivalents, short-term investments, and property, plant and equipment.

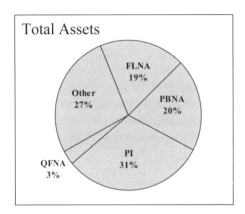

Total Assets

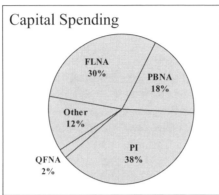

Capital Spending

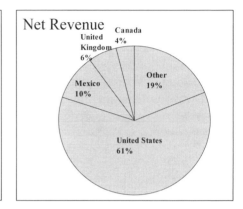

Net Revenue

		2005		2004		2003		2005		2004		2003
			Amortization of Intangible Assets					Depreciation and Other Amortization			
FLNA	$	3	$	3	$	3	$	419	$	420	$	416
PBNA		76		75		75		264		258		245
PI		71		68		66		420		382		350
QFNA				1		1		34		36		36
Total division		150		147		145		1,137		1,096		1,047
Corporate								21		21		29
	$	150	$	147	$	145	$	1,158	$	1,117	$	1,076

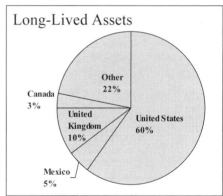

Long-Lived Assets

		2005		2004		2003		2005		2004		2003
			Net Revenue[a]					Long-Lived Assets[b]			
U.S.	$	19,937	$	18,329	$	17,377	$	10,723	$	10,212	$	9,907
Mexico		3,095		2,724		2,642		902		878		869
United Kingdom		1,821		1,692		1,510		1,715		1,896		1,724
Canada		1,509		1,309		1,147		582		548		508
All other countries		6,200		5,207		4,295		3,948		3,339		3,123
	$	32,562	$	29,261	$	26,971	$	17,870	$	16,873	$	16,131

(a) Represents net revenue from businesses operating in these countries.

(b) Long-lived assets represent net property, plant and equipment, nonamortizable and net amortizable intangible assets and
   investments in noncontrolled affiliates. These assets are reported in the country where they are primarily used.

INDEX

–A–

ABC (activity-based costing)	2–19, 2–20, 6–1, 6–2, 6–8, 9–14
ABM (activity-based management)	6–1, 6–3
Absorbed overhead	2–12, 3–12
Accounting for inventories	3–2
Accounts and notes receivable	B–3
Accounts payable and other current liabilities	7–32, B–4
Accumulated other comprehensive loss	B–6
Activity analysis	6–3, 6–8
Activity capacity	6–8
Activity cost	6–7
Activity drivers	2–23, 6–6
Activity management	6–4
Activity matrix	6–8
Activity-based management (ABM)	6–1, 6–3
Activity-based costing (ABC)	2–19, 2–20, 6–1, 6–2, 6–8, 9–14
Actual costs	2–2, 3–6, 4–13, 9–15
Actual, job, full costing	4–13
Actual, process, full costing	4–14
Allocated costs	5–22
Allocating overhead	2–9, 2–11, 2–13, 3–7
Allocation base	2–11, 2–12, 2–20, 2–26
Allocation of overhead	2–9, 2–11, 2–13, 3–7
Amortizable intangible assets, net	B–4
Amortization table	7–26
Artificial economic life	7–34
Asset efficiency ratio	B–14
Asset turnover	B–14
Assigning costs to products or services	2–10, 4–1

–B–

Balance sheet	B–1
Balanced scorecard	8–10, 10–8
Basic earnings per share	B–1
Bonus plans	10–10
Bonus system	10–10
Bottling equity income	B–9
Bottom-up budgeting	8–11, 9–15
Breakeven	4–4, 5–14
Breakeven equations	5–18
Budget revision	8–11, 9–8, 9–16
Budgeting	8–1, 8–11, 9–1
Budgeting process	9–1, 9–2, 9–15

| Budgets | 3–1, 3–17, 8–9, 9–1 |
| Burden | 2–9, 2–28 |

–C–

CAPEX (capital expenditure)	7–1, B–17, B–18
Capital budgeting	7–1
Capital budgets	7–1, 9–1
Capital expenditure ratios	B–17
Capital expenditure (CAPEX)	7–1, B–17, B–18
Capital in excess of par value	B–1
Capitalized	A–3, A–5, B–6
Cash and cash equivalents	B–3
Cash budgets	9–1
Cash flows from financing activities	B–11
Cash flows from investing activities	B–11
Cash flows from operations	B–10
Chart of accounts	2–3
Collecting ideas	7–2
Considering risk	7–29
Consolidated financial statement	B–2
Consumer price index (CPI)	7–32
Contingency planning	9–16
Continuous improvement	3–17, 6–10
Contribution	4–2, 4–4, 4–11, 5–9, 10–4
Control system design	8–3
Control system elements	8–9
Control system evaluation	8–11
Control system framework	8–3
Control system implementation	8–11
Control systems	1–1, 8–1
Controllability	3–16, 8–13
Controllable cost	2–29, 9–13, 9–14
Cost assignment	4–1
Cost behavior	4–1, 4–2, 5–1, 9–8, 9–10, 9–12
Cost center	3–2, 3–4, 8–5
Cost drivers	2–19, 2–23
Cost matching	B–6
Cost modeling	6–10
Cost object	2–6, 2–7, 2–17
Cost pool	2–9, 2–11, 6–2
CPI (consumer price index)	7–32
Credit	3–4, A–2, A–5
Critical performance variables	8–12
Cross-functional involvement	6–9
Current ratio	A–6, B–13
Customer profitability	2–25, 6–8

–D–

Days of receivables	B–3
Debit	3–4, A–2, A–5
Debt ratio	B–13
Debt-to-equity ratio	A–6
Deferred income taxes	B–5
Defining activities	6–2, 6–4, 6–5
Depreciation	5–3, B–4
Depreciation tax savings foregone	7–19, 7–32
Depreciation tax shield	7–14
Design for manufacturing assembly	6–10
Design-to-cost approach	6–10
Developing alternatives	7–2
Diagnostic control system	8–9
Differential analysis	5–11
Differential costs	2–29, 5–20, 5–22, 7–4
Direct cost	2–1, 2–7, 2–8, 2–10, 2–17, 2–27, 2–29, 4–2, 5–2, 5–21, 5–22
Direct costing	2–9, 4–1, 5–2
Direct labor	2–7, 3–7, 4–2, 5–2, 6–2
Direct labor variance	3–8
Direct material	2–8, 2–27
Direct material variance	3–8
Discounting	7–9
Discretionary cost	2–29
Discretionary expense center	8–6
Dividend payout ratio	B–17

–E–

Earnings per share (EPS)	B–1, B–17
Earnings per shared growth rate	B–17
Economic lives	7–33
Economic value added (EVA)	8–10, 10–4, 10–7
Efficiency variance	3–14, 3–15
Engineered cost	2–29
EPS (earnings per share)	B–1, B–17
Equity method	B–4
Equivalent units of production	2–16
Estimates and judgment	B–7
Estimating results	7–3
EVA (economic value added)	8–10, 10–4, 10–7
Evaluating alternatives	7–4
Expense versus capitalized cost	B–7

–F–

Fairness	2–11, 8–13
Feasibility	8–13
Financial leverage	B–13, B–15
Financial planning volume	4–4
Fixed cost	2–19, 2–20, 2–29, 4–2, 5–1, 5–2, 5–22, 9–10
Flexible budget	9–8, 9–10, 9–13
Focus on customers	6–9
Focus on design	6–9
Free cash flow	B–11
Fringe benefits	2–7, 9–6
Full absorption costing	4–1
Full costing	4–3
Full costs	5–2, 10–3

–G–

GAAP (generally accepted accounting principles)	1–1, 2–6, 4–10, B–5
General administrative overhead	2–9
Generally accepted accounting principles (GAAP)	1–1, 2–6, 4–10, B–5
GNP implicit price deflator	7–32
Goal congruence	8–12, 10–3, 10–6, 10–10
Goldratt, Eliyahu	4–12
Goodwill	10–8, B–4
Gross margin percentage	8–6, B–8
Gross national product (GNP)	7–32

–H–

Hewlett-Packard 12C (HP)	7–10
High-low method	9–11
Hurdle rate	7–10, 7–25, 7–29

–I–

Impact of taxes	5–19
Impairs	B–4, B–9
Imputed cost	2–29
Incentive systems	8–11, 10–10, 10–11
Incentives	8–3, 8–11, 10–10
Income statement	A–3, A–5, B–1, B–6, B–8
Income taxes payable	B–4

Income yield basis	B–17
Incremental costs	1–1, 2–29, 5–22
Indirect cost	2–1, 2–5, 2–7, 2–9, 2–17, 2–18, 2–19, 2–20, 2–21, 2–29, 4–2, 5–2
Indirect labor	2–7, 5–2
Indirect material	2–8
Inflation	7–8, 7–32, B–17
Inflation tax	7–32
Interactive control system	8–9
Internal control	8–2, 8–3
Internal control systems	8–3
Internal rate of return	7–24
Interpreting variances	3–16
Inventories	2–6, B–3
Inventory accounting	3–2
Inventory valuation	3–1
Investment center	8–5, 8–7, 8–10, 10–1, 10–5, 10–6

–J–

Job costing	2–12, 2–13, 2–14, 2–18, 4–13
Joint cost	2–27

–K–

Keep or drop problem	5–11
Key success factors	8–10, 8–12

–l–

Labor efficiency variance	3–15
Labor rate variance	3–10, 3–15
Labor variance	3–10, 3–15
Learning curves	6–10
Lifecycle orientation	6–10
Long-term debt obligations	B–5

–M–

Managed cost	2–29
Management control	1–1, 8–1, 8–4, 8–8
Manufacturing costs	2–4, 2–6, 2–7, 2–27, 9–6
Manufacturing overhead	2–9, 2–10, 3–10, 3–14
Marginal contribution	5–9
Marginal cost	2–29, 5–22

Market value added (MVA)	8–10, 10–7
Material price variance	3–10, 3–15
Material usage variance	3–15
Material variance	3–10, 3–15
Matrix costing	2–18
Measuring performance	1–4, 10–1
Microsoft Excel	7–10
Minority interest	B–3
MVA (market value added)	8–10, 10–7

–N–

Negative variances	3–4, 3–16, 3–18
Net assets	8–7, A–1
Net present value (NPV)	7–11
Noncash income	B–11
Nonfinancial performance measures	8–10, 10–4, 10–8

–O–

Objectives of control systems	8–1
Operating budgets	3–1, 9–1, 9–2, 9–4
Operating income	10–1, A–5, B–8
Opportunity cost	2–29, 5–21
Organizational design	8–3, 8–4
Organizational strategy	8–3, 8–4, 8–8
Organizational structure	8–8
Other liabilities	B–5
Other non-amortizable intangible assets	B–4
Out-of-pocket cost	2–29, 5–22
Overabsorbed cost	4–5
Overhead	2–1, 2–9, 2–28, 4–2
Overhead absorption rate	3–11
Overhead allocation	2–9, 2–11, 2–13, 3–7
Overhead costs	2–1, 2–9, 2–24, 2–27, 3–10, 6–2, 9–6
Overhead efficiency variance	3–14, 3–15
Overhead rate	2–12, 6–2, 9–2
Overhead spending variance	3–12, 3–14, 3–15
Overhead variance	3–10
Overhead volume variance	3–15

–P–

P/E (price–earnings ratio)	B–16
Partially completed production	2–15
Payback	7–4
Performance measurement	8–3, 8–8, 8–10, 10–1

Period cost   2–28
Planning   1–2, 3–1, 5–5, 8–1, 8–9, 8–11, 9–1
Positive variances   3–4
Preferred stock, no par value and repurchased   B–2, B–5
    preferred stock
Prepaid expenses and other current assets   B–4
Preparation of the budget   9–4
Present value   7–8, 7–32, 7–35, 10–6
Price changes   7–32
Price–earnings ratio (P/E)   B–16
Price variance   3–8, 3–9, 3–10
Price-led costing   6–9
Pricing   1–2, 4–6, 6–9
Prime cost   2–27
Process costing   2–13, 2–14, 2–15, 2–16, 2–18, 4–13
Process-value analysis   6–3
Product complexity   2–24, 6–6
Product cost   2–1, 2–28
Product profitability   2–18, 4–3, 4–11
Production costs   4–1, A–5
Product's lifecycle   6–11
Profit and loss account   3–4, A–1, A–3,
Profit center   8–5, 8–6
Profitability ratio   7–24
Property, plant, and equipment   B–4

–Q–

Quantity variance   3–8, 3–9, 3–10

–R–

Rate variance   3–8, 3–9
Ratios of liquidity and financial position   B–12
Ratios of performance   B–14
Ratios reflecting general strategy   B–12
Relevant cost   2–29, 5–1
Relevant cost analysis   5–1
Repurchased common stock   B–2, B–6, B–12
Request for proposal (RFP)   6–9
Reserves   B–7
Residual income   8–5, 8–10, 10–6, 10–7
Residual values   7–34
Responsibility centers   8–4, 8–5, 8–10
Return of investment   7–6, 7–26
Return on assets (ROA)   7–7, 8–7, B–5, B–15, B–16
Return on capital employed (ROCE)   8–7
Return on equity (ROE)   B–15

Return on investment (ROI)	7–6, 7–7, 7–26, 8–5, 8–7, 8–10, 10–1, 10–4
Return on net assets (RONA)	8–7
Return on sales (ROS)	8–10, B–14
Revenue center	8–5, 8–6
Revenue recognition	B–6
Reward systems	8–11, 10–10
Rewards	8–3
RFP (request for proposal)	6–9
Risk	7–6, 7–10, 7–29, B–14, B–19
ROA (return on assets)	7–7, 8–7, B–5, B–15, B–16
ROCE (return on capital employed)	8–7
ROE (return on equity)	B–15
ROI (return on investment)	7–6, 7–7, 7–26, 8–5, 8–7, 8–10, 10–1, 10–4
RONA (return on net assets)	8–7
ROS (return on sales)	8–10, B–14

–S–

Segment reporting	B–18
Semivariable cost	2–29, 5–20, 9–10
Sensitivity	7–30
Service cost	2–17
Short-term investments	B–3
Short-term obligation	B–4
Standard cost	2–28, 3–1, 9–15
Standard cost sheet	3–2, 3–3, 3–5
Standard costing systems	3–1
Standard, job, full costing	4–14
Standard, process, full costing	4–14
Standard product costs	3–1, 3–2, 4–13, 9–15
Standard volume	3–11, 4–4
Statement of cash flows	A–7, B–1, B–10
Statement of shareholders' equity	B–1
Static budget	9–8
Strategic costing	2–19
Sunk cost	5–12, 7–4
Supplies	2–8, 5–2

–T–

Target costing	1–4, 6–9
Target price	6–9
Tax shield	5–19
Taxes	5–19, 7–13, 7–35, A–6, B–4
TCS (traditional cost system)	2–2, 2–22, 6–2
Throughput accounting	4–12
Time value of money	7–7, 7–17

Top-down budgeting 8–11, 9–15
Total quality management 6–3
Traditional cost system (TCS) 2–2, 2–22, 6–2
Transfer price 4–9, 10–2

–U–

Unabsorbed cost 4–5
Unadjusted rate of return 7–7
Understandability 8–13
Usage variance 3–15

–V–

Value engineering/analysis 6–10
Value-chain analysis 6–3, 6–10
Value-chain involvement 6–9
Variable cost 2–1, 2–19, 2–20, 2–29, 4–2, 5–1, 9–10, 10–3
Variable costing 4–1
Variable overhead budget 3–11
Variance analysis 3–1, 3–7
Variances 3–1, 3–7
Voice of the customer 6–10

–W–

Working capital 7–32, 10–2, B–2